MW00719139

Securing Systems with the Solaris™ Security Toolkit

Alex Noordergraaf
Glenn Brunette

Sun Microsystems Press
A Prentice Hall Title

2003 Sun Microsystems, Inc.—
4150 Network Circle
Santa Clara, CA 95045 U.S.A. All rights reserved.

This product or document is protected by copyright under licenses restricting its use, copying, distribution, and decompilation. No part of this product or document may be reproduced in any form by any means without prior written authorization of Sun and its licensors, if any. Third-party software, including font technology, is copyrighted and licensed from Sun suppliers.

Parts of the product may be derived from Berkeley BSD systems, licensed from the University of California. UNIX is a registered trademark in the U.S. and other countries, exclusively licensed through X/Open Company, Ltd.

Sun, Sun Microsystems, the Sun logo, Sun BluePrints, Sun Cluster, SunDocs, Sun Enterprise, Sun Fire, Sun ONE, SunOS, Sun StorEdge, SunTone, iPlanet, J2EE Java, JumpStart, OpenBoot, Solaris, StarOffice, and SunSolve Online are trademarks, registered trademarks, or service marks of Sun Microsystems, Inc. in the U.S. and other countries. All SPARC trademarks are used under license and are trademarks or registered trademarks of SPARC International, Inc. in the U.S. and other countries. Products bearing SPARC trademarks are based upon an architecture developed by Sun Microsystems, Inc.

The OPEN LOOK and Sun™ Graphical User Interface was developed by Sun Microsystems, Inc. for its users and licensees. Sun acknowledges the pioneering efforts of Xerox in researching and developing the concept of visual or graphical user interfaces for the computer industry. Sun holds a non-exclusive license from Xerox to the Xerox Graphical User Interface, which license also covers Sun's licensees who implement OPEN LOOK GUIs and otherwise comply with Sun's written license agreements.

RESTRICTED RIGHTS: Use, duplication, or disclosure by the U.S. Government is subject to restrictions of FAR 52.227-14(g)(2)(6/87) and FAR 52.227-19(6/87), or DFAR 252.227-7015(b)(6/95) and DFAR 227.7202-2(a).

DOCUMENTATION IS PROVIDED "AS IS" AND ALL EXPRESS OR IMPLIED CONDITIONS, REPRESENTATIONS AND WARRANTIES, INCLUDING ANY IMPLIED WARRANTY OF MERCHANTABILITY, FITNESS FOR A PARTICULAR PURPOSE OR NONINFRINGEMENT, ARE DISCLAIMED, EXCEPT TO THE EXTENT THAT SUCH DISCLAIMERS ARE HELD TO BE LEGALLY INVALID.

The publishers offers discounts on this book when ordered in bulk quantities. For more information, contact: Corporate Sales Department, Phone: 800-382-3419; Fax: 201-236-7141; E-mail: corpsales@prenhall.com; or write: Prentice Hall PTR, Corp. Sales Dept., One Lake Street, Upper Saddle River, NJ 07458.

Production Supervision: *Mary Sudul*
Acquisitions Editor: *Gregory G. Doench*
Cover Design Director: *Jerry Votta*
Cover Designer: *Kavish & Kavish Digital Publishing and Design*
Manufacturing Manager: *Alexis R. Heydt*
Marketing Manager: *Debby vanDijk*

Sun Microsystems Press:
Publisher: *Myrna Rivera*

1st Printing

ISBN 0-13-141071-7

Sun Microsystems Press
A Prentice Hall Title

Acknowledgments

This book would not exist without the hard work, dedication, and skill of Rex Casey. His attention to detail and ability to consistently meet and exceed our expectations was essential to the success of this project.

Many thanks also to the reviewers of this book who provided many valuable comments and suggestions: Nicholas Nevin, Hal Flynn, Nicholas O'Donnell, Bart Blanquart, Eric Halil, Jason M. Reid, Kevin Song, Warren Belfer, and Darren Moffat. We would like to extend a special thank you to Christopher Jackson whose review comments and criticisms were particularly detailed and helpful.

Much of the work done in this book would not have been possible without the support of our various managers. In particular, we would like to thank Jeff Anderson, Michael Habeck, Bill Nesheim, and all the other managers who helped make this possible.

Finally, we would like to thank our families.

Alex Noordergraaf would like to say that without the encouragement and love of his wife, Lisa, the contents of this book would never have gotten done. Her understanding and tolerance during the frequent deadlines was invaluable.

A heartfelt thanks to his father, Abraham, for helping him see what he could do, and to his mother, Gertrude, for always being there and believing in him. Thanks also to his brother and sisters, Gerrit Jan, Annemiek, and Jeske for helping and encouraging their baby brother.

Glenn Brunette would like say that if not for the boundless love, support, and encouragement of his wife, Beth, this dream would never have become a reality. Thank you. She is and always has been his inspiration and his everything. Thank you to his son, Alex, whose smile and endless enthusiasm never fail to fill his days with happiness and pride.

A profound thanks to his parents, Glenn and Mary. Their love, support, and guidance have made him the man he is today. Thank you for providing him with countless opportunities and for instilling in him not only the drive to excel but also the belief that anything was possible.

Contents

Part II. Reference

Figures

Tables

Code Samples

Preface

This book is one of an on-going series of books collectively known as the Sun BluePrints™ program. This *Securing Systems with the Solaris™ Security Toolkit* BluePrint details best practices for securing the Solaris™ Operating Environment (Solaris OE) by using the Solaris Security Toolkit software.

About This Book

This book provides readers with a single documentation source for features, capabilities, how-to instructions, security recommendations, and best practices for securing systems using the Solaris Security Toolkit software. This book consolidates and restructures for ease of use three previously published Sun BluePrint OnLine articles into one comprehensive user and reference guide. And, it provides significant new content that extends and compliments the previous content.

Note – This book omits information about private software features and functions used by Solaris Security Toolkit software developers.

Securing computer systems against unauthorized access is one of the most pressing issues facing today's data center administrators. Recent studies suggest that unauthorized accesses continue to rise, as do the monetary losses associated with these security breaches.

As with any security decision, a balance must be attained between system manageability and security.

Many attacks have preventative solutions available; however, every day, hackers compromise systems using well-known attack methods. Hardening systems and minimizing entry points to intruders can increase security.

Sun BluePrints Program

The mission of the Sun BluePrints Program is to empower Sun's customers with the technical knowledge required to implement reliable, extensible, and secure information systems within the data center using Sun products. This program provides a framework to identify, develop, and distribute best practices information that applies across the Sun product lines. Experts in technical subjects in various areas contribute to the program and focus on the scope and usefulness of the information.

The Sun BluePrints Program includes books, guides, and online articles. Through these vehicles, Sun provides guidance, installation and implementation experiences, real-life scenarios, and late-breaking technical information.

The monthly electronic magazine, Sun BluePrints OnLine, is located on the Web at http://www.sun.com/blueprints. To be notified about updates to the Sun BluePrints Program, please register yourself on this site.

Who Should Use This Book

This book is primarily intended for persons who use the Solaris Security Toolkit software to secure Solaris OE versions 2.5.1 and newer. This audience includes individuals using the software in either its JumpStart™ mode or standalone mode. This audience is comprised of individuals such as administrators, consultants, and others who are deploying new Sun systems or securing deployed systems.

Before You Read This Book

You should be a Sun certified system administrator or Sun certified network administrator for the Solaris OE. You should also have an understanding of standard network protocols and topologies.

Because this book is designed to be useful to people with varying degrees of experience or knowledge of security, your experience and knowledge are the determining factors of the way you use this book.

How This Book Is Organized

This book serves as both a user guide and a reference guide. Chapters in Part I contain information, instructions, and recommendations for using the software to secure systems. Chapters in Part II contain reference information about the software components. This book is structured as follows:

Part I "Getting Started and Using the Software" The chapters in this Part contain information and procedures for installing and using the Solaris Security Toolkit software to secure systems.

Chapter 1 "Introduction" This chapter describes the design and purpose of the Solaris Security Toolkit software. It covers the key components, features, benefits, and supported platforms.

Chapter 2 "Securing Systems: Applying a Methodology" This chapter recommends a methodology for securing systems. It provides a process that you can apply before securing your systems using the Solaris Security Toolkit software.

Chapter 3 "Installing and Running Security Software" This chapter provides instructions for downloading, installing, and running the Solaris Security Toolkit software and other security-related software.

Chapter 4 "Reversing System Changes" This chapter provides information and procedures for reversing (undoing) the changes made by the Solaris Security Toolkit software during hardening runs.

Chapter 5 "Configuring and Managing JumpStart Servers" This chapter provides information for configuring and managing JumpStart servers to use the Solaris Security Toolkit software.

Chapter 6 "Auditing System Security" This chapter describes how to audit (validate) a system's security using the Solaris Security Toolkit software. Use the information and procedures in this chapter for maintaining an established security profile after hardening.

Chapter 7 "Securing a System" This chapter describes how to apply the information and expertise provided in earlier chapters to a realistic scenario for installing and securing a new system.

Part II "Reference" The chapters in this Part contain reference information for understanding and using the internals of the Solaris Security Toolkit software.

Chapter 8 "Using Framework Functions" This chapter provides reference information for using, adding, modifying, and removing framework functions. Framework functions provide flexibility for you to change the behavior of the Solaris Security Toolkit software without modifying source code.

Chapter 9 "Using File Templates" This chapter provides reference information about how to use, modify, and customize the file templates included in the Solaris Security Toolkit software.

Chapter 10 "Using Drivers" This chapter provides reference information about using, adding, modifying, and removing drivers. This chapter describes the drivers used by the Solaris Security Toolkit software to harden, minimize, and audit Solaris OE systems.

Chapter 11 "Using Finish Scripts" This chapter provides reference information about using, adding, modifying, and removing finish scripts. This chapter describes the scripts used by the Solaris Security Toolkit software to harden and minimize Solaris OE systems.

Chapter 12 "Using Audit Scripts" This chapter provides reference information for using, adding, modifying, and removing audit scripts.

Chapter 13 "Using Environment Variables" This chapter provides reference information about using environment variables. This chapter describes all of the variables used by the Solaris Security Toolkit software and provides tips and techniques for customizing their values.

Ordering Sun Documents

The SunDocs℠ program provides more than 250 manuals from Sun Microsystems, Inc. If you live in the United States, Canada, Europe, or Japan, you can purchase documentation sets or individual manuals through this program.

Accessing Sun Documentation Online

The docs.sun.com web site enables you to access most Sun technical documentation online. You can browse the docs.sun.com archive or search for a specific book title or subject. The URL is http://docs.sun.com/.

Related Resources

Publications

Andert, Donna, Wakefield, Robin, and Weise, Joel. "Trust Modeling for Security Architecture Development," Sun BluePrints OnLine, December 2002, http://www.sun.com/blueprints/1202/817-0775.pdf.

Dasan, Vasanthan, Noordergraaf, Alex, and Ordica, Lou. "The Solaris Fingerprint Database - A Security Tool for Solaris Software and Files," Sun BluePrints OnLine, May 2001, http://www.sun.com/blueprints/0501/Fingerprint.pdf.

Englund, Martin, "Securing Systems with Host-Based Firewalls - Implemented With SunScreen Lite 3.1 Software," Sun BluePrints OnLine, September 2001, http://sun.com/blueprints/0901/sunscreenlite.pdf.

Garfinkel, Simon, and Spafford, Gene. *Practical UNIX and Internet Security*, 2nd Edition, O'Reilly & Associates, April 1996.

Howard, John S., and Noodergraaf, Alex. *JumpStart™ Technology: Effective Use in the Solaris™ Operating Environment*, The Official Sun Microsystems Resource Series, Prentice Hall, October 2001.

Moffat, Darren J., *Solaris BSM Auditing*, http://www.securityfocus.com/focus/sun/articles/bsmaudit1.html.

Noordergraaf, Alex. "Minimizing the Solaris Operating Environment for Security: Updated for Solaris 9 Operating Environment," Sun BluePrints OnLine, November 2000, http://sun.com/blueprints/1100/minimize-updt1.pdf.

Noordergraaf, Alex. "Securing the Sun Cluster 3.x Software," Sun BluePrints OnLine article, February 2003, http://www.sun.com/solutions/blueprints/0203/817-1079.pdf.

Noordergraaf, Alex, "Securing the Sun Enterprise 10000 System Service Processors," Sun BluePrint OnLine article, March 2002, http://www.sun.com/solutions/blueprints/0302/securingenter.pdf.

Noordergraaf, Alex, et. al. *Enterprise Security: Solaris Operating Environment Security Journal, Solaris Operating Environment Versions 2.5.1, 2.6, 7, and 8*, Sun Microsystems, Prentice Hall Press, ISBN 0-13-100092-6, June 2002.

Noordergraaf, Alex and Nimeh, Dina. "Securing the Sun Fire 12K and 15K Domains," Sun BluePrints OnLine article, February 2003, http://www.sun.com/solutions/blueprints/0203/817-1357.pdf.

Noordergraaf, Alex and Nimeh, Dina. "Securing the Sun Fire 12K and 15K System Controllers," Sun BluePrints OnLine article, February 2003, http://www.sun.com/solutions/blueprints/0203/817-1358.pdf.

Noordergraaf, Alex and Watson, Keith. "Solaris Operating Environment Security: Updated for the Solaris 9 Operating Environment," Sun BluePrints OnLine, December 2002, http://www.sun.com/solutions/blueprints/1202/816-5242.pdf.

Osser, William and Noordergraaf, Alex. "Auditing in the Solaris 8 Operating Environment," Sun BluePrints OnLine, February 2001 http://www.sun.com/solutions/blueprints/0201/audit_config.pdf.

Reid, Jason M. and Watson, Keith. "Building and Deploying OpenSSH in the Solaris Operating Environment," Sun BluePrints OnLine, July 2001, http://sun.com/blueprints/0701/openSSH.pdf.

Reid, Jason M. "Configuring OpenSSH for the Solaris Operating Environment," Sun BluePrints OnLine article, January 2002, http://www.sun.com/solutions/blueprints/0102/configssh.pdf.

Reid, Jason. *Secure Shell in the Enterprise*, The Official Sun Microsystems Resource Series, Prentice Hall, June 2003

Solaris Advanced Installation Guide, Sun Microsystems, http://docs.sun.com.

SunSHIELD Basic Security Module Guide, Sun Microsystems, Inc., http://docs.sun.com.

Watson, Keith and Noordergraaf, Alex. "Solaris Operating Environment Network Settings for Security: Updated for Solaris 9 Operating Environment," Sun BluePrints OnLine, June 2003, http://www.sun.com/solutions/blueprints/0603/816-5240.html.

Weise, Joel, and Martin, Charles R. "Developing a Security Policy," Sun BluePrints OnLine article, December 2001, http://www.sun.com/solutions/blueprints/1201/secpolicy.pdf.

Web Sites

Note – Sun is not responsible for the availability of third-party Web sites mentioned in this document. Sun does not endorse and is not responsible or liable for any content, advertising, products, or other material on or available from such sites or resources. Sun will not be responsible or liable for any damage or loss caused or alleged to be caused by or in connection with use of or reliance on any such content, goods, or services that are available on or through any such sites or resources.

AUSCERT, *UNIX Security Checklist,*
`ftp://ftp.auscert.org.au/pub/auscert/papers/unix_security_checklist`

CERT/CC at `http://www.cert.org` is a federally funded research and development center working with computer security issues.

Chkrootkit, `http://www.chkrootkit.org`

Galvin, Peter Baer, *The Solaris Security FAQ,*
`http://www.sunworld.com/common/security-faq.html`

HoneyNet Project, "Know Your Enemy: Motives"
`http://project.honeynet.org/papers/motives/`

List open files software,
`ftp://vic.cc.purdue.edu/pub/tools/unix/lsof/`

Nmap Port Scanner, `http://www.insecure.org`

OpenSSH tool, `http://www.openssh.com/`

Pomeranz, Hal, *Solaris Security Step by Step,* `http://www.sans.org/`

Rhoads, Jason, *Solaris Security Guide,*
`http://www.sabernet.net/papers/Solaris.html`

Security Focus at `http://www.securityfocus.org` is a Web site dedicated to discussing pertinent security topics.

Sendmail Consortium, `sendmail` configuration information,
`http://www.sendmail.org/`

Spitzner, Lance, *Armoring Solaris,*
`http://www.enteract.com/~lspitz/armoring.html`

SSH Communications Security, Secure Shell (SSH) tool, `http://www.ssh.com/`

Sun BluePrints OnLine, `http://sun.com/blueprints`

Sun BluePrints OnLine Tools:

    FixModes software, `http://sun.com/blueprints/tools/FixModes_license.html`

    MD5 software, `http://sun.com/blueprints/tools/md5_license.html`

Sun Enterprise Authentication Mechanism information,
http://www.sun.com/software/solaris/ds/ds-seam

SunSolve – http://sunsolve.sun.com

Typographic Conventions

Typeface	Meaning	Examples
AaBbCc123	The names of commands, files, and directories; on-screen computer output	Edit your .login file. Use ls -a to list all files. % You have mail.
AaBbCc123	What you type, when contrasted with on-screen computer output	% **su** Password:
AaBbCc123	Book titles, new words or terms, words to be emphasized	Read Chapter 6 in the *User's Guide*. These are called *class* options. You *must* be superuser to do this.
	Command-line variable; replace with a real name or value	To delete a file, type rm *filename*.

Shell Prompts in Command Examples

The following table shows the default system prompt and superuser prompt for the C shell, Bourne shell, and Korn shell.

Shell	Prompt
C shell prompt	machine_name%
C shell superuser prompt	machine_name#
Bourne shell and Korn shell prompt	$
Bourne shell and Korn shell superuser prompt	#

Sun Welcomes Your Comments

Sun is interested in improving its documentation and welcomes your comments and suggestions. You can submit your comments to us at:

```
http://www.sun.com/hwdocs/feedback
```

Please include the part number (817-0074-10) of this document in the subject line of your email.

## PART I

Getting Started and Using the Software

The chapters in this Part contain information and procedures for installing and using the Solaris Security Toolkit software to secure systems.

This Part contains the following chapters:

## CHAPTER 1

Introduction

This chapter describes the design and purpose of the Solaris Security Toolkit software. It covers the key components, features, benefits, and supported platforms. This chapter provides recommendations for maintaining version control of modifications and deployments, and it sets forth important guidelines for customizing the Solaris Security Toolkit software.

This chapter contains the following topics:

"Securing Systems with the Solaris Security Toolkit Software" on page 2

"Understanding the Software Components" on page 4

"Maintaining Version Control" on page 14

"Running Supported Solaris OE Versions" on page 14

"Configuring and Customizing the Solaris Security Toolkit Software" on page 15

Securing Systems with the Solaris Security Toolkit Software

The Solaris Security Toolkit software, informally known as the JASS (JumpStart™ Architecture and Security Scripts) toolkit, provides an automated, extensible, and scalable mechanism to build and maintain secure Solaris OE systems. Using the Solaris Security Toolkit software, you can harden, minimize, and audit the security of systems.

The Solaris Security Toolkit software was developed by Sun teams in the Enterprise Server Products and the Professional Services organizations; it is based on proven security best practices and practical customer-site experience gathered over many years. The Solaris Security Toolkit software was developed after noticing that many customers were investing resources to develop and maintain their own security tools. Because these tools were frequently out-of-date, often not extensible, and not well integrated with Solaris installation technologies, the Solaris Security Toolkit software was developed. It provides an up-to-date, extensible, and scalable solution.

Use the Solaris Security Toolkit software to secure and maintain the security of Solaris OE systems in your environment, whether there are ten or ten-thousand systems. The Solaris Security Toolkit software automates and simplifies the process of minimizing, hardening, and auditing secured Solaris OE systems.

Hardening is the modification of Solaris OE configurations to improve the security of a system.

Minimizing is the removal of Solaris OE packages that are not needed on a particular system. (Because each system's requirements vary, what is deemed unnecessary also varies and has to be evaluated.) This removal reduces the number of components to be patched and made secure, which, in turn, reduces entry points available to a possible intruder.

Auditing is the process of determining if a system's configuration is in compliance with a predefined security profile.

System installation and configuration should be as automated as possible (ideally, 100 percent). This recommendation includes OS installation and configuration, network configuration, user accounts, applications, and security modifications. The security modification may include hardening and/or minimization, depending on the purpose of the system. One technology available to automate Solaris OE installations is JumpStart software. The JumpStart software provides a mechanism to install systems, over a network, with little or no human intervention required. The Solaris Security Toolkit software provides a framework and scripts to implement and automate most of the tasks associated with hardening and minimizing Solaris OE systems in JumpStart software-based installations.

In addition, the Solaris Security Toolkit software has a standalone mode. This mode provides the ability to perform all the same hardening functionality as in JumpStart mode, but on deployed systems. In either mode, the security modifications made can, and should, be customized to match security requirements for your system.

Regardless of how a system is installed, we recommend that you use the Solaris Security Toolkit software initially to harden and minimize your systems. Then, periodically use the Solaris Security Toolkit software to audit that the security profile of secured systems is not accidently or maliciously modified. The frequency of auditing your systems is discretionary; however, we recommend that at a minimum, you perform auditing after software updates or patch installations.

Note – The term *audit* is used in this book to define the Solaris Security Toolkit software's automated process of validating a security posture by comparing it with a predefined security profile. The use of this term in this publication does not represent a guarantee that a system is completely secure after using the audit option.

Understanding the Software Components

This section provides an overview of the structure of the Solaris Security Toolkit software components. The Solaris Security Toolkit software is a collection of files and directories. FIGURE 1-1 shows an illustration of the structure.

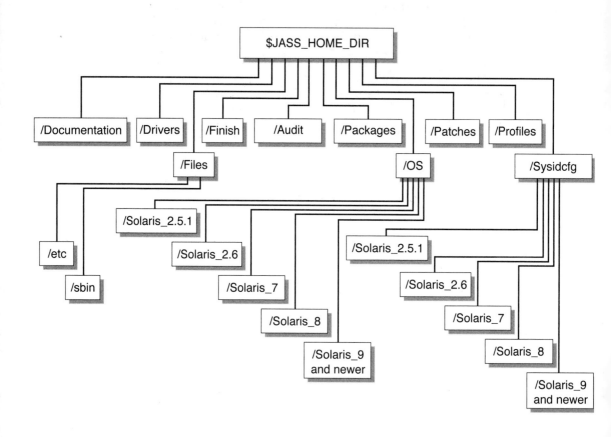

FIGURE 1-1   Software Component Structure

In addition to these directories and subdirectories, the following files are in the top-level of the Solaris Security Toolkit software structure:

add-client – A JumpStart helper program for adding clients into a JumpStart environment.

rm-client – A JumpStart helper program for removing clients from a JumpStart environment.

make-jass-pkg – A command that provides the ability to create a Solaris OE package from the contents of the Solaris Security Toolkit directory, to simplify internal distribution of a customized Solaris Security Toolkit configuration.

jass-check-sum – A command that provides the ability to determine if any files modified by the Solaris Security Toolkit software have been changed, based on a checksum created during each Solaris Security Toolkit run.

Directories

The components of the Solaris Security Toolkit architecture are organized in the following directories:

Audit
Documentation
Drivers
Files
Finish
OS
Packages
Patches
Profiles
Sysidcfg

Each directory is described in this section. Where appropriate, each script, configuration file, or subdirectory is listed, and references to other chapters are provided for detailed information.

The Solaris Security Toolkit directory structure is based on the recommendations made in the Sun BluePrint book *JumpStart™ Technology: Effective Use in the Solaris™ Operating Environment*.

Audit Directory

This directory contains the audit scripts that evaluate a system's compliance with a defined security profile or set of audit scripts. The scripts in this directory are organized into the following categories:

Disable
Enable
Install
Minimize
Print
Remove
Set
Update

For detailed listings of the scripts in each of these categories and descriptions of each script, refer to Chapter 12.

Documentation Directory

This directory contains Sun BluePrints OnLine documentation providing security recommendations for the Solaris Security Toolkit software. Also, these documents and the most recent updates are available at:

```
http://www.sun.com/security/blueprints
```

The documentation in this directory is in PDF format, which requires a PDF viewer such as Adobe Acrobat.

Drivers Directory

This directory contains files of configuration information specifying which files are executed and installed when you run the Solaris Security Toolkit software. This directory contains drivers, scripts, and configuration files.

The following is an example of the drivers and scripts in the Drivers directory:

```
common_{log|misc}.funcs
config.driver
desktop-{config|hardening|secure}.driver
driver.{funcs|init|run}
hardening.driver
finish.init
install-Sun_ONE-WS.driver
jumpstart-{config|hardening|secure}.driver
secure.driver
starfire-{config|hardening|secure}.driver
suncluster3x-{config|hardening|secure}.driver
sunfire_15k_domain-{config|hardening|secure}.driver
sunfire_15k_sc-{config|hardening|secure}.driver
sunfire_mf_msp-{config|hardening|secure}.driver
undo.{funcs|init|run}
hardening.driver
user.init.SAMPLE
user.run.SAMPLE
audit_{private|public}.funcs
```

All product-specific drivers and some others include three files for each driver:

```
name-secure.driver
name-config.driver
name-hardening.driver
```

These three files are indicated in brackets in the previous list, for example, `sunfire_15k_sc-{config|hardening|secure}.driver`. These files are listed for completeness. Use only the `name-secure.driver` when you want to execute a driver. That driver automatically calls the related drivers.

The Solaris Security Toolkit architecture includes configuration information to enable driver, finish, and audit scripts to be used in different environments, while not modifying the actual scripts themselves. All variables used in the finish and audit scripts are maintained in a set of configuration files—these configuration files are imported by drivers, which make the variables available to the finish and audit scripts as they are called by the drivers.

The Solaris Security Toolkit software has three main configuration files, all of which are stored in the Drivers directory:

```
driver.init
finish.init
user.init
```

Finish scripts called by the drivers are located in the Finish directory. Audit scripts called by the drivers are located in the Audit directory. Files installed by the drivers are read from the Files directory. For more information about finish and audit scripts, refer to the respective chapters in this book.

FIGURE 1-2 shows a flow chart of the driver control flow.

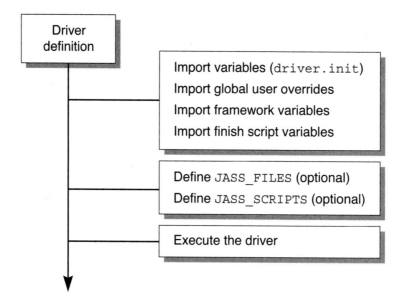

FIGURE 1-2   Driver Control Flow

All of the environment variables from the various .init files are imported first. Once this is complete, the driver moves on to part two, which defines JASS_FILES and JASS_SCRIPTS. The definition of these are optional; either a single environment can be defined, or both, or none. Part three of the driver calls driver.run to perform the tasks defined by the JASS_FILE and JASS_SCRIPTS environment variables.

The following code is an excerpt demonstrating driver control flow.

```
DIR="`/bin/dirname $0`"

export DIR
. ${DIR}/driver.init

JASS_FILES="
                /etc/cron.d/cron.allow
                /etc/default/ftpd
                /etc/default/telnetd
"

JASS_SCRIPTS="
                install-at-allow.fin
                remove-unneeded-accounts.fin
"
. ${DIR}/driver.run
```

This sample code sets and exports the DIR environment variable so that the drivers recognize the starting directory. Next, the JASS_FILES environment variable is defined as containing those files that are copied from the JASS_HOME_DIR/Files directory onto the client. The JASS_SCRIPTS environment variable is then defined with the finish scripts that are run by the Solaris Security Toolkit software. Finally, the execution of the hardening run is started by calling the driver.run driver. Once called, driver.run copies the files specified by JASS_FILES, and runs the scripts specified by JASS_SCRIPTS.

Files Directory

This directory is used by the JASS_FILES environment variable and the driver.run script. This directory stores files that are copied to the JumpStart client.

The following files are in this directory:

```
/.cshrc
/.profile
/etc/default/sendmail
/etc/defaultrouter
/etc/dt/config/Xaccess
/etc/hosts.{allow|deny}
/etc/init.d/inetsvc
/etc/init.d/nddconfig
/etc/init.d/set-tmp-permissions
/etc/init.d/sms_arpconfig
/etc/issue
```

```
/etc/motd
/etc/notrouter
/etc/rc2.d/S00set-tmp-permissions
/etc/rc2.d/S07set-tmp-permissions
/etc/rc2.d/S70nddconfig
/etc/rc2.d/S73sms_arpconfig
/etc/security/audit_class
/etc/security/audit_control
/etc/security/audit_event
/etc/sms_domain_arp
/etc/sms_sc_arp
/etc/syslog.conf
/sbin/noshell
```

Finish Directory

This directory contains the finish scripts that perform system modifications and updates during installation. The scripts in this directory are organized into the following categories:

Disable
Enable
Install
Minimize
Print
Remove
Set
Update

For detailed listings of the scripts in each of these categories and descriptions of each script, refer to Chapter 11.

OS Directory

This directory contains only Solaris OE images. These are used by the JumpStart software installation process as the source of the client installation and to provide the add_install_client and rm_install_client scripts. The add_client script accepts these additional directory names.

For more information about loading and modifying Solaris OE images, refer to the Sun BluePrints book titled *JumpStart™ Technology: Effective Use in the Solaris™ Operating Environment*.

The standard installation naming convention recommended is as follows.

Solaris OE

Use the following naming standard for Solaris OE:

`Solaris_<os version_4 digit year_2 digit month of CD release>`

For example, the Solaris 8 Operating Environment CD, dated April 2001, would have a directory name of `Solaris_8_2001-04`. By separating updates and releases of the Solaris OE, very fine control can be maintained for testing and deployment purposes.

Trusted Solaris OE

Use the following directory naming standard for Trusted Solaris:

`Trusted_Solaris_<os version_4 digit year_2 digit month of CD release>`

For example, if the Trusted Solaris software release were dated February of 2000, the directory name would be: `Trusted_Solaris_8_2000-02`.

Solaris OE Intel Platform Edition

Use the following directory naming for Solaris OE Intel Platform Edition:

`Solaris_<os version_4 digit year_2 digit month of CD release>_ia`

For example, if the Solaris OE Intel Platform Edition release were dated April 2001, the directory name would be: `Solaris_8_2001-04_ia`.

Packages Directory

This directory contains software packages that can be installed with a finish script. For example, the SunONE™ Web Server (formerly iPlanet™ Web Server) software package could be stored in the Packages directory so that the appropriate finish script installs the software as required.

Several finish scripts included in the Solaris Security Toolkit software perform software installation and basic configuration functions. The scripts that install software from the Packages directory include:

```
install-fix-modes.fin
install-Sun_ONE-WS.fin
install-jass.fin
install-md5.fin
install-openssh.fin
```

Patches Directory

This directory is for storing Recommended and Security Patch Clusters for the Solaris OE. We strongly recommend that you download and extract required patches into this directory.

By placing and extracting the patches in this directory, you streamline installation. When the patches are extracted into this directory, the Solaris Security Toolkit software's patch installation script automates installation so that you do not have to manually extract the patch clusters for each system installation.

We recommend that you create subdirectories for each of the Solaris OE versions used. For example, you might have directories `2.5.1_Recommended` and `2.6_Recommended` within the Patches directory.

Solaris Security Toolkit software supports Solaris OE Intel Platform Edition patch clusters. The supported naming convention for these patch clusters is the same as made available through SunSolve OnLine℠ service.

The format is `Solaris_<release>_x86_Recommended`. The Solaris OE Intel Platform Edition patch cluster for Solaris 8 OE would be in a directory named: `Solaris_8_x86_Recommended`.

Profiles Directory

This directory contains all JumpStart profiles. These profiles contain configuration information used by JumpStart software to determine Solaris OE clusters for installation (for example, Core, End User, Developer, or Entire Distribution), disk layout, and installation type (for example, standalone) to perform.

JumpStart profiles are listed and used in the `rules` file to define how specific systems or groups of systems are built.

Sysidcfg Directory

Similar to the Profiles directory, the Sysidcfg directory contains files that are only used during JumpStart mode installations. These files automate Solaris OE installations by providing the required installation information. A separate directory tree stores OE-specific information.

Each Solaris OE has a separate directory. For each release, there is a directory named `Solaris_OE Version`. The Solaris Security Toolkit software includes sample `sysidcfg` files for Solaris OE versions 2.5.1 and newer.

The sample `sysidcfg` files can be extended to other types such as per network, host, etc. The Solaris Security Toolkit software supports arbitrary `sysidcfg` files.

For additional information on `sysidcfg` files, refer to the Sun BluePrint book *JumpStart™ Technology: Effective Use in the Solaris™ Operating Environment*.

Data Repository

The data repository is an environment variable in the `JASS_REPOSITORY` directory that supports Solaris Security Toolkit undo runs, saves data on how each run is executed, maintains a manifest of files modified by the software, and saves data for the execution log. The undo feature relies on the information stored in the data repository.

Maintaining Version Control

Maintaining version control for all files and scripts used by the Solaris Security Toolkit software is critical for two reasons. First, one of the goals of this environment is to be able to recreate a system installation. This goal would be impossible without having a snapshot of all file versions used during an installation. Second, because these scripts are performing security functions—which is a critical process for many organizations—extreme caution must be exercised to ensure only appropriate and tested changes are implemented.

A Source Code Control System (SCCS) version control package is provided in the Solaris OE SUNWsprot package. Also, you can use other version control software available from freeware and commercial vendors to manage version information. Whichever version control product you use, we recommend that you have a process in place to manage updates and capture version information for future system re-creation.

We recommend that in addition to version control, that you use an integrity management solution to determine if the contents of files were modified. Although privileged users of a system may be able to bypass the version control system, they would not be able easily to bypass an integrity management system, which maintains its integrity database on a remote system. Integrity management solutions are best when centralized, because locally-stored databases could be maliciously modified.

Running Supported Solaris OE Versions

The current release of the Solaris Security Toolkit software works with Solaris OE versions 2.5.1 and newer. The Solaris Security Toolkit software automatically detects which version of the Solaris OE software is installed, then only runs tasks appropriate for that version.

Configuring and Customizing the Solaris Security Toolkit Software

Every attempt is made to deliver the Solaris Security Toolkit software with sensible out-of-the box default values for scripts, framework functions, and variables. These default settings implement all security recommendations contained in the Sun BluePrint book titled *Enterprise Security: Solaris Operating Environment Security Journal, Solaris Operating Environment Versions 2.5.1, 2.6, 7, and 8* and Sun BluePrint OnLine articles about security. These settings will not be appropriate for all systems and will mandate customizing of the Solaris Security Toolkit software to meet the security requirements for your systems.

One of the most significant characteristics of the Solaris Security Toolkit software is that you can easily customize it to fit your environment, systems, and requirements. One of the early design goals of the Solaris Security Toolkit was that users must be able to both configure and extend it, because there is no single default that fits all.

To customize the Solaris Security Toolkit software, adjust its actions through drivers, finish scripts, audit scripts, framework functions, environment variables, and file templates.

We recommend that you do not modify the Solaris Security Toolkit code, because your changes may negatively impact supportability and upgrades. If code modifications are absolutely necessary for using the Solaris Security Toolkit software in your environment, we recommend that you copy the code to a unique file or function name, so that you can easily track changes as in "Recommendations" on page 16.

Throughout this book, recommendations and instructions for customizing the Solaris Security Toolkit software are provided where applicable in each chapter. For example, in Chapter 10, you'll find information helpful about customizing the drivers. Customizing includes modifying and creating files or variables.

Also, the chapters provide examples for customizing the Solaris Security Toolkit software. The examples highlight some ways that you can customize the Solaris Security Toolkit software; however, there are many possibilities.

The following sections present information that must be clearly understood before attempting to customize the Solaris Security Toolkit software. The information is based on shared experiences collected from many deployments, so that you can avoid common pitfalls.

Policies and Requirements

When customizing and deploying the Solaris Security Toolkit software, it is crucial that proper planning be done to ensure that the resulting platform configuration is correct and in line with your organization's expectations.

In your planning phase, be sure to obtain input from a variety of sources, including security policies and standards, industry regulations and guidelines, and vendor-supplied preferred practices.

In addition to this information, it is essential that you consider application and operational requirements to ensure that the resulting configuration does not impact a platform's ability to serve its intended business function.

Recommendations

When customizing the Solaris Security Toolkit software, consider the following recommendations. Understanding and observing these recommendations helps to make the process of sustaining a deployment much simpler and effective.

As a general rule, never alter any of the *original* files (drivers, scripts, files, etc.) provided with the Solaris Security Toolkit software. Changing the original files inhibits and restricts your organization's ability to upgrade to newer versions of the Solaris Security Toolkit software, because any changes to the original files may be overwritten by new versions of the files. (All of your custom changes would be lost, and your system's configuration might change in undesirable ways.) To customize any of the files, first make a copy, then modify the copy, leaving the original intact. Only three exceptions exist to this recommendation, the `sysidcfg` files, templates in the Files directory, and when recommended by Sun BluePrint OnLine articles.

Name your copy of a driver or script appropriately, so that it can be distinguished from the original. Also, we recommend that you use a prefix or keyword that is indicative of the purpose of the script. For example, a prefix that contains the name or stock symbol of the company, a department identifier, or even a platform or application type are all excellent naming standards. TABLE 1-1 lists a few examples of recommended naming standards.

TABLE 1-1   Naming Standards for Custom Files

`abccorp-secure.driver`	Company prefix

TABLE 1-1   Naming Standards for Custom Files

`abcc-nj-secure.driver`	Company stock symbol, location
`abbcorp-nj-webserver.driver`	Company, location, application type
`abc-nj-trading-webserver.driver`	Company, location, organization, application type

Review the following Solaris Security Toolkit files for suitability to your system. To customize these files, copy the original files, rename the copies to `user.init` and `user.run`, then modify or add content to the copies.

`Drivers/user.init.SAMPLE`	Used for customizing global parameters.
`Drivers/user.run.SAMPLE`	Used for customizing global functions.

If necessary, modify the following original files. These files are the *only* original Solaris Security Toolkit files that you should ever modify directly.

`Sysidcfg/*/sysidcfg`	Used for JumpStart automatic configuration.
`Files/*`	Used as file templates and copied to systems.

Note – Be aware that if `SUNWjass` is removed using the `pkrgm` command, the `user.init` and `user.run` files, if created, are not removed. This behavior is true for any customer files that are added to the Solaris Security Toolkit directory structure and are not included in the distribution. The files in the Files directory included in the Solaris Security Toolkit distribution and `sysidcfg` files exist, and would therefore be removed.

## CHAPTER 2

Securing Systems: Applying a Methodology

This chapter recommends a methodology for securing systems. It provides a process that you can apply before securing your systems using the Solaris Security Toolkit software.

This chapter contains the following topics:

Planning and Preparing

Proper planning is key to successfully using the Solaris Security Toolkit software to secure systems. The planning phase constructs a Solaris Security Toolkit profile for the system, based on an organization's security policies and standards, as well as the application and operation requirements of the system. This phase is divided into the following tasks:

"Consider Risks and Benefits" on page 20

"Review Security Policy, Standards, and Related Documentation" on page 22

"Determine Application and Service Requirements" on page 23

Although not covered in this book, other considerations for this phase might include understanding risks and exposures, understanding infrastructure and its security requirements, and considering accountability, logging, and usage auditing.

Consider Risks and Benefits

This section presents considerations that must be clearly understood before you attempt to secure a system. Carefully weigh the risks with the benefits to determine which actions are appropriate for your organization.

When hardening systems, special precautions must be taken to help ensure that the system is functional after the Solaris Security Toolkit software is implemented. Further, it is important that the process be optimized to ensure any downtime is as minimal as possible.

Note – When securing a deployed system, in some cases, it may be more effective for an organization to rebuild the system, hardening it at installation time, followed by reloading all of the software necessary for operation.

---

1. Understand the requirements of the services and applications on the system.

   It is critical that the services and applications running on a system be identified prior to running the Solaris Security Toolkit software. Any dependencies associated with the services and applications must be enumerated so that the configuration of the Solaris Security Toolkit software can be sufficiently adjusted. Failure to do so may inadvertently disable or prevent necessary services from starting. While the changes made by the Solaris Security Toolkit software can in most cases be undone, it is better to develop a correct profile before installation, to limit the potential downtime associated with the Solaris Security Toolkit software implementation.

2. Take into account that the system has to be taken offline and rebooted.

   While this may seem an obvious point, it needs to be made. For the changes made by the Solaris Security Toolkit software to take effect, the system must be rebooted. Depending on the criticality of the system, the services that it provides, and the availability of a maintenance window, an organization may face difficulties implementing the software. If this is a problem for your organization, a decision must be made after carefully weighing the cost of downtime versus the risks of not enhancing security.

3. A system might require multiple reboots to verify functionality.

   It is strongly recommended that all changes be made on nonproduction systems prior to being implemented in a mission-critical setting. For a variety of reasons, this is not always possible; for example, due to lack of sufficient hardware or software that effectively mirrors the target environment. Testing must still be conducted both before and after the installation of the Solaris Security Toolkit software. Recognize that there could still be unidentified dependencies that require troubleshooting after a system is hardened. In most cases, these issues can be resolved fairly quickly using the techniques described in this chapter. If functionality problems are discovered after the Solaris Security Toolkit software installation, additional platform reboots might be necessary to either undo the effects of the Solaris Security Toolkit software run or to make further changes to the security configuration of the system to support and enable the missing functionality.

4. Platform security entails more than just hardening and minimizing.

   When considering retrofitting a system's configuration to enhance its security posture, it is critical to understand that platform hardening and minimizing represent only a fraction of what can and should be done to protect a system, services, and data. A treatment of the additional measures and controls is outside the scope of this chapter, but the reader is encouraged to consider issues related to account management, privilege management, file system and data integrity, host-based access control, intrusion detection, vulnerability scanning and analysis, and application security.

5. System might already have been exploited or has exploitable vulnerabilities.

   This grim possibility must be considered. The platform being hardened might have already been exploited by an attacker. The Solaris Security Toolkit software is probably being implemented too late to offer protection for an exploited vulnerability. In this case, you would most likely reinstall the system, then install and use the Solaris Security Toolkit software to enhance security.

Review Security Policy, Standards, and Related Documentation

The first task in securing a system is to understand your organization's relevant security policies, standards, and guidelines with respect to platform security. Use these documents to form your foundation of the Solaris Security Toolkit's profile, because these documents communicate mandatory requirements and recommended practices to be followed for all systems in your organization. If your organization does not have documentation, we strongly recommend that it be developed.

Note – When looking for these documents, remember that the information might be spread over multiple related documents. Also, keep in mind that some material might be listed in best practices or other documentation.

For more information on security policies, refer to the Sun BluePrint OnLine article "Developing a Security Policy." This document can be used to gain a greater understanding of the role that security policies play in an organization's security posture.

The following two examples illustrate how policy statements can directly impact the way that the Solaris Security Toolkit's profile is configured.

Example 1

Policy – An organization must use management protocols that support strong authentication of users and encryption of transmitted data.

Profile Impact – Clear-text protocols such as Telnet, FTP, SNMPv1, and others should not be used. By default, the Solaris Security Toolkit disables such services, so no additional configuration is needed.

Note – Both Telnet and FTP services can be configured to support stronger authentication and encryption using extensions such as Kerberos. These services are listed as examples, however, because their default configurations do not support these added levels of security.

Example 2

Policy: All users are forced to change their passwords every 30 days.

Profile Impact: The Solaris Security Toolkit software can be configured to enable password aging. By default, the Solaris Security Toolkit software sets a password maximum age to 8 weeks (56 days). To comply with the policy, the Solaris Security Toolkit software's profile must be changed. Refer to Chapter 11, "Set Finish Scripts" on page 252.

Although the Solaris Security Toolkit software enables password aging by default when run on a system, this change does not affect existing users. To enable password aging for existing users, invoke the passwd(1) command on each user account.

Determine Application and Service Requirements

This task is necessary to ensure that services remain functional after a system is hardened. This task is comprised of the following steps:

"Identifying Application and Operational Service Inventory" on page 23

"Determining Service Requirements" on page 24

Identifying Application and Operational Service Inventory

Inventory the applications, services, and operational or management functions. This inventory is necessary to determine the software that is actually being used on a system. In many cases, systems are configured with more software than is used and with software that does not support business functions.

Sun recommends that systems be constructed minimally whenever possible. That is, software that is not required to support a business function should not be installed. Unnecessary software applications on a system increase the number of opportunities that an attacker can use to exploit the system. Additionally, more software on a system usually equates to more patches that must be applied. For information on minimizing the Solaris OE, refer to the Sun BluePrint OnLine article "Minimizing the Solaris Operating Environment for Security."

When building the inventory of software, be sure to include infrastructure components such as management, monitoring, and backup software in addition to applications residing on the system.

Determining Service Requirements

After you complete an application and service inventory, review each of the components to determine if any have dependencies that could be impacted by the hardening process. While this at first might sound like a daunting process, based on actual deployment of the Solaris Security Toolkit software over the last several years, there were only a few special cases that had to be considered. This experience is due to the fact that many third-party applications do not directly use services provided by the Solaris OE. For those applications that do, the following sections provide helpful information.

"Shared Libraries" on page 24

"Configuration Files" on page 27

"Service Frameworks" on page 28

Shared Libraries

It is important to understand which libraries are needed to support an application. This knowledge is most useful in debugging circumstances, but also is useful in preparing a system to be hardened. When the state of a system is unknown, it is important to gather as much information as possible so that issues such as software dependencies are clearly understood.

Three methods can be used to determine the libraries that are in use by an application, depending upon the Solaris OE version you install.

The first is used against a file system object (for example, application binary).

The second is used when analyzing a running application.

The third is used to trace a program when it is started.

Example: Determine the libraries that are needed to support the DNS server software.

To collect information about a file system object, use the `/usr/bin/1dd` command.

CODE EXAMPLE 2-1 Obtaining Information About File System Objects

```
# ldd /usr/sbin/in.named
libresolv.so.2 => /usr/lib/libresolv.so.2
libsocket.so.1 => /usr/lib/libsocket.so.1
libnsl.so.1 =>    /usr/lib/libnsl.so.1
libc.so.1 =>      /usr/lib/libc.so.1
libdl.so.1 =>     /usr/lib/libdl.so.1
libmp.so.2 =>     /usr/lib/libmp.so.2
/usr/platform/SUNW,Ultra-5_10/lib/libc_psr.so.1
```

To collect the information from a running process, use the `/usr/proc/bin/pldd` command (available on Solaris 8 OE and newer versions).

CODE EXAMPLE 2-2 Collecting Information From a Running Process

```
# pldd 20307
20307:  /usr/sbin/in.named
/usr/lib/libresolv.so.2
/usr/lib/libsocket.so.1
/usr/lib/libnsl.so.1
/usr/lib/libc.so.1
/usr/lib/libdl.so.1
/usr/lib/libmp.so.2
/usr/platform/sun4u/lib/libc_psr.so.1
/usr/lib/dns/dnssafe.so.1
/usr/lib/dns/cylink.so.1
```

Note that the `pldd` command shows the shared libraries that are loaded dynamically by the application, in addition to those against which the application is linked. This information can also be gathered using the following `truss` command.

Note – The following output is truncated for brevity.

CODE EXAMPLE 2-3 Identifying Dynamically Loaded Applications

```
# truss -f -topen,open64 /usr/sbin/in.named
20357:   open("/usr/lib/libresolv.so.2", O_RDONLY)        = 3
20357:   open("/usr/lib/libsocket.so.1", O_RDONLY)        = 3
20357:   open("/usr/lib/libnsl.so.1", O_RDONLY)           = 3
20357:   open("/usr/lib/libc.so.1", O_RDONLY)             = 3
20357:   open("/usr/lib/libdl.so.1", O_RDONLY)            = 3
20357:   open("/usr/lib/libmp.so.2", O_RDONLY)            = 3
20357:   open("/usr/lib/nss_files.so.1", O_RDONLY)        = 4
20357:   open("/usr/lib/nss_files.so.1", O_RDONLY)        = 4
20357:   open("/usr/lib/dns/dnssafe.so.1", O_RDONLY)      = 4
20357:   open("/usr/lib/dns/cylink.so.1", O_RDONLY)       = 4
20357:   open("/usr/lib/dns/sparcv9/cylink.so.1", O_RDONLY) = 4
```

This version of the output contains the process identifier, the system call (in this case open) and its arguments, as well as the system call's return value. Using the return value, it is clear when the system call is successful in finding and opening the shared library.

Also note that once the list of shared libraries are well known, it is trivial to determine the Solaris OE packages to which they belong. This task is done using the following command.

```
# grep '/usr/lib/dns/cylink.so.1' /var/sadm/install/contents
/usr/lib/dns/cylink.so.1 f none 0755 root bin 63532 24346 \
   1018126408 SUNWcsl
```

From the resulting output, it is clear that this shared library belongs to the SUNWcsl (Core, Shared Libs) package. This process is especially useful when performing platform minimization, because this process helps to identify the packages that are required to support an application or service.

Configuration Files

Another way to gather requirements is through configuration files. This process has a more direct impact on how a system is hardened, because configuration files can be renamed or removed to disable services. For more information, refer to Chapter 13, "This variable defines the approach used by the Solaris Security Toolkit software to disable services that are started from run-control scripts. For Solaris OE versions 9 and newer, this variable is assigned the default value of conf, whereas all earlier releases default to the value of script." on page 304.

To determine if a configuration file is in use, employ the same technique shown earlier (the truss command).

Note – The following output is truncated for brevity.

CODE EXAMPLE 2-4   Determining if a Configuration File is In Use

```
# truss -f -topen,open64 /usr/sbin/in.named 2>&1 | \
grep -v "/usr/lib/.*.so.*"
20384:  open("/etc/resolv.conf", O_RDONLY)                = 3
20384:  open("/dev/conslog", O_WRONLY)                    = 3
20384:  open("/usr/share/lib/zoneinfo/US/Eastern", O_RDONLY) = 4
20384:  open("/var/run/syslog_door", O_RDONLY)            = 4
20384:  open("/etc/nsswitch.conf", O_RDONLY)              = 4
20384:  open("/etc/services", O_RDONLY)                   = 4
20384:  open("/etc/protocols", O_RDONLY)                  = 4
20384:  open("/etc/named.conf", O_RDONLY)                 = 4
20384:  open("named.ca", O_RDONLY)                        = 5
20384:  open("named.local", O_RDONLY)                     = 5
20384:  open("db.192.168.1", O_RDONLY)                    = 5
20384:  open("db.internal.net", O_RDONLY)                 = 5
```

In this case, it is clear that the DNS service is using configuration files such as /etc/named.conf. As with the previous example, if a service has a return value indicating an error, that might be an indication of a problem. Carefully documenting the results both before and after hardening can help to speed the entire validation process.

Service Frameworks

This category includes frameworks or meta-services on which larger, more complex applications are built. The types of frameworks typically found in this category are naming services (for example, NIS, NIS+, and LDAP), authentication services (for example, Kerberos and LDAP), and services such as port mapper used by the RPC facility.

The fact that an application depends on these types of services might not always be clear. When special adjustments are needed to configure an application such as to add it to a Kerberos realm, the dependency is known. There are cases, however, where application dependencies do not require any added tasks and the actual dependency might not be documented by the vendor.

One such example is the RPC port mapper. By default, the Solaris Security Toolkit software disables the RPC port mapper from starting. This action may cause unexpected behavior in services relying on this service. Based on past experiences, services abort, hang, or fail depending on how well the application's code is written to handle exception cases. To determine if an application is using the RPC port mapper, use the `rpcinfo` command. For example:

CODE EXAMPLE 2-5   Determining Applications That Use RPC

```
# rpcinfo -p
100000    3    tcp     111    rpcbind

100000    4    udp     111    rpcbind

100000    2    udp     111    rpcbind

100024    1    udp    32777   status

100024    1    tcp    32772   status

100133    1    udp    32777

100133    1    tcp    32772

100021    1    udp    4045    nlockmgr

100021    2    udp    4045    nlockmgr

100021    3    udp    4045    nlockmgr

100021    4    udp    4045    nlockmgr

100021    1    tcp    4045    nlockmgr
```

Note that the service column is populated with information from the /etc/rpc file and/or a configured naming service such as LDAP.

If this file does not have an entry for a service, as is often the case for third-party products, the service field might be empty, thereby making it more difficult to identify applications registered by other applications.

For example, consider the `rusers` command. This command relies on the RPC port mapping service. If the RPC port mapper is not running, the `rusers` command appears to hang. The program eventually times out with the following error message:

```
# rusers -a localhost
localhost: RPC: Rpcbind failure
```

This problem occurs because the program cannot communicate with the service. After starting the RPC port mapping service from /etc/init.d/rpc, however, the program immediately yields its result.

As another example, consider the case where the RPC port mapping service is running, and the `rusers` service is not configured to run. In this case, a completely different response is generated, and it is relatively straightforward to validate.

CODE EXAMPLE 2-6   Validating `rusers` Service

```
# rusers -a localhost
localhost: RPC: Program not registered
# grep rusers /etc/rpc
rusersd          100002   rusers
# rpcinfo -p | grep rusers
<No output generated>
```

Given that the `rpcinfo` command does not have a registry for the `rusers` service, it is safe to assume that the service is not configured to run. This assumption is validated by looking at the service entry in the /etc/inet/inetd.conf.

```
# grep rusers /etc/inet/inetd.conf
# rusersd/2-3   tli     rpc/datagram_v,circuit_v         wait root /
usr/lib/netsvc/rusers/rpc.rusersd      rpc.rusersd
```

The comment mark (#) at the beginning of the service line indicates that the `rusers` service is disabled. To enable the service, simply uncomment the line and send a SIGHUP signal to the `/usr/sbin/inetd` process as follows.

```
# pkill -HUP inetd
```

Note – The `pkill` command is only available in Solaris OE versions 7 and newer. For other versions, use the combination of `ps` and `kill` commands respectively to find and signal the process.

Another way to determine if an application uses the RPC facility is to use the `ldd` command described earlier.

CODE EXAMPLE 2-7   Alternative Method for Determining Applications That Use RPC

```
# ldd /usr/lib/netsvc/rusers/rpc.rusersd
libnsl.so.1 =>     /usr/lib/libnsl.so.1
librpcsvc.so.1 =>            /usr/lib/librpcsvc.so.1
libc.so.1 =>       /usr/lib/libc.so.1
libdl.so.1 =>      /usr/lib/libdl.so.1
libmp.so.2 =>      /usr/lib/libmp.so.2
/usr/platform/SUNW,Ultra-250/lib/libc_psr.so.1
```

Note the entry for "`librpcsvc.so.1`." This entry is a clear indication, with the file name, that this service does rely on the RPC port mapping service.

In addition to the RPC port mapper, applications may rely on other common OS services such as FTP, SNMP, or NFS. You can use similar techniques to debug these services and to determine if they are actually needed to support a business function. One simple method involves the use of the `netstat` command as follows.

```
# netstat -a | egrep "ESTABLISHED|TIME_WAIT"
```

This command returns a list of services that are or were recently in use, for example.

TABLE 2-1 Listing Services Recently In Use

localhost.32827 ESTABLISHED	localhost.32828	49152	0 49152	0
localhost.35044 ESTABLISHED	localhost.32784	49152	0 49152	0
localhost.32784 ESTABLISHED	localhost.35044	49152	0 49152	0
localhost.35047 ESTABLISHED	localhost.35046	49152	0 49152	0
localhost.35046 ESTABLISHED	localhost.35047	49152	0 49152	0
filefly.ssh 192.168.0.3.2969	17615	1 50320	0 ESTABLISHED	

In this case, it is clear that there are many services in use, but it is unclear which ports are owned by which services or applications. This information can be collected, albeit by brute force, by inspecting the processes using the pfiles command (available on Solaris OE versions 8 and newer).

CODE EXAMPLE 2-8 Determining Which Ports Are Owned by Services or Applications

```
# for pid in `ps -aeo pid | grep -v PID`; do
> pfiles ${pid} | egrep "^${pid}:|sockname:"
> done
```

A much more effective and efficient way to determine these dependencies is by using the lsof (list open files) program. This program determines which processes are using which files and ports. For example, to determine what is using port 35047 from the previous example, use the following command.

CODE EXAMPLE 2-9 Determining Which Processes are Using Files and Ports

```
# ./lsof -i | grep 35047
ttsession   600 root 9u  IPv4 0x3000b4d47e8    0t1  TCP
localhost:35047->localhost:35046 (ESTABLISHED)
dtexec    5614 root 9u  IPv4 0x3000b4d59e8    0t0  TCP
localhost:35046->localhost:35047 (ESTABLISHED)
```

The output of lsof indicates that port 35047 is in use for communication between the dtexec and ttsession processes.

Using the lsof program, you may be able to more rapidly determine intersystem or interapplication dependencies that require file system or network usage. Nearly everything that is addressed in this section can be captured using various options of the lsof program.

To obtain the lsof program, download it from:

    ftp://vic.cc.purdue.edu/pub/tools/unix/lsof/

Note – The methods described for determining dependencies might not find those items that are rarely used; therefore, we recommend that in addition to using these methods, review documentation and vendor documentation.

Developing and Implementing a Solaris Security Toolkit Profile

After you complete the planning and preparation phase, develop and implement a security profile. A security profile consists of a hardening driver, for example, *name*-hardening.driver, and all related drivers, scripts, and files to implement your site-specific security policies.

Customize one of the security profiles provided with the Solaris Security Toolkit software, or develop your own. Although some users implement one of the standard profiles as is, we recommend that you at least customize one of the standard security profiles provided with the software. Each organization's policies, standards, and application requirements differ, even if only slightly.

To customize a security profile, adjust its actions through finish scripts, audit scripts, environment variables, framework functions, and file templates.

Refer to the following chapters for more information:

For important guidelines about customizing the software, refer to Chapter 1, "Configuring and Customizing the Solaris Security Toolkit Software" on page 15.

For an example scenario where a security profile is created, refer to Chapter 7, "Creating a Security Profile" on page 110.

For information about customizing drivers, refer to Chapter 10.

As needed, refer to the other applicable chapters for information about scripts, framework functions, environment variables, and files.

Two key environment variables you might want to customize are JASS_FILES and JASS_SCRIPTS. For detailed information, refer to Chapter 13.

If you need to enforce standards across a majority of platforms while still providing for platform-specific differences, you might want to employ a technique known as nested or hierarchical security profiles. For more information, refer to Chapter 10, "Customizing Drivers" on page 208.

It is important to compare the resulting security profile with the policies, standards, and requirements of your organization to ensure that changes are not inadvertently or erroneously made. It is always better to "measure twice and cut once." The same is true for profile development.

Installing the Software

The installation of the Solaris Security Toolkit software is the same for both deployed and new systems that are being installed. For detailed instructions, refer to Chapter 3.

For deployed systems, a few special cases exist that, if followed, can help to make this process simpler and faster. These cases are not directly focused on the hardening process, but are focused on pre-installation and post-installation tasks.

Perform Pre-Installation Tasks

Before hardening a deployed system, consider and plan two significant tasks: back up and verification. These tasks help to determine the state of the deployed system and to work out any potential configuration problems before the system is hardened.

Backing Up Data

This task focuses on contingency planning. In the event of a problem, it is necessary to ensure that the system's configuration and data are archived in some form. For this reason, it is necessary to back up the system, ensure that the backup media can be read, and validate that its contents can be restored. This precaution is a necessary and prudent step that should be executed prior to any significant change to a system's configuration.

Verifying System Stability

The verification task is nearly as important as the backup task. This task ensures that the system is in a stable and working state prior to the implementation of any configuration changes, such as those done by the hardening process. This verification process typically involves a reboot followed by the successful testing of any applications or services. While having a well-defined test and acceptance plan is recommended, documentation might not always be available. If such a plan is not available, test the system in a reasonable way based on how it is used. The goal of this effort is to ensure that the running configuration, in fact, matches the saved configuration.

If any error messages or warnings are displayed at either system boot or application start, they should be investigated and corrected, if possible. Otherwise, they should be logged so that during the hardening process they are not included as potential causes of problems. When looking at the log files, be sure to include system, service, and application logs such as:

```
/var/adm/messages
/var/adm/sulog
/var/log/syslog
/var/cron/log
```

This task is complete when you can restart the system without encountering errors or warning messages, or without encountering any unknown errors or warnings (all known ones are documented). Further, the system should restart to a known and stable state, ideally ready to offer its services. If, during the course of verification, you discover that the running and stored configuration of the system differs, it is strongly recommended that your organization revisit its change control policies and processes to identify the gap that leads to that condition.

Perform Post-Installation Tasks

The post-installation task is an extension of the pre-installation tasks. The goal is to ensure that the hardening process did not cause any new faults to the system or applications. This task is primarily conducted by reviewing system and application log files. Ideally, the log files created after hardening and the subsequent reboot are similar to those collected before the system was hardened. In some cases, there might be fewer messages, because there are fewer services started. Most importantly, there should be no new error or warning messages.

In addition to reviewing log files, test the functionality, because some applications might fail without generating a log entry. Refer to the following section for detailed information.

Verifying Application and Service Functionality

The final task in the process of securing a system involves verifying that the applications and services offered by the system are functioning correctly. Also, this task verifies that the security profile successfully implemented the requirements of the security policies. It is important that this task be done thoroughly and soon after the reboot of the hardened platform, to ensure that any anomalies or problems are detected and corrected immediately. This process is divided into two tasks: verifying security profile installation and verifying application and service functionality.

Verify Security Profile Installation

To verify that the Solaris Security Toolkit software installed the security profile correctly and without error, review the installation log file. This file is installed in `JASS_REPOSITORY/jass-install-log.txt`.

Note – This log file can be used as a reference to understand exactly what the Solaris Security Toolkit software did to a system. For each run on a system, there is a new log file stored in a directory based on the start time of the run.

In addition to verifying that the profile is installed, assess the security configuration of the system. This task can be accomplished through manual inspection or by using a tool to automate the process.

Verify Application and Service Functionality

The verification process for applications and services typically involves the execution of a well-defined test and acceptance plan. This plan is used to exercise the various components of a system or application to determine that they are in an available and working order. While using this type of plan is strongly recommended, it might not always be available. If such a plan is not available, test the system in a reasonable way based on how it is used. The goal of this effort is to ensure that the hardening process in no way affected the ability of applications or services to perform their functions.

If you discover that an application or service malfunctions after a system was hardened, determine the problem by reviewing the application log files. Also, in many cases, you can use the `truss` command to determine at what point an application is having difficulty. Once this is known, you can target the problem and trace it back to a change made by the Solaris Security Toolkit software.

Maintaining System Security

A common mistake that many organizations make is addressing security only during installation, then rarely or never revisiting it. Maintaining security is an ongoing process and must be reviewed and revisited periodically.

Maintaining a secure system requires vigilance, because the default security configuration for any system tends to become increasingly open over time. For example, system vulnerabilities become known. An in-depth coverage of ongoing system maintenance is beyond the scope of this guide. However, the following basic guidelines are offered to raise your awareness.

Keep in mind that Solaris OE patches might install additional software packages as part of their installation and could overwrite your system configuration files. Be sure to review the security posture of a system after, and ideally before, any patch installation is performed. Also, it's important to keep your systems updated with the latest patches.

The Solaris Security Toolkit software can assist you with applying patches, because it was built to support repetitive runs on a system, so that you can secure the system after installing patches. Run it after any patch installation, with the applicable drivers, to ensure that your configuration remains consistent with your defined security policies. Also, perform a manual review of the system, because the version of the Solaris Security Toolkit software being used might not support the new features added by the installed patches.

Monitor the system on an ongoing basis to ensure that unauthorized behavior is not taking place. Review system accounts, passwords, and access patterns; they can provide a great deal of information about what is being done on a system.

Deploy and maintain a centralized `syslog` repository to collect and parse `syslog` messages. A tremendous amount of information can be logged and valuable information obtained by gathering and reviewing these logs. We highly recommend that you observe this guideline.

Your organization needs to have a comprehensive vulnerability and audit strategy in place to monitor and maintain system configurations. This requirement is particularly important in the context of maintaining systems in secure configurations over time.

Periodically update your systems with the latest version of the Solaris Security Toolkit software.

The Solaris Security Toolkit software includes default security profiles for use as a starting point.

## CHAPTER 3

Installing and Running Security Software

This chapter provides instructions for downloading, installing, and running the Solaris Security Toolkit software and other security-related software. Included are instructions for configuring your environment for either standalone or JumpStart mode, and obtaining support. Also in this chapter is a fast-track approach for users who want to quickly install and run the Solaris Security Toolkit software.

This chapter contains the following topics:

Obtaining Support

The configurations for Sun systems implemented by the Solaris Security Toolkit software are Sun supported configurations. Support calls to Sun's support services are handled the same as other cases.

Note – The Solaris Security Toolkit software itself is not a supported Sun product. Sun's support services cannot accept calls about the Solaris Security Toolkit's scripts.

To obtain Solaris Security Toolkit software assistance and to submit bug reports, questions, suggestions, and feedback, please use the Solaris Security Toolkit Support Forum at the following Web site:

```
http://supportforum.sun.com/cgi-bin/WebX.cgi?/
security.jass.toolkit
```

Feedback on how the Solaris Security Toolkit software works and words of encouragement to the developers are appreciated.

Taking the Recommended Track

We *highly* recommend that you follow the instructions and process provided in this section to install, configure, and execute the software. By following the recommended approach, you'll be guided through the process, including downloading additional security software, with detailed instructions, helpful examples, and useful recommendations.

Although the Solaris Security Toolkit software is a standalone product, it is most effective when used with the additional security software we recommend and provide for downloading. This software includes the latest Recommended and Security Patch Cluster from SunSolve OnLine, Secure Shell software for Solaris OE releases that do not include it, permission and ownership modification software to tighten Solaris OE and third-party software permissions, and integrity validation binaries to validate the integrity of Sun files and executables.

This section contains the following tasks:

"Perform Planning and Pre-Installation Tasks" on page 41

"Determine Which Mode to Use" on page 42

"Download Security Software" on page 43

"Customize Security Profiles" on page 51

"Install and Execute the Software" on page 51

"Validate the System Modifications" on page 61

Perform Planning and Pre-Installation Tasks

Proper planning is key to successfully using the Solaris Security Toolkit software to secure systems. Refer to Chapter 2 for detailed information about planning and other tasks recommended before you install the software.

If you are installing the software on a deployed system, refer to Chapter 2, "Perform Pre-Installation Tasks" on page 33, for information about performing pre-installation tasks to install the software on deployed systems.

Determine Which Mode to Use

We recommend that you harden systems either during or immediately after installation, to limit the period a system might be exposed to attack while in an unsecured state. Before using the Solaris Security Toolkit software to secure a system, configure the Solaris Security Toolkit software to run properly in your environment.

The Solaris Security Toolkit software has a modular framework. For customers not yet using the JumpStart product, the flexibility of the Solaris Security Toolkit software's framework allows them to efficiently prepare for using JumpStart later. Customers with existing JumpStart installations benefit from the Solaris Security Toolkit software's ability to integrate into existing JumpStart architectures.

The following sections describe each mode.

Standalone Mode

The Solaris Security Toolkit software runs directly from a Solaris OE shell prompt in standalone mode. The standalone mode allows you to use the Solaris Security Toolkit software on systems that require security modifications or updates, yet cannot be taken out of service to re-install the OS from scratch. Ideally, however, we recommend that systems be reinstalled from scratch to secure them.

Standalone mode is particularly useful when hardening a system after installing patches. You can run the Solaris Security Toolkit software multiple times on a system with no ill effects. Patches might overwrite or modify files the Solaris Security Toolkit software has modified; by rerunning the Solaris Security Toolkit software, any security modifications undone by the patch installation can be reimplemented.

Note – In production environments, we recommend that patches always be staged in test and development environments before installation in live environments.

The standalone mode is one of the best options to harden a deployed system as quickly as possible. No special steps are required to integrate the Solaris Security Toolkit software into a non-JumpStart architecture, other than those provided in the downloading and installing instructions provided in "Download Security Software" on page 43.

JumpStart Mode

JumpStart technology, which is Sun's network-based Solaris OE installation mechanism, can run Solaris Security Toolkit scripts during the installation process. This book assumes that the reader is familiar with JumpStart technology and has an existing JumpStart environment available. For more information about JumpStart technology, refer to the Sun BluePrints book *JumpStart™ Technology: Effective Use in the Solaris™ Operating Environment*.

For use in a JumpStart environment, the Solaris Security Toolkit source in either the JASS_HOME_DIR (for tar downloads) or /opt/SUNWjass (for pkg downloads) has to be copied into the base directory of the JumpStart server. Typically, this is /jumpstart on the JumpStart server. After this task is done, JASS_HOME_DIR becomes the base directory of the JumpStart server.

Only a few steps are required to integrate the Solaris Security Toolkit software into a JumpStart architecture. Refer to Chapter 5 for instructions on how to configure a JumpStart Server.

Download Security Software

The first stage in hardening a system requires downloading additional software security packages onto the system you want to secure. This section covers the following tasks:

"Downloading Solaris Security Toolkit Software" on page 44

"Downloading Recommended Patch Cluster Software" on page 45

"Downloading FixModes Software" on page 47

"Downloading OpenSSH Software" on page 48

"Downloading the MD5 Software" on page 50

Note – Of the software described in this section, the Solaris Security Toolkit software, Recommended and Security Patch Cluster, FixModes, and MD5 software are strongly recommended. Instead of OpenSSH, you can substitute a commercial version of Secure Shell, available from a variety of vendors. We strongly recommend that you install and use a Secure Shell product on all systems. With the release of Solaris 9 OE, a version of Solaris Secure Shell is included. If using Solaris 9 OE, we strongly recommend using this Secure Shell version.

Downloading Solaris Security Toolkit Software

The Solaris Security Toolkit software must be downloaded first, then installed on either the server on which you are using the Solaris Security Toolkit software in standalone mode or on a JumpStart server for JumpStart mode.

The primary function of the Solaris Security Toolkit software is to automate and simplify building secured Solaris OE systems based on the recommendations contained in this guide and security-related Sun BluePrints OnLine articles.

Note – The following instructions use filenames that do not reference the version number. Always download the latest version available from the Web site.

Throughout the rest of this guide, the JASS_HOME_DIR environment variable refers to the root directory of the Solaris Security Toolkit software. When the Solaris Security Toolkit software is installed from the tar archive, JASS_HOME_DIR is defined to be the path up to, and including, jass-*n.n*. If you install the tar version of the distribution in the /opt directory, the JASS_HOME_DIR environment variable is defined as /opt/jass-*n.n*.

The Solaris Security Toolkit software is distributed in Solaris OE package format, in addition to the traditional compressed tar archive. The same software is included in both archives.

Choose the format most appropriate for your situation. Typically, the pkg format is best for clients and the tar is best for JumpStart systems and for developing custom packages.

Procedures for downloading and installing these two different archive types are provided in the following sections.

To Download the tar Version

1. **Download the software distribution file** (jass-*n.n*.tar.Z).

   The source file is located at the following Web site:

   http://www.sun.com/security/jass

2. **Extract the software distribution file into a directory on the server using the** zcat **and** tar **commands as shown**:

   ```
   # zcat jass-n.n.tar.Z | tar xvf -
   ```

   Where *n.n* is the most current version that you are downloading.

Executing this command creates the `jass-`*n.n* subdirectory in the current working directory. This subdirectory contains all the Solaris Security Toolkit directories and associated files.

To Download the `pkg` Version

1. **Download the software distribution file (**`SUNWjass-`*n.n*`.pkg.Z`**).**

   The source file is located at:

   `http://www.sun.com/security/jass`

Note – If you encounter difficulty downloading the software, use your browser's integrated Save As option.

---

2. **Extract the software distribution file into a directory on the server by using the** `uncompress` **command:**

   ```
   # uncompress SUNWjass-n.n.pkg.Z
   ```

3. **Install the software distribution file into a directory on the server using the** `pkgadd` **command as shown:**

   ```
   # pkgadd -d SUNWjass-n.n.pkg SUNWjass
   ```

   Where *n.n* is the most current version that you are downloading.

   Executing this command creates the `SUNWjass` directory in `/opt/jass-`*n.n*. This subdirectory contains all the Solaris Security Toolkit directories and associated files.

Downloading Recommended Patch Cluster Software

Patches are released by Sun to provide Solaris OE fixes for performance, stability, functionality, and security. It is critical to the security of a system that the most up-to-date patch cluster is installed. To ensure that the latest Solaris OE Recommended and Security Patch Cluster is installed on your system, this section describes how to download the latest patch cluster.

Note – Apply standard best practices to all patch cluster installations. Before installing any patches, evaluate and test them on nonproduction systems or during scheduled maintenance windows.

To Download Recommended Patch Cluster Software

Before you install a patch cluster, we recommend that you review individual patch README files and other information provided. The information often contains suggestions and information helpful to know before installing a patch cluster.

1. **Download the latest patch cluster from the SunSolve OnLine Web site at:**

   `http://sunsolve.sun.com`

2. **Click on the Patches link at the top of the left navigation bar.**

3. **Click on the Recommended and Security Patches link.**

   The license agreement is displayed.

4. **Select the appropriate Solaris OE version in the Recommended Solaris Patch Clusters box.**

   In our example, we select Solaris 8 OE.

5. **Select the best download option, either HTTP or FTP, with the associated radio button, then click Go.**

   A Save As dialog box is displayed in your browser window.

6. **Save the file locally.**

7. **Move the file securely to the system being hardened by using the** `scp` **command, or another method that provides secure file transfer.**

   The `scp` command used should be similar to the following:

```
# scp 8_Recommended.zip target01:
```

8. **Move the file to the** `/opt/SUNWjass/Patches` **directory and uncompress it.**

For example:

CODE EXAMPLE 3-1   Moving a Patch File to `/opt/SUNWjass/Patches` Directory

```
# cd /opt/SUNWjass/Patches
# mv /<directory in which file was saved>/8_Recommended.zip .
# unzip 8_Recommended.zip
Archive:      8_Recommended.zip
   creating: 8_Recommended/
  inflating: 8_Recommended/CLUSTER_README
  inflating: 8_Recommended/copyright
  inflating: 8_Recommended/install_cluster
[. . .]
```

Later, the patch cluster software is installed automatically after downloading all the other security packages and executing the Solaris Security Toolkit software.

Note – If you do not place the Recommended and Security Patch Cluster software into the `/opt/SUNWjass/Patches` directory, a warning message displays when you execute the Solaris Security Toolkit software. You can safely ignore this message if no patch clusters apply, as is often the case with new releases of the OS.

Downloading FixModes Software

FixModes is a software package that tightens the default Solaris OE directory and file permissions. Tightening these permissions can significantly improve overall security. More restrictive permissions make it even more difficult for malicious users to gain privileges on a system.

Note – With the Solaris 9 OE release, changes were made to improve the default permissions of objects previously altered by the FixModes software. However, the FixModes software is still necessary, because third-party and unbundled software typically requires tightening of file and directory permissions.

To Download FixModes Software

1. **Download the FixModes precompiled binaries from:**

   `http://www.sun.com/blueprints/tools/FixModes_license.html`

   The FixModes software is distributed as a precompiled and compressed package version file formatted for Solaris OE systems. The file name is `SUNBEfixm.pkg.Z`.

2. **Once downloaded, move the file securely to the system being hardened by using the `scp` command, or another method that provides secure file transfer.**

   The `scp` command used should be similar to the following command:

   ```
   # scp SUNBEfixm.pkg.Z target01:
   ```

3. **Save the file, `SUNBEfixm.pkg.Z`, in the Solaris Security Toolkit `Packages` directory in `/opt/SUNWjass/Packages`, with the following commands:**

   ```
   # cd /opt/SUNWjass/Packages
   # mv /<directory in which file was saved>/SUNBEfixm.pkg.Z .
   ```

   Later, the FixModes software is installed automatically after downloading all the other security packages and executing the Solaris Security Toolkit software.

4. **Uncompress the `pkg` file with the following command:**

   ```
   # uncompress SUNWBEfixm.pkg.Z
   ```

Downloading OpenSSH Software

In any secured environment, the use of encryption in combination with strong authentication is required to protect user-interactive sessions. At a minimum, network access must be encrypted.

The tool most commonly used to implement encryption is Secure Shell software, whether a version bundled with the Solaris OE, a third-party commercial, or freeware version. To implement all the security modifications performed by the Solaris Security Toolkit software, you must include a Secure Shell software product.

Note – With the release of Solaris 9 OE, a version of Secure Shell is included. If using Solaris 9 OE, we strongly recommend using this Secure Shell version due to its integration with other Solaris OE security features such as the Basic Security Module (BSM) as well as its support by Sun's support organization.

Information on where to obtain commercial versions of Secure Shell is provided in the Preface under "Related Resources" on page xxix.

The Solaris Security Toolkit software disables all nonencrypted user-interactive services and daemons on the system, in particular daemons such as `in.telnetd`, `in.ftpd`, `in.rshd`, and `in.rlogind`.

Access to the system can be gained with Secure Shell similarly to what is provided by Telnet and FTP.

To Download OpenSSH Software

Note – If the server is running Solaris 9 OE, you can use the bundled Secure Shell software and skip the OpenSSH installation steps in this section.

Obtain the following Sun BluePrints OnLine article, and use the instructions in the article for downloading the software.

A Sun BluePrints OnLine article about how to compile and deploy OpenSSH titled "Building and Deploying OpenSSH on the Solaris Operating Environment" is available at:

  `http://www.sun.com/blueprints`

Or, obtain the Sun BluePrints publication *Secure Shell in the Enterprise*, which is available at book stores.

Later, the OpenSSH software is installed automatically after downloading all the other security packages and executing the Solaris Security Toolkit software.

Caution – Do not compile OpenSSH on the system being hardened and do not install the compilers on the system being hardened. Use a separate Solaris OE system—running the same Solaris OE version, architecture, and mode (for example, Solaris 8 OE, Sun4U™ (sun4u), and 64-bit)—to compile OpenSSH. If you implement a commercial version of SSH, then no compilation is required. The goal is to limit the availability of compilers to potential intruders. Understand, however, that refraining from installing compilers locally on a system does not provide significant protection against determined attackers, because they can still install pre-compiled tools.

Downloading the MD5 Software

The MD5 software generates MD5 digital fingerprints on the system being hardened. Generate the digital fingerprints, then compare them with what Sun has published as correct, to detect system binaries that are altered or *trojaned* (hidden inside something that appears safe) by unauthorized users. By modifying system binaries, attackers provide themselves with backdoor access onto a system; they hide their presence and could cause systems to operate in unstable manners.

To Download the MD5 Software

1. Download the MD5 binaries from the following web site:

    http://www.sun.com/blueprints/tools/md5_license.html

The MD5 programs are distributed as a compressed package version file.

2. Move the file SUNBEmd5.pkg.Z **securely to the system being hardened with the** scp **command, or another method that provides secure file transfer.**

The scp command used should be similar to the following command:

```
# scp SUNBEmd5.pkg.Z target01:
```

3. Move the file, SUNBEmd5.pkg.Z, **to the Solaris Security Toolkit** Packages **directory in** /opt/SUNWjass/Packages **with a command similar to the following:**

```
# cd /opt/SUNWjass/Packages
# mv /<directory in which file was saved>/SUNWBEmd5.Z .
```

After the MD5 software is saved to the /opt/SUNWjass/Packages directory, the execution of the Solaris Security Toolkit software installs the software.

After the MD5 binaries are installed, you can use them to verify the integrity of executables on the system through the Solaris fingerprint database. More information on the Solaris fingerprint database is available in the Sun BluePrints OnLine article titled "The Solaris™ Fingerprint Database - A Security Tool for Solaris Software and Files."

4. (Optional) Download and install Solaris Fingerprint Database Companion and Solaris Fingerprint Database Sidekick software from the Sun BluePrint Web site at:

    http://www.sun.com/blueprints/tools

We strongly recommend that you install these optional tools and use them with the MD5 software. These tools simplify the process of validating system binaries against the database of MD5 checksums. Use these tools frequently to validate the integrity of the Solaris OE binaries and files on a secured system.

These tools and instructions for downloading them are in the Sun BluePrints OnLine article titled "The Solaris™ Fingerprint Database - A Security Tool for Solaris Software and Files."

The integrity of the security tools downloaded should be verified. On the download page of the Solaris Security Toolkit, MD5 checksums are available for this purpose. Before installing and running the Solaris Security Toolkit software and additional security software, validate integrity through the use of MD5 checksums.

Customize Security Profiles

A variety of security profile templates are included with the Solaris Security Toolkit software distribution as drivers. As mentioned in the previous chapter, the default security profile and changes made by these drivers may not be appropriate for your systems. Typically, the security profiles implemented by these drivers are "high-water" marks for security. By this, we mean that they disable services that are not required, and they enable optional security features disabled by default.

Before running the Solaris Security Toolkit software, review and customize the default security profiles for your environment, or develop new ones. Techniques and recommendations for customizing security profiles are provided in Chapter 10.

Install and Execute the Software

It is important that the following preliminary tasks be completed prior to executing the Solaris Security Toolkit software. Most of the hardening is done automatically when you execute the Solaris Security Toolkit software.

Download the additional security software and the Solaris Security Toolkit software on the system you want to harden or on the JumpStart server. (Refer to "Download Security Software" on page 43.)

Configure your system for standalone or JumpStart mode. (Refer to "Determine Which Mode to Use" on page 42.)

If applicable, customize the Solaris Security Toolkit software for your environment.

Before installing and running the Solaris Security Toolkit software and additional security software, validate integrity through the use of MD5 checksums.

You can execute the Solaris Security Toolkit software directly from the command line or a JumpStart server.

For command line options and other information about executing the software, refer to one of the following:

"Executing the Software in Standalone Mode" on page 52

"Executing the Software in JumpStart Mode" on page 60

Executing the Software in Standalone Mode

Example command line usage in standalone mode:

```
# jass-execute [-r root_directory -p os_version ] [ -q | -o
output_file ] [ -m e-mail_address ] -d driver
```

TABLE 3-1 lists the command line options available and describes each.

TABLE 3-1   Using Command Line Options With `jass-execute`

Option	Description
-a	Determines if a system is in compliance with its security profile.
-d	Specifies the driver to be run in standalone mode.
-h	Displays the `jass-execute` help message, which provides an overview of the available options.
-H	Provides a simple mechanism to determine how many times the Solaris Security Toolkit software has been run on a system.
-l	Provides a mechanism to determine the most recent run.
-m	Mails output to an email address.
-o	Directs output to a file.
-q	Prevents the display of output to the screen. Also known as the quiet option.
-r	Specifies the root directory used during `jass-execute` runs.
-u	Runs undo option with interactive prompts that ask you what action you want to take when exceptions are encountered.

For detailed information about the options available with jass-execute command in standalone mode, refer to the following sections:

"Audit Option" on page 54

"Display Help Option" on page 55

"Driver Option" on page 55

"Email Notification Option" on page 56

"Execute History Option" on page 57

"Most Recent Execute Option" on page 57

"Output File Option" on page 58

"Quiet Output Option" on page 58

"Root Directory Option" on page 59

"Undo Option" on page 59

For a complete listing of available drivers, refer to the Drivers directory. Newer versions of the software may contain additional drivers.

To Execute the Software in Standalone Mode

1. **Execute the** secure.driver **(or a product specific script such as** sunfire_15k_sc-secure.driver**) as follows.**

   CODE EXAMPLE 3-2   Executing the Software in Standalone Mode

   ```
   # cd /opt/SUNWjass
   # ./jass-execute -d secure.driver
   [NOTE] Executing driver, secure.driver


   ================================================================
   secure.driver: Driver started.
   ================================================================


   ================================================================
   JASS Version:   4.0
   Node name:      ufudu
   Host ID:        8085816e
   Host address:   10.8.31.115
   MAC address:    8:0:20:85:81:6e
   OS version:     5.9
   Date:           Tue Dec 31 16:28:24 EST 2002
   ================================================================
   [...]
   ```

For a complete listing of available drivers, refer to the Drivers directory. Newer versions of the software may contain additional drivers.

2. **After running the Solaris Security Toolkit software on a system, reboot the system to implement the changes.**

   During hardening, a variety of modifications are made to the configuration of the client. These modifications could include disabling startup scripts for services, disabling options for services, and installing new binaries or libraries through patches. Until the client is restarted, these modifications might not be effective.

3. **After rebooting the system, verify the correctness and completeness of the modifications. (Refer to "Validate the System Modifications" on page 61.)**

4. **If any errors are encountered, fix them and run the Solaris Security Toolkit software again in standalone mode.**

Audit Option

Through the -a option, the Solaris Security Toolkit software can perform an audit run to determine if a system is in compliance with its security profile. This run validates not only if system file modifications made are still active, but also if previously disabled processes are running or removed software packages are reinstalled. For more information on this function, refer to Chapter 6.

Example usage to audit a system against a security profile:

```
# jass-execute -a driver [ -V verbosity ] [ -q | -o output_file ]
[ -m e-mail_address ]
```

Display Help Option

The -h option displays the jass-execute help message, which provides an overview of the available options.

The -h option produces output similar to the following:

CODE EXAMPLE 3-3   Sample -h Option Output

```
# ./jass-execute -h

To apply this Toolkit to a system, using the syntax:
   ./jass-execute [-r root_directory -p os_version ]
[ -q | -o output_file ] [ -m e-mail_address ] -d driver

To undo a previous application of the Toolkit from a system:
   ./jass-execute -u [ -n ] [ -q | -o output_file ]
[ -m e-mail_address ]

To audit a system against a pre-defined profile:
   ./jass-execute -a driver [ -V verbosity ]
[ -q | -o output_file ] [ -m e-mail_address ]

To display the history of Toolkit applications on a system:
   ./jass-execute -H

To display the last application of the Toolkit on a system:
   ./jass-execute -l

To display this help message:
   ./jass-execute -h
```

Driver Option

The -d <driver> option specifies the driver to be run in standalone mode.

You must specify a driver with the -d option. The Solaris Security Toolkit software prepends Drivers/ to the name of the script added. You need to enter only the script name on the command line.

Note – You cannot use the -d option with the -u, -H, -h, or -a options.

A `jass-execute` hardening run using the `-d <driver>` option produces output similar to the following:

CODE EXAMPLE 3-4 Sample `-d <driver>` Option Output

```
# ./jass-execute -d secure.driver
[NOTE] Executing driver, secure.driver


================================================================
secure.driver: Driver started.
================================================================


================================================================
JASS Version:   4.0
Node name:      ufudu
Host ID:        8085816e
Host address:   10.8.31.115
MAC address:    8:0:20:85:81:6e
OS version:     5.9
Date:           Tue Dec 31 16:28:24 EST 2002
================================================================
[...]
```

Email Notification Option

The `-m <email address>` option provides a mechanism by which standalone hardening and undo output can be emailed automatically by the Solaris Security Toolkit software when the run completes. The email report is in addition to any logs generated on the system using other options.

A Solaris Security Toolkit run calling `sunfire_15k_sc-config.driver` using the email option would be similar to the following:

```
# ./jass-execute -m root -d sunfire_15k_sc-config.driver
[...]
```

Execute History Option

The -H option provides a simple mechanism to determine how many times the Solaris Security Toolkit software has been run on a system. All runs are listed regardless of whether they have been undone.

The -H option produces output similar to the following:

CODE EXAMPLE 3-5   Sample -H Option Output

```
# ./jass-execute -H
Note: This information is only applicable for applications of
       the Solaris Security Toolkit starting with version 0.3.

The following is a listing of the applications of the Solaris
Security Toolkit on this system.  This list is provided in
reverse chronological order:

1.    December 31, 2002 at 12:20:19 (20021231122019) (UNDONE)
2.    December 31, 2002 at 12:10:29 (20021231121029)
3.    December 31, 2002 at 12:04:15 (20021231120415)
```

From the output, it is clear that the Solaris Security Toolkit software was run on this system three times and that the last run was undone.

Most Recent Execute Option

The -l option provides a mechanism to determine the most recent run. This is always the last run listed by the -H option as well.

The -l option provide outputs similar to the following:

CODE EXAMPLE 3-6   Sample -l Option Output

```
# ./jass-execute -l

Note: This information is only applicable for applications of
       the Solaris Security Toolkit starting with version 0.3.

The last application of the Solaris Security Toolkit was:

1.    December 31, 2002 at 12:20:19 (20021231122019) (UNDONE)
```

Output File Option

The `-o <output_file>` option redirects the console output of `jass-execute` runs to a separate file, `output_file`.

This option has no effect on the logs kept in the `JASS_REPOSITORY` directory. This option is particularly helpful when performed over a slow terminal connection, because there is a significant amount of output generated by a Solaris Security Toolkit run.

This option can be used with either the `-d`, `-u`, or `-a` options.

The `-o` option produces output similar to the following:

CODE EXAMPLE 3-7   Sample `-o` Option Output

```
# ./jass-execute -o jass-output.txt -d secure.driver
[NOTE] Executing driver, secure.driver
[NOTE] Recording output to jass-output.txt
```

Quiet Output Option

The `-q` option disables Solaris Security Toolkit output to standard input output (stdio) stream during a hardening run.

This option has no effect on the logs kept in the `JASS_REPOSITORY` directory. Similar to the `-o` option, this option is particularly helpful when running the Solaris Security Toolkit software through a cron job or over slow network connections.

This option can be used with either the `-d`, `-u`, or `-a` options.

The `-q` option produces output similar to the following:

CODE EXAMPLE 3-8   Sample `-q` Option Output

```
# ./jass-execute -q -d secure.driver
[NOTE] Executing driver, secure.driver
```

Root Directory Option

The -r <root directory> option is for specifying the root directory used during jass-execute runs. Using the -r option also requires using the -p option to specify the platform (OS) version. The format of the -p option is equivalent to that produced by uname -r.

By default, the root filesystem directory is /. This root directory is defined by the Solaris Security Toolkit environment variable JASS_ROOT_DIR. The Solaris OE being secured is available through /. For example, if you want to secure a separate OS directory, temporarily mounted under /mnt, then use the -r option to specify /mnt, and all the scripts are applied to that OS image.

Undo Option

Through the -u option, the Solaris Security Toolkit software can undo system modifications performed during hardening. Each finish script can be undone with the -u option. In addition, the Solaris Security Toolkit's undo ability is tightly integrated with the checksums generated during each run. For more information on this capability, refer to Chapter 4.

Example command line usage of an undo command:

```
# jass-execute -u [ -f | -b | -k] [ -q | -o output_file ] [ -m e-
mail_address ]
```

Executing the Software in JumpStart Mode

The JumpStart mode is controlled by the Solaris Security Toolkit driver inserted in the `rules` file on the JumpStart server.

If you have not configured your environment to use JumpStart mode, refer to Chapter 5.

For more information on the JumpStart technology, refer to the Sun BluePrint book *JumpStart™ Technology: Effective Use in the Solaris™ Operating Environment*.

To Execute the Software in JumpStart Mode

To execute the Solaris Security Toolkit software in JumpStart mode, it must be integrated into your JumpStart environment and called as part of the finish scripts associated with a JumpStart installation. For information about how to integrate the Solaris Security Toolkit software into your environment, refer to Chapter 5.

1. **After making all of the required modifications to the drivers, install the client using the JumpStart infrastructure.**

   This task is done using the following command from the client's ok prompt.

   ```
   ok> boot net - install
   ```

   Once the installation is completed, the system is rebooted by the JumpStart software.

   The system should be in its correct configuration. During hardening, a variety of modifications are made to the configuration of the client. These modifications could include disabling startup scripts for services, disabling options for services, and installing new binaries or libraries through patches. Until the client is restarted, these modifications might not be effective.

2. **After the system is rebooted, verify the correctness and completeness of the modifications. (Refer to "Validate the System Modifications" on page 61.)**

3. **If any errors are encountered, fix them and reinstall the client's OE.**

Validate the System Modifications

After rebooting the system, validate the correctness and completeness of the modifications as described in the following sections.

Performing QA Checks of Services

One of the significant challenges involved in securing systems is determining what OE services must be left enabled for the system to function properly. Solaris OE services might be needed because they are used directly, such as Secure Shell to log into a system. Or, they could be used indirectly, such as the Remote Procedure Call (RPC) daemon for the graphical user interface of third-party software management tools.

Most of these requirements should be determined before running the Solaris Security Toolkit software. (Refer to Chapter 2, "Determine Application and Service Requirements" on page 23.) However, the only definitive mechanism is to install and secure the system, then perform thorough testing of its required functionality through quality assurance (QA) testing. Ideally, there should be a QA plan in place for any new system being deployed. If so, this plan should be executed after the system is hardened. Similarly, for deployed systems being hardened, thorough testing must be performed to ensure that all required and expected functionality is present.

If the QA process uncovers any discrepancies, perform the following:

1. Determine the problem area, based on the recommendations in Chapter 2.

2. Validate that the application runs in the modified configuration.

3. Undo the Solaris Security Toolkit run.

4. Modify the security profile (driver), based on the problem resolution.

5. Run the Solaris Security Toolkit software again.

The end result should be a security profile that can be run on the system without adversely impacting any required functionality.

Performing Security Assessments of Configuration

While validating that the system performs all required functions, also evaluate the security configuration to determine if the system is secured to the desired level. Depending on what hardening or minimization was performed on the system, this may involve different aspects.

At a minimum, the configuration of the system should be reviewed in the following ways:

Ensure that all appropriate Security and Recommended Patches are installed.

Verify that only required and appropriate processes are running, and that they are running with the appropriate arguments.

Ensure that only required daemons are running, and that they are running with the appropriate arguments.

Verify that only required ports are open on the system by checking locally (for example, `netstat -a`) and remotely by using a port scanner such as Nmap, which can determine which ports are available on a network interface.

Make sure that only required Solaris OE packages were installed if the system was minimized.

This review should be considered a minimum for newly built and secured systems. When hardening legacy systems, the underlying OE should be verified to determine if unauthorized modifications were made. Integrity checking of this nature is best done by mounting the system's file system in read-only mode and running integrity checking software from a known OE instance. The tools described in the Sun BluePrints OnLine article titled "The Solaris™ Fingerprint Database - A Security Tool for Solaris Software and Files" are useful in these scenarios.

Validating Security Profile

After a system is secured and you validate its required services and capabilities, use the audit function to make sure that the security profile was applied properly and completely. This task is critical for two reasons. The first is to ensure that the system is hardened as required. The second is to ensure that the security profile defined for the system is properly reflected in the Solaris Security Toolkit configuration. This check is critical because the configuration information is used to maintain the security profile of the system over its entire deployed lifecycle.

For more information about the audit function, refer to Chapter 6.

Perform Post-installation Tasks

If you installed the software on a deployed system, refer to Chapter 2, "Perform Post-Installation Tasks" on page 34, for information about performing post-installation tasks on deployed systems.

Taking the Fast Track

This section provides a fast track approach to using the Solaris Security Toolkit software. Although we strongly recommend that you follow the standard methods presented in "Taking the Recommended Track" on page 41, we empathize with users who are terminally impatient and want to execute the Solaris Security Toolkit software immediately to see what happens. Review the following key considerations to determine if this characterization fits you:

The approach in this section assumes that you are willing to break things and are able to fix them.

Because there are potentially serious consequences that could result, it is important that you read and carefully consider the notes, cautions, and recommendations in this section.

Note – Only notes and cautions critical to successfully installing and configuring the Solaris Security Toolkit software are included in this section. Refer to "Taking the Recommended Track" on page 41 for complete information on configuring and executing the Solaris Security Toolkit software.

Evaluate your security policy and requirements against the default drivers before executing the Solaris Security Toolkit software.

We strongly recommend that you have console access.

A reboot is required for the changes to take affect.

If you run into problems with a hardening run, use the undo feature. For detailed information, refer to Chapter 4.

Note – The information in this section applies to using the Solaris Security Toolkit software in standalone mode only. For details on the differences between standalone mode and JumpStart mode, refer to "Determine Which Mode to Use" on page 42.

This section contains the following topics:

"Download Software" on page 64

"Install and Execute the Software" on page 66

Download Software

Note – The following instructions use filenames that do not reference the version number. Always download the latest version available from the Web site.

To Download the Solaris Security Toolkit Software

The Solaris Security Toolkit software is distributed in Solaris OE package format, in addition to the traditional compressed `tar` archive. The same software is included in both archives. Choose the format most appropriate for your scenario. Downloading and installing these two different archive types are addressed in the following procedures.

To Download the `pkg` Version

1. **Download the software distribution file** (`SUNWjass-n.n.pkg.Z`).

   The source file is located at:

   ```
   http://www.sun.com/blueprints/tools/license.html
   ```

2. **Extract the software distribution file into a directory on the server by using the** `uncompress` **command**:

   ```
   # uncompress SUNWjass-n.n.pkg.Z
   ```

3. **Install the software distribution file into a directory on the server using the** `pkgadd` **command as shown**:

   ```
   # pkgadd -d SUNWjass-n.n.pkg SUNWjass
   ```

   Executing this command creates the `SUNWjass` directory in `/opt`. This subdirectory contains all the Solaris Security Toolkit directories and associated files.

To Download the `tar` Version

1. Download the software distribution file (`jass-n.n.tar.Z`).

The source file is located at the following Web site:

```
http://www.sun.com/security/jass
```

2. Extract the software distribution file into a directory on the server using the `zcat` and `tar` commands as shown:

```
# zcat jass-n.n.tar.Z | tar xvf -
```

Where `n.n` is the most current version that you downloaded.

Executing this command creates the `jass-n.n` subdirectory in the current working directory. This subdirectory contains all the Solaris Security Toolkit directories and associated files.

Throughout the rest of this document, the `JASS_HOME_DIR` environment variable refers to the root directory of the Solaris Security Toolkit software. When the Solaris Security Toolkit software is installed from the `tar` archive, `JASS_HOME_DIR` is defined to be the path up to, and including, `jass-n.n`.

If you invoke the command from the `/opt` directory, then the `JASS_HOME_DIR` variable is defined as `/opt/jass-n.n`, where `n.n` is the Solaris Security Toolkit version.

To Download Additional Security Software

In "Taking the Recommended Track" on page 41, we provide instructions for downloading other security software. Of the software described, the Recommended and Security Patch Cluster, FixModes, and MD5 software are required. We strongly recommend that you use a Secure Shell product on the internal servers to protect user and administrative network traffic from disclosure, modification, and hijacking.

Refer to "Taking the Recommended Track" on page 41 for instructions if you want to download the additional security software at this time.

Install and Execute the Software

After you download the Solaris Security Toolkit software, install it on the server you are hardening in standalone mode.

The Solaris Security Toolkit software provides a default driver named `secure.driver` for automating the implementation of Solaris OE modifications and installation of security software. This default driver implements Solaris OE security modifications based on the recommendations in Sun BluePrint OnLine articles. Also, if you downloaded the additional security software, it performs the following tasks:

Installs the Recommended and Security Patch Cluster software

Installs and executes the FixModes software to tighten file system permissions

Installs the MD5 software

Note – During the modifications implemented in this section, all nonencrypted access mechanisms to the system being hardened—such as Telnet and FTP—are disabled. The hardening steps do not disable console access over serial ports, or directly attached video cards, monitors, and keyboards.

In addition to the default `secure.driver` driver, we provide product-specific drivers. You can use the default driver, use any of the product-specific drivers, or customize and create your own drivers. For more information, refer to Chapter 10.

To Install Downloaded Software and Implement Changes

Caution – A Solaris Security Toolkit standalone run, on a pre-existing system, should only be performed after the machine has been backed up and rebooted to verify that it is in a known, working, and consistent configuration. Any errors or warnings detected during this preliminary reboot should be corrected or noted.

---

1. **From the list of hardening drivers, choose the one that applies to your system and purpose.**

   For a complete and up-to-date listing of available drivers, download the most recent version of the Solaris Security Toolkit software from the following Web site:

   ```
   http://www.sun.com/security/jass
   ```

   Refer to Chapter 10 for information about standard and product-specific drivers. For the most current listing of drivers, refer to the `Drivers` directory.

   Caution – The following command executes all of the hardening scripts included in `secure.driver`. This action might not be appropriate for all environments. Evaluate which security modifications are required for your system before executing the Solaris Security Toolkit software.

   ---

2. **Execute the** `secure.driver` **(or a product-specific such as** `sunfire_15k_sc-secure.driver`**) as follows.**

   CODE EXAMPLE 3-9   Executing a Driver

   ```
   # cd /opt/SUNWjass
   # ./jass-execute -d sunfire_15k_sc-secure.driver
   [NOTE] Executing driver, sunfire_15k_sc-secure.driver


   ================================================================
   sunfire_15k_sc-secure.driver: Driver started.
   ================================================================


   ================================================================
   JASS Version:   4.0
   Node name:      ufudu
   Host ID:        8085816e
   Host address:   10.8.31.115
   MAC address:    8:0:20:85:81:6e
   OS version:     5.9
   Date:           Tue Dec 31 16:28:24 EST 2002
   ================================================================
   [...]
   ```

Note – The `secure.driver` disables all remote access capabilities, such as Telnet, RSH, and RLOGIN, with the exception of Secure Shell in the Solaris 9 OE. Do not reboot the system without at least one of those services being enabled, having serial or console access to the system, or having an alternate remote access mechanism available such as Secure Shell.

---

3. **After running the Solaris Security Toolkit software on a system, reboot the system to implement the changes.**

   During hardening, a variety of modifications are made to the configuration of the client. These modifications could include disabling startup scripts for services, disabling options for services, and installing new binaries or libraries through patches. Until the client is restarted, these modifications might not be effective.

4. **After rebooting the system, verify the correctness and completeness of the modifications. (Refer to "Validate the System Modifications" on page 61.)**

5. **If any errors are encountered, fix them and run the Solaris Security Toolkit software again.**

## CHAPTER 4

Reversing System Changes

This chapter provides information and procedures for reversing (undoing) the changes made by the Solaris Security Toolkit software during hardening runs. This option provides an automated mechanism by which you can return a system to its state prior to a Solaris Security Toolkit hardening run or sequence of runs.

This chapter contains the following topics:

Understanding How Changes Are Logged and Reversed

Each Solaris Security Toolkit hardening run creates a run directory in JASS_REPOSITORY. The names of these directories are based on the date and time the run is initiated. In addition to displaying the output to a screen, the Solaris Security Toolkit software creates a set of files in the directory to track the changes and log the operations.

The files stored in the directory track modifications performed on the system and enable the undo feature to work.

Caution – The contents of the files in the JASS_REPOSITORY should never be modified by an administrator.

When you use the Solaris Security Toolkit software to harden a system, either in JumpStart or standalone mode, the software logs the changes in the JASS_REPOSITORY/jass-manifest.txt file. This file is a list of operations that the undo feature uses to reverse changes. It contains information about the hardening operations implemented by the Solaris Security Toolkit software, including files created, copied, moved, or removed. In addition, this file may contain both standard and custom entries that are required when reversing more complex changes, such as software package installations. A separate jass-manifest.txt file is created for each hardening run.

Note – The Solaris Security Toolkit software undo feature only reverses changes for which there are entries in manifest files.

The undo run goes through the manifest files generated during a Solaris Security Toolkit run and stored in the JASS_REPOSITORY. It restores the backed-up files to their original locations. If files were not backed up, then the undo function is not available.

When a Solaris Security Toolkit run is undone, the associated directory is not removed. Instead, two files are created in the JASS_REPOSITORY directory: jass-undo-log.txt and reverse-jass-manifest.txt. Afterward, the run that was undone is not listed the next time jass-execute -u is executed. A hardening run can be undone only once.

Requirements for Undoing System Changes

Be aware of the following limitations and requirements for using the undo feature of the Solaris Security Toolkit software.

In Solaris Security Toolkit versions 0.3 and newer, you can use the undo feature for runs that were initiated in either standalone or JumpStart mode. However, you can undo changes only in standalone mode. The undo feature cannot be used during a JumpStart installation.

If the Solaris Security Toolkit option not to create backup files is selected, either through JumpStart or standalone modes, the undo feature is not available. (The creation of back-up file copies is disabled by setting the JASS_SAVE_BACKUP parameter to 0.)

A run can only be undone once.

If you develop a new finish script that does not use the Solaris Security Toolkit framework functions, you must create a matching audit script and add entries to the manifest file by using the add_to_manifest function. Otherwise, the Solaris Security Toolkit has no way of knowing about your custom development.

Do not modify the contents of the JASS_REPOSITORY directories under any circumstances. Modifying the files can corrupt the contents and cause unexpected errors or system corruption when you use the undo feature.

Customizing Scripts to Undo Changes

The Solaris Security Toolkit framework provides flexibility for designing and building finish scripts. The framework allows you to extend the capabilities of the Solaris Security Toolkit software to better meet the needs of your organization while also helping you to better manage the configuration of systems over their life cycles.

When customizing scripts, it is important to understand how the actions you take can affect the undo feature. To simplify customizing scripts, we provide helper functions that make the appropriate changes to the manifest files. (The undo feature relies on the contents of manifest files to reverse hardening runs.) In most cases, these helper functions provide what you need to customize scripts for your organization.

For a list of helper functions and information about using them, refer to Chapter 8. Use these helper functions in place of their system command counterparts, so that undo runs can reference the related entries in manifest files.

In some rare cases, you may need to perform a function for which there is not a helper function. In these cases, we strongly recommend that you use the special function called add_to_manifest. Using this function, you can manually insert entries into manifest files without needing to call one of the helper functions. Use this special function with care, so that you protect the integrity of the system and the Solaris Security Toolkit repository. An example of when you might use this special function is when you want to add software packages that are not in Sun's pkg format. In this example, you would need to tell the undo feature how to remove the packages that were added in another format during the hardening run.

With the helper functions and the special add_to_manifest function, the Solaris Security Toolkit software provides a simple and flexible way to customize scripts and have the changes extended to undo runs.

If you make changes to a finish script's behavior without using these functions, there is no way for the Solaris Security Toolkit software to know that a change was made. Therefore, you would have to manually undo any changes that are not referenced in manifest files.

Here's another example. Before modifying a file on the system, the original version of the file should first be saved. Outside the context of the Solaris Security Toolkit software, typically users accomplish this task by executing the /bin/cp command. However, within the context of the Solaris Security Toolkit software, if you use this command directly, the Solaris Security Toolkit software has no way of knowing that a manifest entry needs to be created. Instead of using the cp command, use the backup_file helper function. This function saves a copy of the original file, with a suffix of JASS_SUFFIX, and adds a manifest entry instructing the Solaris Security

Toolkit software that a copy of the file was made. Also, this function causes the file checksums to be calculated. File checksums are used both by the undo feature as well as the `jass-check-sum` command.

Checking for Files That Were Manually Changed

Although using the `jass-execute -u` command automatically checks for files that were changed manually after a hardening run, sometimes you might find it helpful to use the `jass-check-sum` command to list and review the files that have been changed.

This command allows you to review the contents of the `JASS_REPOSITORY` and perform checksums on all of the files listed in manifest files to determine which files listed have changed since their checksums were recorded during a hardening run. Performing this check before proceeding with a forced undo run provides valuable information that may save many hours of needless troubleshooting.

The following is an example output.

CODE EXAMPLE 4-1   Sample Output of Files That Were Manually Changed

```
# ./jass-check-sum

File Name               Saved CkSum           Current CkSum

- - - - - - - - - - - - - - - - - - - - - - - - - - - - - -

/etc/inet/inetd.conf    1643619259:6883       2801102257:6879

/etc/logadm.conf        2362963540:1042       640364414:1071

/etc/default/inetd      3677377803:719        2078997873:720
```

From the output, we see that three files were changed after the hardening run was completed.

Using Options With Undo

This section describes the jass-execute -u command and options that you can use when executing an undo run.

Note – You cannot use the -d, -a, -h, -l or -H options with the undo command.

The jass-execute -u command is the standard for executing an undo run. This command automatically discovers any files that were manually modified since the last hardening run. If the Solaris Security Toolkit software discovers files that were manually changed after a hardening run, it asks you to choose a response:

1. Back up the most current file before restoring the original (the one that existed before the hardening run).

2. Keep the most current file, and do not restore the original file.

3. Force an overwrite to any manually changed file (might loose data) and restore original file.

If you want to change the default undo behavior, use the -b, -k, and -f options when executing the undo command.

TABLE 4-1 lists command line options you can use with undo. For detailed information about each option, refer to the sections that follow.

TABLE 4-1 Using Command Line Options With Undo Command

Option	Description
-b	Backs up any files that have been manually changed since the last hardening run, then restores system to original state.
-f	Reverses changes made during a hardening run without asking you about exceptions, even if files were manually changed after a hardening run.
-k	Keeps any manual changes you made to files after a hardening run.
-m	Mails output to an email address.
-o	Directs output to a file.
-q	Prevents the display of output to the screen. Also known as the quiet option. Output is stored in JASS_REPOSITORY/jass-undo-log.txt.

Backup Option

The -b option automatically backs up any files that have been manually changed since the last hardening run, then restores the files to their original state prior to the hardening run. To implement the manual changes, you need to compare the restored files with the backed up files, and reconcile the differences manually. If a file is backed up using this option, it appears similar to the following example.

```
/etc/motd.BACKUP.<JASS_SUFFIX>
```

Force Option

The -f option reverses the changes made during a hardening run with no exceptions, even if files were manually changed after a hardening run. The undo run does not compare the saved file checksums to the current versions of the files. As a result, if you manually changed files after a hardening run, the changes would be overwritten and lost after the undo run.

It may be necessary to manually re-implement changes after the undo run completes. Furthermore, it may be necessary to reconcile differences between groups of files depending on the types of changes made. To help prevent these problems, use the jass-check-sum command or the -b command line option mentioned previously.

Keep Option

The -k option automatically keeps any manual changes you made to files after a hardening run instead of restoring the original files. The -k option discovers any mismatches in files, causes a notice to be generated and logged, and does not overwrite the file with the original. The only changes reversed are those for which the saved checksums in jass-checksums.txt file are valid.

This option is not without its drawbacks. For example, a system can be rendered into an inconsistent state if a subset of files modified by a finish script are later modified.

Consider the remove-unneeded-accounts.fin finish script. This script modifies both the /etc/passwd and /etc/shadow files on the system. If a user manually changes a password after a hardening run is finished, then the checksum associated with the /etc/shadow file does not match the value saved by the Solaris Security Toolkit software. As a result, if the keep option is used, then only the /etc/passwd file is copied back to its original state. The /etc/shadow file remains in its current form. The two files are no longer consistent.

Output File Option

The -o <*output_file*> option redirects the console output of jass-execute runs to a separate file, *output_file*.

This option has no affect on the logs kept in the JASS_REPOSITORY directory. This option is particularly helpful when performed over a slow terminal connection, because there is a significant amount of output generated by a Solaris Security Toolkit undo run.

Quiet Output Option

The -q option prevents the Solaris Security Toolkit software from displaying output to the screen. This option has no affect on the logs kept in the JASS_REPOSITORY directory. Similar to the -o option, this option is particularly helpful when running the Solaris Security Toolkit through a cron job or over slow network connections.

Email Notification Option

The -m <email address> option instructs the Solaris Security Toolkit software to e-mail a copy of the completed run to an email address. The email report is in addition to any logs generated on the system using other options.

Undoing System Changes

Sometimes it's necessary to reverse the changes made during one or multiple Solaris Security Toolkit hardening runs. If you find that the changes made during a hardening run have negatively impacted your system, undo the changes.

For example, if after a hardening run you discover that a required service such as NFS was disabled, undo the hardening run. Then, enable NFS and repeat the hardening run with the revised security profile.

This section provides instructions for reversing changes made during one or multiple hardening runs. Note that there are limitations and requirements for effectively reversing a hardening run. Refer to "Requirements for Undoing System Changes" on page 71.

To Undo a Solaris Security Toolkit Run

1. **Back up your system, then reboot it before performing an undo run.**

   We recommend that you always reboot and back up the system to ensure that it returns to or can be brought back to a known and working state.

2. **Determine which options you want to use with the** `jass-execute -u` **command. (Refer to "Using Options With Undo" on page 74.)**

   The following instructions assume that you are using the `jass-execute -u` command.

3. **To undo one or more hardening runs using the standard** `-u` **option, enter the following command from** `JASS_HOME_DIR`:

   ```
   # ./jass-execute -u
   ```

The Solaris Security Toolkit software collects information about each hardening run by finding all of the manifest files located in `JASS_REPOSITORY`. If a manifest file is empty or nonexistent, it is assumed that there are no changes to be undone and that run is omitted. In addition, if a file called `jass-undo-log.txt` exists in the same directory as the manifest file, it is assumed that the run has already been reversed, so that run is omitted. After the collection process is completed, the results are displayed. The following is an example output.

CODE EXAMPLE 4-2   Sample Output of Runs Available to Undo

```
# ./jass-execute -u
[NOTE] Executing driver, undo.driver
Please select a JASS run to restore through:
1. January 24, 2003 at 13:57:27 (/var/opt/SUNWjass/run/20030124135727)
2. January 24, 2003 at 13:44:18 (/var/opt/SUNWjass/run/20030124134418)
3. January 24, 2003 at 13:42:45 (/var/opt/SUNWjass/run/20030124134245)
4. January 24, 2003 at 12:57:30 (/var/opt/SUNWjass/run/20030124125730)

Choice? ('q' to exit)?
```

In this example, four separate hardening runs are found. These runs made changes to the system and have not been undone. The list of hardening runs is always presented in reverse chronological order. The first entry in the list is the most recent hardening run.

4. **Review the output to determine which run(s) you want to undo, then enter the corresponding number.**

For any entry selected, the Solaris Security Toolkit software reverses each run with an index number equal to or less than the value selected. That is, the undo run undoes the changes in the reverse order that they were originally made, starting with the most recent hardening run and continuing to the one you select. Using the previous example as a guide, if you select run 3, then the undo run first reverses changes for run 3, then moves on to reverse changes for run 2, then finishes by reversing changes to run 1.

The following example shows output generated when the undo run processes two manifest file entries.

CODE EXAMPLE 4-3 Sample Output of an Undo Run Processing Multiple Manifest File Entries

```
[...]


=================================================================
undo.driver: Performing UNDO of //var/opt/SUNWjass/run/
20030124135727.
=================================================================

[...]


=================================================================
undo.driver: Undoing Finish Script: update-cron-allow.fin
=================================================================

[NOTE] Undoing operation COPY.
cp -p /etc/cron.d/cron.allow.JASS.20030125223417
/etc/cron.d/cron.allow
rm -f /etc/cron.d/cron.allow.JASS.20030125223417

[NOTE] Removing a JASS-created file.
rm -f /etc/cron.d/cron.allow

[...]
```

In this example, the Solaris Security Toolkit software undoes a copy operation and removes a file that was added during the hardening run. The output of an undo run documents the actual commands that are taken to restore the system, so that the process can be clearly understood and referenced in case you need to troubleshoot a system's configuration.

The undo run continues until all runs and corresponding manifest files are processed and the changes reversed.

In addition to the Solaris Security Toolkit software collecting information about each hardening run by finding all of the manifest files located in JASS_REPOSITORY, the Solaris Security Toolkit software compares the checksum of each modified file. Any mismatches in the checksum files cause a notice to be generated and logged. For these files, the undo run asks you what action you want to take.

5. **If the undo run discovers an exception (a file that was manually changed after the hardening run), enter one of the options.**

The following is an example output showing an exception and the choices for handling the exception.

CODE EXAMPLE 4-4   Sample Output of Undo Exception

```
[...]


======================================================================
undo.driver: Undoing Finish Script: install-templates.fin
======================================================================

[NOTE] Undoing operation COPY.
cp -p /etc/skel/local.login.JASS.20030125223413
/etc/skel/local.login
rm -f /etc/skel/local.login.JASS.20030125223413

[NOTE] Undoing operation COPY.
[WARN] Checksum of current file does not match the saved value.
[WARN]     filename = /etc/.login
[WARN]     current = 3198795829:585, saved = 1288382808:584

Please select the course of action:

1. Backup.  Save current file before restoring original.
2. Keep.    Keep the current file, making no changes.
3. Force.   Ignore manual changes and overwrite current file.

Enter 1, 2, or 3:
```

In our example, if we choose item 1, the following output is displayed.

CODE EXAMPLE 4-5   Sample Output of Choosing Backup Option During Undo

```
Enter 1, 2, or 3: 1

[NOTE] BACKUP specified, creating backup copy of /etc/.login.
[NOTE] File to be backed up is from an undo operation.
[NOTE] Copying /etc/.login to /etc.login.BACKUP.JASS.20030125224926
cp -p /etc/.login.JASS.20030125223413 /etc/.login
rm -f /etc/.login.JASS.20030125223413

[...]
```

Take appropriate action regarding files that were manually modified after any hardening runs.

When an undo run encounters modified files and you choose to not overwrite them, reconcile these before rebooting the system.

Note – In our example, the file that was modified is saved with the new name: `/etc/.login.BACKUP.JASS.20030125224926`. After the undo run is complete, we would compare that file to `/etc/.login` to determine if any further reconciliation is needed.

---

6. **Reconcile any exceptions.**

   We strongly recommend that you reconcile all exceptions before continuing.

7. **After reconciling any exceptions, reboot the system.**

   Rebooting the system is necessary for the system to provide services available before it was hardened. The reboot is necessary because the Solaris Security Toolkit software neither stops running processes nor restarts them when you perform undo runs.

## CHAPTER 5

Configuring and Managing JumpStart Servers

This chapter provides information for configuring and managing JumpStart servers to use the Solaris Security Toolkit software. JumpStart technology, which is Sun's network-based Solaris OE installation mechanism, can run Solaris Security Toolkit software during the installation process.

The Solaris Security Toolkit's JumpStart mode is based on JumpStart technology, available for the Solaris OE product since version 2.1. JumpStart technology helps you manage complexity by fully automating the Solaris OE and system software installation, facilitating the correctness and standardization of systems. It provides a way to meet the requirements of rapidly installing and deploying systems.

The advantages of using JumpStart technology are apparent in the area of system security. By using JumpStart technology with the Solaris Security Toolkit software, you can secure systems during automated Solaris OE installations. This practice helps ensure that system security is standardized and addressed at the time of system installation. For more information about JumpStart technology, refer to the Sun BluePrints book *JumpStart™ Technology: Effective Use in the Solaris™ Operating Environment*.

This chapter contains the following topics:

Configuring JumpStart Servers and Environments

For use in a JumpStart environment, the Solaris Security Toolkit source in either the JASS_HOME_DIR (for tar downloads) or /opt/SUNWjass (for pkg downloads) has to be copied into the base directory of the JumpStart server. Typically, this is /jumpstart on a JumpStart server. After this task is done, JASS_HOME_DIR becomes the base directory of the JumpStart server.

This section assumes that the reader is familiar with JumpStart technology and has an existing JumpStart environment available.

Only a few steps are required to integrate the Solaris Security Toolkit software into a JumpStart architecture.

To Configure for JumpStart Mode

1. **Copy the Solaris Security Toolkit source into the root directory of the JumpStart server.**

   For example, if the Solaris Security Toolkit archive was extracted to JASS_REPOSITORY, and the JumpStart server root directory is /jumpstart, the following command copies the Solaris Security Toolkit source:

   ```
   # pwd
   /opt/SUNWjass
   # tar cf - . | (cd /jumpstart; tar xf -)
   ```

   Typically, the Solaris Security Toolkit software is installed in the SI_CONFIG_DIR of the JumpStart server, which would normally also be JASS_HOME_DIR.

2. **If you make any modifications to the Solaris 2.5.1 OE** sysidcfg **file, make them to the one in the** JASS_HOME_DIR/Sysidcfg/Solaris_2.5.1 **directory.**

   If you are using Solaris 2.5.1 OE, the sysidcfg file in JASS_HOME_DIR/Sysidcfg/ Solaris_2.5.1 cannot be used directly because this version of Solaris only supports sysidcfg files in SI_CONFIG_DIR and not in separate subdirectories. To address this limitation on Solaris 2.5.1 OE, the Solaris Security Toolkit software has SI_CONFIG_DIR/sysidcfg, which is linked to the JASS_HOME_DIR/Sysidcfg/ Solaris_2.5.1/sysidcfg file.

3. **Copy the** `JASS_HOME_DIR/Drivers/user.init.SAMPLE` **to** `JASS_HOME_DIR/Drivers/user.init` **with the following command:**

```
# pwd
/jumpstart/Drivers
# cp user.init.SAMPLE user.init
```

4. **If you experience problems with a multihomed JumpStart server, modify the two entries for** `JASS_PACKAGE_MOUNT` **and** `JASS_PATCH_MOUNT` **to the correct path to the** `JASS_HOME_DIR/Patches` **and** `JASS_HOME_DIR/Packages` **directories.**

5. **If you want to install the Solaris Security Toolkit software under a subdirectory of** `SI_CONFIG_DIR`, **such as** `SI_CONFIG_DIR/path/to/JASS`, **then add the following to the** `user.init` **file:**

```
if [ -z "${JASS_HOME_DIR}" ] ; then
    if [ "${JASS_STANDALONE}" = 0 ] ; then
        JASS_HOME_DIR="${SI_CONFIG_DIR}/path/to/JASS"
    fi
fi
export JASS_HOME_DIR
```

6. **Select or create a Solaris Security Toolkit driver (for example, the default** `secure.driver`).

   If all the scripts listed in the `hardening.driver` and `config.driver` are to be used, then add the `Drivers/secure.driver` path to the `rules` file.

   If only selected scripts are to be used, make copies of those files, then modify the copies.

7. **After completing the driver, make the appropriate entry in the** `rules` **file.**

   The entry should be similar to the following:

```
hostname imbulu - Profiles/core.profile Drivers/secure.driver
```

Caution – Never modify the original scripts included with the Solaris Security Toolkit software. To allow for efficient migration to new releases of the Solaris Security Toolkit software, maintain the original files and your custom files separately.

One other modification may be required to successfully integrate the Solaris Security Toolkit software into the existing JumpStart environment.

8. **If the** `sysidcfg` **files provided with the Solaris Security Toolkit software are used to automate the JumpStart client installation, review them for applicability.**

If the JumpStart server encounters any errors while parsing the `sysidcfg` file, the entire content of the file is ignored.

After completing all the configuration steps in this section, you are able to use JumpStart technology on the client and successfully harden or minimize the OS during the installation process.

Using JumpStart Profile Templates

JumpStart profile templates are files used only with JumpStart mode. The required and optional contents of profiles are described in the Sun BluePrint book *JumpStart™ Technology: Effective Use in the Solaris™ Operating Environment*.

We recommend that you use the JumpStart profile templates as samples from which to make your individual site modifications. Review the profiles to determine what changes are necessary, if any, to use in your environment.

Make copies of the profiles, then modify them for your site. Do not modify the originals, because updates to the Solaris Security Toolkit software may overwrite your customization.

The following JumpStart profiles are included with the Solaris Security Toolkit software:

```
32-bit-minimal.profile
core.profile
end-user.profile
developer.profile
entire-distribution.profile
oem.profile
minimal-Sun_ONE-WS-Solaris*.profile
```

The following subsections describe these profiles.

32-bit-minimal.profile

This JumpStart profile is a relatively generic JumpStart profile for a 32-bit minimized system. It is a reasonable starting point for the development of minimized systems and was used as the starting point for the `minimal-Sun_ONE-WS-Solaris*.profile` minimization scripts.

core.profile

This JumpStart profile installs the smallest Solaris OE cluster, `SUNWCreq`. Other than specifying that the partitioning of the disk include a root and swap partitions, no other configuration modifications are made.

end-user.profile

This JumpStart profile installs the End User Solaris OE cluster, `SUNWCuser`, and the two Solaris OE packages required for process accounting to work properly. In addition, disk partitioning is defined to include only root and swap partitions.

developer.profile

This JumpStart profile installs the Developer Solaris OE cluster, `SUNWCprog`, and the two Solaris OE packages required for process accounting to work properly. As in the `core.profile` definition, the only other configuration definitions made, in addition to the Solaris OE cluster, are for the disk partitioning to include root and swap.

entire-distribution.profile

This JumpStart profile installs the Entire Distribution Solaris OE cluster, `SUNWCall`. As with the other profiles, disk partitioning is defined to include root and swap partitions.

oem.profile

This JumpStart profile installs the OEM Solaris OE cluster, `SUNWCXall`. This cluster is a superset of the Entire Distribution cluster, and it installs OEM-provided software.

minimal-Sun_ONE-WS-Solaris*.profile

All of the following profiles are based on the Sun BluePrint OnLine article titled "Minimizing the Solaris™ Operating Environment for Security." All the Solaris OE versions addressed in this article have specific profiles. The following JumpStart profiles are the same as those referenced in the article.

```
minimal-Sun_ONE-WS-Solaris.26.profile
minimal-Sun_ONE-WS-Solaris7-32bit.profile
minimal-Sun_ONE-WS-Solaris7-64bit.profile
minimal-Sun_ONE-WS-Solaris8-32bit.profile
minimal-Sun_ONE-WS-Solaris8-64bit.profile
minimal-Sun_ONE-WS-Solaris9-64bit.profile
```

Adding and Removing Clients

The following information describes the scripts available for use in JumpStart mode. The mode is controlled by the Solaris Security Toolkit driver inserted in the `rules` file on the JumpStart server.

If you have not configured your environment to use JumpStart mode, refer to "Configuring JumpStart Servers and Environments" on page 84.

add-client Script

To simplify adding clients from JumpStart servers, use this script included with the Solaris Security Toolkit software. The command and options are described in the following paragraphs, however, the underlying JumpStart technology is not. Refer to the Sun BluePrint book *JumpStart™ Technology: Effective Use in the Solaris™ Operating Environment* for information about JumpStart technology.

The `add-client` script is a wrapper around the `add_install_client` command, which accepts the following arguments.

Example Usage:

```
# add-client <client> <client OS> <client class> <server>
<sysidcfg>
```

TABLE 5-1 describes the valid input for the add-client command.

TABLE 5-1   JumpStart add-client Command

Value	Description
client	Is the resolvable host name of the JumpStart client.
client OS	Is the revision of the Solaris OE, available in the JASS_HOME_DIR/OS directory, that is to be installed on the client. If no value is specified, a list of available Solaris OE versions in the JASS_HOME_DIR/OS directory are displayed.
client class	Is the machine class of the JumpStart client. This value is in the same format as the output of the uname -m command.
server	Is the IP address or resolveable host name of the JumpStart server interface for this JumpStart client. If no value is specified, a list of interfaces available on the local host are displayed.
sysidcfg	Is an optional path name to an alternate directory containing a sysidcfg file that you want to use for system identification and configuration. By default, this value is set to the JASS_HOME_DIR/Sysidcfg/Solaris_version/ directory, where the version is extracted from the OS specified for this client. If specified, a path name relative to the JASS_HOME_DIR directory must be used. Only specify the path to the sysidcfg file.

To add a JumpStart client called jordan to a JumpStart server called nomex using Solaris 8 OE (4/01) on an interface called nomex-jumpstart, we would use the following add-client command:

```
# ./add-client jordan Solaris_8_2001-04 sun4u nomex-jumpstart
updating /etc/bootparams
```

To add the same JumpStart client (jordan) using the sysidcfg option, we would use the following command:

```
# ./add-client jordan Solaris_8_2001-04 sun4u nomex-jumpstart\
Hosts/jordan
updating /etc/bootparams
```

rm-client Script

To simplify removing clients from JumpStart servers, use this script included with the Solaris Security Toolkit software. The command and options are described in the following paragraphs; however, the underlying JumpStart technology is not. Refer to *JumpStart™ Technology: Effective Use in the Solaris™ Operating Environment* for information about JumpStart technology.

The rm-client script is a wrapper around the rm_install_client command in much the same way as add-client:

Example Usage: rm-client <*client*>

Where *client* is the resolvable host name of the JumpStart client.

To remove a JumpStart client called jordan, we would use the following rm-client command:

```
# ./rm-client jordan
removing jordan from bootparams
```

## CHAPTER 6

Auditing System Security

This chapter describes how to audit (validate) a system's security using the Solaris Security Toolkit software. Use the information and procedures in this chapter for maintaining an established security profile after hardening. For systems that are already deployed, you may want to use the information in this chapter to assess security before hardening.

Note – The term *audit* is used in this chapter and book to define the Solaris Security Toolkit software's automated process of validating a security posture by comparing it with a predefined security profile. The use of this term in this publication does not represent a guarantee that a system is completely secure after using the audit option.

This chapter contains the following topics:

Maintaining Security

Maintaining security is an ongoing process and is something that must be reviewed and revisited periodically. Maintaining a secure system requires vigilance, because the default security configuration for any system tends to become increasingly open over time. (For more information about maintaining security, refer to Chapter 2, "Maintaining System Security" on page 36.)

Based upon user experience and requests, we developed an automated method for the Solaris Security Toolkit software to audit the security posture of a system, by determining its level of compliance with a specified security profile.

Note – This method is only available in standalone mode using the `jass-execute -a` command and cannot be used during a JumpStart installation.

We recommend that you audit the security posture of your systems periodically, either manually or automatically (for example, via `cron` job or an `rc` script). For example, after hardening a new installation, execute the Solaris Security Toolkit software audit command (`jass-execute -a <driver-name>`) five days later to determine if the system security has changed from the state defined by the security profile.

How often you audit security depends on the criticality of the environment and your security policy. Some users run an audit every hour, every day, or only once a month. Some users run a mini-scan (limited number of checks) every hour, and a full scan (with all the possible checks) once a day.

Consider auditing an essential component to maintain the security posture of deployed systems. If security posture is not periodically audited, then configurations often drift over time due to entropy or modifications that unknowingly or maliciously change the desired security posture. Without periodic review, these changes go undetected and corrective measures are not taken. The result is a system that becomes less secure and, correspondingly, more vulnerable.

In addition to periodic audits, we recommend that you perform audits after upgrades, patches, and other significant system configuration changes.

Reviewing Security Prior to Hardening

In some cases, you may find it useful to review the security posture on deployed systems *before* hardening them. For example, if you assume responsibility for deployed systems that another person administrated, inspect the state of the systems so that you know their posture and, if necessary, can bring them into compliance with the same security profiles used on your other systems.

Another example that commonly applies is when a consultant, such as a Sun Professional Services consultant, wants to determine the security posture of a deployed system for a customer before securing the system. In this scenario, the consultant typically executes one of the Solaris Security Toolkit security profiles in audit mode to determine what changes would be made to a system without actually making the changes. Of course, without customizing the security profile, the result is a high-water mark, and the output might contain false-positive vulnerabilities. However, consultants may find the output useful as a starting point from which to develop and implement custom security profiles for the customer's systems.

Customizing Security Audits

The audit option provides a highly flexible and extensible mechanism for evaluating the state of a system. As with hardening scripts, you can customize the actions of audit scripts. For example, you can customize environment variables, customize framework and helper functions, add new checks, and add functionality to the audit framework.

Typically, most users find the standard and product-specific audit scripts are suitable as templates from which to customize auditing for their environments. For this scenario, customize audit script actions through drivers, finish scripts, environment variables, and file templates. These custom changes can be made with little effort and without modifying the code. Whatever changes you make for hardening are automatically known by the Solaris Security Toolkit software when you perform auditing.

Occasionally, some users find it necessary to add checks or functionality that the Solaris Security Toolkit software does not provide. For this scenario, add the checks or new functionality to the audit script. (You may want to make related changes in the corresponding finish script.) In some cases, you may need to modify the code. Use extreme care when performing code additions and modifications, to avoid introducing bugs and failures.

Rarely, some users find that they need to create entirely new proprietary, or site-specific, drivers and scripts. For this scenario, we recommend that you use the templates and samples as guidelines when coding the new drivers and scripts. Also, be advised that site-specific drivers, finish scripts, variables, and functions are *not* automatically known to the Solaris Security Toolkit software when you use the audit option. For example, if you add a site-specific driver named `abcc-nj-secure.driver` that contains a site-specific finish script, `abcc-nj-install-foo.fin`, then you need to create a site-specific audit script, `abcc-nj-install-foo.aud`. Similarly, if you start with only the audit script, you should create the matching finish script.

To customize or create new drivers, scripts, variables, and functions, use the following information:

For drivers, refer to Chapter 10.

For finish scripts, refer to Chapter 11.

For audit scripts, refer to Chapter 12.

For variables, refer to Chapter 13.

For functions, Chapter 8.

For example, what if you need to add a patch that the Solaris Security Toolkit software does not install? You can extend one of the standard or product-specific templates, or you can create your own. If you create your own, create a finish script to add the patch, then create the corresponding audit script to check for the patch installation.

Preparing to Audit Security

To use the instructions and recommendations in this chapter, you need a security profile. For information about developing and implementing a security profile, refer to Chapter 2.

A variety of security profile templates are included with the Solaris Security Toolkit distribution as drivers. As mentioned earlier in this book, the default security profile and changes made by these drivers might not be appropriate for your systems. Typically, the security profiles implemented by these drivers are "high-water" marks for security. By this, we mean that they disable services that are not required, and they enable optional security features disabled by default.

Many Solaris Security Toolkit software users find that the standard and product-specific security profile templates are acceptable for their environments. If this applies to your situation, then determine which security profile is closest to the security posture you want, and use it for both assessing and hardening your systems.

The preferred practice we recommend, however, is that you review and customize the security profile templates for your environment, or develop new ones. Techniques and recommendations for customizing security profiles are provided in Chapter 10. This approach provides a security posture tailored for your organization, and it minimizes the amount of false errors returned during a security assessment. For example, if you know that Telnet needs to be enabled, you can customize the security profile so that when performing a security assessment, the software does not consider Telnet a vulnerability. For example, a site using Telnet with Kerberos, for authentication and encryption, would not consider the use of Telnet a vulnerability.

Using Options and Controlling Audit Output

This section describes the options available for executing an audit run and the options for controlling output. This section contains the following topics:

"Command Line Options" on page 96

"Banners and Messages Output" on page 100

"Host Name, Script Name, and Timestamp Output" on page 102

Command Line Options

Example usage to audit a system against a security profile:

```
# jass-execute -a driver [ -V verbosity ] [ -q | -o output_file ]
[ -m e-mail_address ]
```

When executing the Solaris Security Toolkit software audit command, you can use the following options listed in TABLE 6-1.

TABLE 6-1 Using Command Line Options With the Audit Command

Option	Description
-h	Displays the jass-execute help message, which provides an overview of the available options.
-m	Mails output to an email address.
-o	Directs output into a file.
-q	Prevents the display of output to the console. Also known as the quiet option.
-V	Specifies the verbosity level for an audit run.

For detailed information about the options available with jass-execute -a command, refer to the following sections:

"Display Help Option" on page 97

"Email Notification Option" on page 98

"Output File Option" on page 98

"Quiet Option" on page 99

"Verbosity Option" on page 99

Display Help Option

The -h option displays the jass-execute help message, which provides an overview of the available options.

The -h option produces output similar to the following:

CODE EXAMPLE 6-1   Sample -h Option Output

```
# ./jass-execute -h

To apply this Toolkit to a system, using the syntax:
    ./jass-execute [-r root_directory -p os_version ]
[ -q | -o output_file ] [ -m e-mail_address ] [-d] driver

To undo a previous application of the Toolkit from a system:
    ./jass-execute -u [ -n ] [ -q | -o output_file ]
[ -m e-mail_address ]

To audit a system against a pre-defined profile:
    ./jass-execute -a driver [ -V verbosity ]
[ -q | -o output_file ] [ -m e-mail_address ]

To display the history of Toolkit applications on a system:
    ./jass-execute -H

To display the last application of the Toolkit on a system:
    ./jass-execute -l

To display this help message:
    ./jass-execute -h
```

Email Notification Option

The -m <email address> option provides a mechanism by which output can be emailed automatically by the Solaris Security Toolkit software when the run completes. The email report is in addition to any logs generated on the system using other options.

A Solaris Security Toolkit run calling sunfire_15k_sc-config.driver using the email option would be similar to the following:

```
# ./jass-execute -m root -a sunfire_15k_sc-config.driver
[...]
```

Output File Option

The -o <output_file> option redirects the console output of jass-execute runs to a separate file, output_file.

This option has no effect on the logs kept in the JASS_REPOSITORY directory. This option is particularly helpful when performed over a slow terminal connection, because there is a significant amount of output generated by a Solaris Security Toolkit run.

This option can be used with either the -d, -u, or -a options.

The -o option produces output similar to the following:

CODE EXAMPLE 6-2   Sample -o Option Output

```
# ./jass-execute -o jass-output.txt -d secure.driver
[NOTE] Executing driver, secure.driver
[NOTE] Recording output to jass-output.txt
```

Quiet Option

The -q option disables Solaris Security Toolkit output to standard input/output (stdio) stream during a hardening run.

This option has no effect on the logs kept in the JASS_REPOSITORY directory. Similar to the -o option, this option is particularly helpful when running the Solaris Security Toolkit software through a cron job or over slow network connections.

This option can be used with either the -d, -u, or -a options.

The -q option produces output similar to the following:

CODE EXAMPLE 6-3   Sample -q Option Output

```
# ./jass-execute -q -a secure.driver
[NOTE] Executing driver, secure.driver
```

Verbosity Option

The -V option specifies the verbosity level for an audit run. This option is only available for auditing. Verbosity levels provide a highly flexible way of displaying the results of an audit run. For example, if you have 100 machines to audit, you may want to limit the output to a single line for each machine to simply determine which machines pass or fail. Then, for the machines that fail, you might want to run an audit that produces expanded output, to focus on the problem areas.

The five verbosity levels (0 through 4) are controlled by the -V option. Each incremental level provides additional detail that you can use to more fully understand which checks are passing and which are failing. TABLE 6-2 describes the verbosity levels.

TABLE 6-2   Audit Verbosity Levels

Level	Output
0	Single line indicating pass or fail.
1	For each script, a single line indicating pass or fail. One grand total score line below all the script lines.
2	For each script, provides results of all checks.
3	Multiple lines providing full output, including banner and header messages.
4	Multiple lines (all data provided from level 3) plus all entries that are generated by the logDebug logging function. This level is for debugging.

Note – The default verbosity level for the `jass-execute -V` command is 3.

For complete descriptions of the verbosity levels, refer to Chapter 13, "`JASS_VERBOSITY`" on page 320.

Banners and Messages Output

You can configure the Solaris Security Toolkit audit option to report or omit banners and messages. The `JASS_LOG_BANNER` variable cannot be used with verbosity levels 0-2. These output options apply to verbosity levels 3 and 4. For example, you might want to eliminate pass messages (`JASS_LOG_SUCCESS` variable) from the output so you can report and focus only on fail messages (`JASS_LOG_FAILURE` variable).

TABLE 6-3 lists the banners and messages that you can control through logging variables. (For detailed information about logging variables, refer to Chapter 13.) If the logging variable is set to 0, then no output is generated for messages of that type. Conversely, if the logging variable is set to 1, then messages are displayed. The default action for each of these variables is to display the output. TABLE 6-3 describes the logging variables.

TABLE 6-3 Displaying Banners and Messages in Audit Output

Logging Variable	Log Prefix	Description
JASS_LOG_BANNER	All Banner Output	This parameter controls the display of banner messages. These messages are usually surrounded by separators comprised of either equal sign ("=") or dash ("-") characters.
JASS_LOG_ERROR	[ERR]	This parameter controls the display of error messages. If set to 0, no error messages will be generated.
JASS_LOG_FAILURE	[FAIL]	This parameter controls the display of failure messages. If set to 0, no failure messages will be generated.

TABLE 6-3   Displaying Banners and Messages in Audit Output *(Continued)*

Logging Variable	Log Prefix	Description
JASS_LOG_NOTICE	[NOTE]	This parameter controls the display of notice messages. If set to 0, no notice messages will be generated.
JASS_LOG_SUCCESS	[PASS]	This parameter controls the display of success or passing status messages. If set to 0, no success messages will be generated.
JASS_LOG_WARNING	[WARN]	This parameter controls the display of warning messages. If set to 0, no warning messages will be generated.

Using these options is very useful when you only need to view specific messages. By setting these options, you can minimize output, yet still focus on areas you deem critical. For example, by setting all logging variables to 0 except for JASS_LOG_FAILURE (leave it at the default of 1), the audit reports only on failures generated by the logFailure function.

CODE EXAMPLE 6-4   Sample Output of Reporting Only Audit Failures

```
# JASS_LOG_FAILURE=1
# export JASS_LOG_FAILURE
[setting of other parameters to 0 omitted]
# ./jass-execute -a secure.driver -V 2
update-at-deny        [FAIL] User test is not listed in
   /etc/cron.d/at.deny.
update-at-deny        [FAIL] Audit Check Total : 1 Error(s)
update-inetd-conf     [FAIL] Service ftp is enabled in
   /etc/inet/inetd.conf.
update-inetd-conf     [FAIL] Service telnet is enabled in
   /etc/inet/inetd.conf.
update-inetd-conf     [FAIL] Service rstatd is enabled in
   /etc/inet/inetd.conf.
update-inetd-conf     [FAIL] Audit Check Total : 3 Error(s)
```

Host Name, Script Name, and Timestamp Output

You can configure the Solaris Security Toolkit audit option to include host name, script name, and timestamp information for verbosity levels 0-2. For example, if you have many machines to audit, you may want to be able to sort the output by host name, script name, or timestamp. TABLE 6-4 lists the variables.

TABLE 6-4   Displaying Host Name, Script Name, and Timestamp Audit Output

Variable Name	Variable Description
JASS_DISPLAY_HOSTNAME	Setting this parameter to 1 causes the Solaris Security Toolkit software to prepend each log entry with the host name of the system. This information is based on the JASS_HOSTNAME parameter. By default, this parameter is empty, so the Toolkit will not display this information.
JASS_DISPLAY_SCRIPTNAME	By default, this parameter is set to 1, so the Solaris Security Toolkit software prepends each log entry with the name of the audit script currently being run. Setting this parameter to any other value causes the Toolkit to not display this information.
JASS_DISPLAY_TIMESTAMP	Setting this parameter to 1 causes the Solaris Security Toolkit software to prepend each log entry with the timestamp associated with the audit run. This information is based on the JASS_TIMESTAMP parameter. By default, this parameter is empty, so the software does not display this information.

By configuring the Solaris Security Toolkit software to prepend host, script, and timestamp information, you can combine many runs from either a single system or group of systems and sort them based on the key data. You can use the information to look for problems that span several systems or that are symptomatic of deployment processes. For example, using the information in this way, an administrator can tell if every system build using a given process always has the same failed checks.

For example, by setting the JASS_DISPLAY_TIMESTAMP parameter to 1 and setting the JASS_DISPLAY_SCRIPTNAME value at 0, output similar to the following would be generated.

CODE EXAMPLE 6-5   Sample Output of Auditing Log Entries

```
# JASS_DISPLAY_SCRIPTNAME=0
# JASS_DISPLAY_TIMESTAMP=1
# export JASS_DISPLAY_SCRIPTNAME JASS_DISPLAY_TIMESTAMP
# ./jass-execute -a secure.driver -V 2
20030101233525 [FAIL] User test is not listed in
    /etc/cron.d/at.deny.
20030101233525 [FAIL] Audit Check Total : 1 Error(s)
20030101233525 [FAIL] Service ftp is enabled in
    /etc/inet/inetd.conf.
20030101233525 [FAIL] Service telnet is enabled in
    /etc/inet/inetd.conf.
20030101233525 [FAIL] Service rstatd is enabled in
    /etc/inet/inetd.conf.
20030101233525 [FAIL] Audit Check Total : 3 Error(s)
```

Performing a Security Audit

Performing a security assessment periodically on your systems provides a benchmark of how closely the security matches the security profile you implemented. The most common scenario for performing security assessments is as a security maintenance task sometime after hardening new installations. We designed the security assessment option so that you simply execute the same hardening driver(s) that you used to harden the system, but that now you use the -a option to check the current state compared to the security profile implemented during hardening. This design eliminates complexity and provides flexibility. For example, when you update your security profile, subsequent security assessments use the updated security profile.

Another possible scenario is that you are responsible for securing systems that are already deployed, and before you harden them, you want to perform a security assessment. In this scenario, you would define your own security profile, customize a Solaris Security Toolkit security profile template, or use one of the security profile templates as is.

To Perform a Security Audit

Before performing an audit, you need to define or choose a security profile. For more information, refer to "Preparing to Audit Security" on page 95.

 Caution – If you are performing a security assessment on a deployed system that you did not harden previously, we recommend that you first back up the machine and reboot it to verify that it is in a known, working, and consistent configuration. Any errors or warnings detected during this preliminary reboot should be corrected or noted before proceeding with security assessment.

1. **Choose the security profile (hardening driver) that you want to use:**

   If you hardened the system previously, use the same security profile.

   For example, `secure.driver`.

   If you have not hardened the system, use one of the standard security profiles or your own.

   For example, `secure.driver or abccorp-secure.driver`.

   For a complete and up-to-date listing of available drivers, download the most recent version of the Solaris Security Toolkit software from the following Web site:

   `http://www.sun.com/security/jass`

   Refer to Chapter 10 for information about standard and product-specific drivers. For the most current listing of drivers, refer to the Drivers directory.

2. **Determine the command line options you want and how you want to control the output. (Refer to "Using Options and Controlling Audit Output" on page 96.)**

3. **Enter the** `jass-execute -a` **command, the name of the security profile, and the options you want.**

The following is a sample audit run using the sunfire_15k_sc-secure.driver.

CODE EXAMPLE 6-6   Sample Output of Audit Run

```
# ./jass-execute -a sunfire_15k_sc-secure.driver
[NOTE] Executing driver, sunfire_15k_sc-secure.driver

[...]

===================================================================
sunfire_15k_sc-secure.driver: Audit script: enable-rfc1948.aud
===================================================================

#------------------------------------------------------------------
# RFC 1948 Sequence Number Generation
#
# Rationale for Audit:
#
# The purpose of this script is to audit that the system is
# configured and is in fact using RFC 1948 for its TCP sequence
# number generation algorithm (unique-per-connection ID). This is
# configured by setting the 'TCP_STRONG_ISS' parameter to '2' in
# the /etc/default/inetinit file.
#
# Determination of Compliance:
#
[...]
#------------------------------------------------------------------

[PASS] TCP_STRONG_ISS is set to '2' in /etc/default/inetinit.
[PASS] System is running with tcp_strong_iss=2.

# The following is the vulnerability total for this audit script.

[PASS] Audit Check Total : 0 Error(s)


===================================================================

# The following is the vulnerability total for this driver profile.

[PASS] Driver Total : 0 Error(s)


===================================================================
sunfire_15k_sc-secure.driver: Driver finished.
===================================================================

[PASS] Grand Total : 0 Error(s)
```

When an audit run is initiated, the Solaris Security Toolkit software accesses files from the JASS_HOME_DIR/Audit directory. Although the files in both the JASS_HOME_DIR/Audit and JASS_HOME_DIR/Finish directories share the same base file names, they have different file name suffixes. The driver.run script automatically translates the finish scripts defined by the JASS_SCRIPTS variable into audit scripts, by changing their suffixes from .fin to .aud.

The audit run starts and initializes the state of the Solaris Security Toolkit software. Each driver that is accessed during the run evaluates the state of all of its file templates and audit scripts. Each check results in a state of success or failure, represented by a vulnerability value of either zero or nonzero, respectively. In most cases, failure is represented by a number 1. Each script that is run produces a total security score, based on the total vulnerability value of each check contained within a script. Furthermore, the total vulnerability value result for each driver is displayed at the completion of a driver's assessment. Lastly, a grand total of all scores is presented at the end of the run.

The security assessment option provides a comprehensive view of the state of a system at the time the assessment run is initiated. The Solaris Security Toolkit software checks the stored state of the system by inspecting configuration files and checks the running state of the system by inspecting process table information, device driver information, etc. The Solaris Security Toolkit software checks not only for the existence of each file or service, but it checks if the software associated with a service is installed, configured, enabled, and running. This holistic approach yields an accurate snapshot of the current state of a system.

## CHAPTER 7

Securing a System

This chapter describes how to apply the information and expertise provided in earlier chapters to a realistic scenario for installing and securing a new system. In this chapter, we illustrate how to deploy the Solaris Security Toolkit software with a Checkpoint Firewall-1 NG for the Solaris 8 OE.

Use the information in this chapter as a guide and case scenario for securing a new system and applications.

Sun BluePrint books and online articles are available to guide you through the process of minimizing and hardening many of Sun's systems. Refer to the following Web site for the latest product-specific books and articles:

    http://www.sun.com/blueprints

This chapter contains the following topics:

Planning and Preparing

To effectively and efficiently deploy minimized and secured systems as described in this case study, it is critical for us to plan and prepare appropriately. The underlying network infrastructure, policies, and procedures must be in place. In addition, support and maintenance of the systems must be defined and communicated. For more information about planning and preparing, refer to Chapter 2. The scenario described in this chapter documents the recommended process and tasks that a system administrator (SA) would perform to achieve a minimized and hardened Solaris OE image for a firewall system.

In this scenario, the SA is tasked with creating an automated and scalable solution for building and deploying Checkpoint Firewall-1 NG systems for a service provider (xSP) that wants to provide firewall service to its customers. For this scenario, xSP's requirements and considerations are as follows:

Because xSP plans to deploy many of these systems, the time to build and deploy each system is critical and must be streamlined for efficiency.

Systems are installed using a dedicated management network connected to the internal Ethernet interface of each system. This network is only used by xSP staff and not by subscribers.

All other interfaces are on separate physical network interfaces and are filtered.

The security of the management network is critical to the overall security of the deployed firewall systems.

Based on these requirements, we decide to automate the installation, minimization, and hardening of the OE images by using JumpStart technology and the Solaris Security Toolkit software.

Assumptions and Limitations

This chapter assumes we are using an already working Solaris Security Toolkit software and JumpStart technology installation. (Other chapters in this book provide instructions and recommendations for installing the software; refer to applicable chapters for that information.)

This chapter assumes we are developing a custom configuration for minimizing and hardening a specific application. The Solaris Security Toolkit software does not have any drivers or JumpStart profiles specifically for the application. Therefore, we need to create custom drivers and profiles for this application. This task is done by copying existing drivers and profiles, then modifying them to fit the application.

For this case scenario, we assume the following about the SA's skill level:

Has enough knowledge and experience to configure the OS and applications.

Knows how to test the configuration and make adjustments to fine tune it.

Knows how to build a JumpStart environment from which the client system is installed. (Refer to the Sun BluePrint book *JumpStart™ Technology: Effective Use in the Solaris™ Operating Environment.*

Is familiar with OE minimization techniques. (Refer to *Enterprise Security: Solaris Operating Environment Security Journal, Solaris Operating Environment Versions 2.5.1, 2.6, 7, and 8.*)

Is familiar with the Solaris Security Toolkit software basics and is ready to focus on building a customized configuration using both minimization and hardening techniques and recommendations. (Refer to Chapter 1.)

System Environment

The example scenario is based on the following hardware and software environment:

Checkpoint Firewall-1 NG

Solaris 8 OE

JumpStart technology

Solaris OE cluster (SUNWCreq)

Solaris Security Toolkit software

Platform based on SPARC technology

At least two Ethernet interfaces

Security Requirements

For this scenario, the high-level requirements and software packages have been identified, but the specific components and services of all the packages need to be identified. Also, the Solaris OE capabilities needed to administer and manage the systems must be identified.

The following list provides a detailed view on how software components will be used:

Secure Shell for remote administration
FTP to copy files
Solstice DiskSuite™ software to mirror disks
SYSLOG messages forward to a central repository

From this list, we can develop a security profile. For detailed information about developing security profiles and using the profile templates, refer to Chapter 2, "Developing and Implementing a Solaris Security Toolkit Profile" on page 32.

Creating a Security Profile

A security profile defines what security modifications the Solaris Security Toolkit software makes when hardening and minimizing the security configuration of a system. None of the standard security profiles or drivers included in the Solaris Security Toolkit software meet the requirements for the minimized Checkpoint Firewall-1 NG systems. Therefore, we must create a custom security profile to implement the appropriate system modifications.

For this scenario, our process for creating a security profile is covered in several sections in this chapter, as the scenario evolves, and is covered where most applicable. First, we create new driver files based on existing drivers. Then we modify the new drivers to comply with the security requirements outlined previously. We describe minimization in "Installing the Software" on page 111, and we customize the hardening modifications in "Customizing the Hardening Configuration" on page 119.

Installing the Software

This section demonstrates the process of installing the software. For the sample scenario, we provide any exceptions or scenario-specific instructions. For general instructions about installing software, use the references to other parts of this book.

Note – In the following sections, we speak directly to the reader as though the reader is performing the tasks. We use this approach to simplify the presentation and to provide instructions in this chapter that readers may use as a template for handling related situations.

This section contains the following tasks:

"Download and Install Security Software" on page 111

"Install Patches" on page 112

"Specify and Install the OE Cluster" on page 113

Download and Install Security Software

Download and install the Solaris Security Toolkit and additional security software, including patches, on the JumpStart server as follows.

To Download and Install the Security Software

1. **Download the Solaris Security Toolkit software and additional security software. (Refer to Chapter 3, "Download Security Software" on page 43.)**

2. **Install the downloaded Solaris Security Toolkit software and additional security software. (Refer to Chapter 3, "Install and Execute the Software" on page 51.)**

Caution – Do not execute the Solaris Security Toolkit software yet. First perform the additional configuration and customizing described in the following sections.

Install Patches

Patches are a critical part of any system installation. Despite best efforts, issues are sometimes encountered after an OE version is released and patches are required.

OE patches may address security vulnerabilities, availability issues, performance concerns, or other aspects of a system. When installing a new OE, and on an ongoing basis after the OE is installed, check to ensure that appropriate patches are installed.

The Solaris Security Toolkit software provides a mechanism to install the Recommended and Security Patch Cluster available from SunSolve OnLine. This OE-specific cluster of patches includes the most commonly needed patches.

To Install Patches

1. **At a minimum, download the Recommended and Security Patch Cluster into the Patches directory and uncompress it.**

   If the `install-recommended-patches.fin` script is included in the hardening driver, then that patch cluster is installed automatically.

   We are aware of an added issue for CheckPoint Firewall-1 NG. This application requires specific patches not included in the Recommended and Security Patch Cluster. The Checkpoint Firewall-1 NG requires the following patches:

   108434
   108435

2. **To automate the installation of patches 108434 and 108435, download the latest versions from SunSolve OnLine, and place them in the Patches directory.**

3. **After the patches are in the `Patches` directory, create a new finish script (for example, `fw1-patch-install.fin`) that calls the `add_patch` helper function, with the name of each patch.**

   This finish script calls the appropriate helper functions with the two Checkpoint Firewall-1 NG required patch IDs. For example:

```
# !/bin/sh
# add_patch 108434-10
# add_patch 108435-10
```

Specify and Install the OE Cluster

After defining a disk layout for the OE installation, the next task is to specify which Solaris OE cluster to install. Choose one of the five installation clusters available with Solaris OE: SUNWCreq, SUNWCuser, SUNWCprog, SUNWCall, and SUNWCXall.

To Specify and Install the OE Cluster

1. Specify the OE cluster to install.

Because the goal of this case scenario is to build a minimized and dedicated firewall device, we choose the smallest of the available Solaris OE clusters, SUNWCreq, also known as Core. Because this cluster includes a relatively small number of packages, other packages are probably required. These other required packages need to be included in the profile with the Solaris OE cluster definition.

The baseline profile definition adds the following to the previously defined profile.

```
cluster          SUNWCreq
```

The SUNWCreq installation cluster includes packages that are not required for a firewall Sun server to function properly. Remove these extra packages after you have a working baseline. (Refer to Sun BluePrints OnLine article "Minimizing the Solaris Operating Environment for Security: Updated for the Solaris 9 Operating Environment.")

2. Run through an installation with the appropriately defined security profile to determine if there are any package dependency issues.

Some package dependencies are encountered during installation, and we determine that the following Solaris OE packages are required for Checkpoint Firewall-1 NG:

SUNWter – Terminal information

SUNWadmc – System administration core libraries

SUNWadmfw – System and network administration framework

SUNWlibC and SUNWlibCx – Required for the CheckPoint NG application

The complete listing of packages in the profile is as follows.

```
cluster      SUNWCreq
package      SUNWter      add
package      SUNWlibC     add
package      SUNWlibCx    add
package      SUNWadmc     add
package      SUNWadmfw    add
```

Although this list is complete for this case study, additional packages may be added or removed based on the actual environment into which this configuration is deployed.

Until the system is verified from both a function and security perspective, as described in "Testing for Quality Assurance" on page 125, the final list of packages may require modification. If so, modify the profile, reinstall the system, and repeat the testing.

3. **Create a** `minimize-firewall.fin` `script,` **based on the package dependencies in the previous two steps.**

Configuring the JumpStart Server and Client

This section demonstrates how to configure the JumpStart server and client to use a custom security profile for minimization. For detailed information about using the the Solaris Security Toolkit software in JumpStart environments, refer to Chapter 5.

This section contains the following tasks:

"Prepare the Infrastructure" on page 115

"Validate and Check the Rules File" on page 118

Prepare the Infrastructure

Perform the following tasks to prepare the infrastructure. The following tasks demonstrate the process of creating a baseline configuration for the client using existing drivers, profiles, and finish scripts. After this baseline is in place, verify that it works properly, then customize it for the chosen application.

To Prepare the Infrastructure

1. **Configure your JumpStart server and environment. (Refer to Chapter 5 for detailed instructions.)**

2. **Add the client to the JumpStart server by using the** add-client **command.**

   CODE EXAMPLE 7-1   Adding a Client to the JumpStart Server

   ```
   # pwd
   /jumpstart
   # ./add-client jordan Solaris_8_2002-02 sun4u nomex-jumpstart
   cleaning up preexisting install client "jordan"
   removing jordan from bootparams
   updating /etc/bootparams
   ```

3. **Create a** rules **file entry for the client, specifying the appropriate JumpStart profile and finish script. For example:**

   ```
   hostname jordan - Profiles/xsp-minimal-firewall.profile \
     Drivers/xsp-firewall-secure.driver
   ```

4. **Create a profile file named** `xsp-minimal-firewall.profile` **and a driver file named** `xsp-firewall-secure.driver` **by copying the files provided with the Solaris Security Toolkit software.**

You must create these files before you can successfully complete the next step. Initially, these files can simply be copies of files distributed with the Solaris Security Toolkit software. Never modify the original files distributed with the Solaris Security Toolkit software. The following example shows how to create the files.

CODE EXAMPLE 7-2 Creating a Profile

```
# pwd
/jumpstart/Drivers
# cp install-Sun_ONE-WS.driver xsp-firewall-secure.driver
# cp hardening.driver xsp-firewall-hardening.driver
[...]
# pwd
/jumpstart/Profiles
# cp minimal-Sun_ONE-WS-Solaris8-64bit.profile \
     xsp-minimal-firewall.profile
```

We base this example on a dedicated web server configuration, because it is a good baseline from which to develop a dedicated firewall.

5. **After creating the profile and driver files, modify the files as follows:**

a. **Replace the** `xsp-firewall-secure.driver` **reference to** `hardening.driver` **with** `xsp-firewall-hardening.driver`.

b. **Replace the two finish scripts defined in** `JASS_SCRIPTS` **with references to** `minimize-firewall.fin` **and your finish script (for example,** `fw1-patch-install.fin`**).**

The modified script should appear similar to the following.

CODE EXAMPLE 7-3 Sample Output of Modified Script

```
DIR="`/bin/dirname $0`"
export DIR
. ${DIR}/driver.init
. ${DIR}/config.driver
JASS_SCRIPTS="
                minimize-firewall.fin
                fw1-patch-install.fin"
. ${DIR}/driver.run
. ${DIR}/xsp-firewall-hardening.driver
```

6. **Check the** `rules` **file entry for correctness using the following command.**

   CODE EXAMPLE 7-4   Checking the `rules` File for Correctness

   ```
   # pwd
   /jumpstart
   # ./check
   Validating rules...
   Validating profile Profiles/end-user.profile...
   Validating profile Profiles/xsp-minimal-firewall.profile...
   Validating profile Profiles/test.profile...
   Validating profile Profiles/entire-distribution.profile...
   Validating profile Profiles/oem.profile...
   The custom JumpStart configuration is ok.
   ```

   At this point, it should be possible to successfully begin the JumpStart installation on the client, `jordan` in this example, using the JumpStart configuration and Solaris Security Toolkit drivers, finish scripts, and profiles that you created.

7. **If you encounter problems when checking the** `rules` **file, refer to "Validate and Check the Rules File" on page 118.**

8. **From the client's** `ok` **prompt, enter the following command to install the client using the JumpStart infrastructure.**

   ```
   ok> boot net - install
   ```

   If the client does not build, review the configuration and modify it until it works properly. Note that all aspects of the JumpStart configuration are not addressed in this section. Refer to the Sun BluePrint book *JumpStart™ Technology: Effective Use in the Solaris™ Operating Environment* for more details.

   After achieving a correct run of the `rules` file and verifying that patches were installed correctly, you can start the base-level installation of the client system and its minimization and hardening.

Validate and Check the Rules File

When validating the `rules` file for correctness, you might encounter a variety of problems. Some of the most common are addressed in this section.

The first run on the `rules` file results in the following output.

CODE EXAMPLE 7-5 Sample Output for `rules` File

```
# pwd
/jumpstart
# ./check
Validating rules...
Validating profile Profiles/xsp-minimal-firewall.profile...
Error in file "rules", line 20
hostname jordan - Profiles/xsp-minimal-firewall.profile Drivers/xsp-
firewall-secure.driver
ERROR: Profile missing:
    Profiles/xsp-minimal-firewall.profile
```

In this example, the profile specified in the `rules` entry for `jordan` does not exist. The profile, `xsp-minimal-firewall.profile`, was not present in the profiles directory. Typically, this error is generated due to a spelling mistake in the file name, forgetting to specify the correct directory for the profiles, or simply not having created the profile yet. Fix the problem and rerun the check.

The second run uncovers two other problems. The first problem is the driver being called in the `xsp-firewall-secure.driver`. Instead of calling `xsp-firewall-hardening.driver`, the `xsp-firewall-secure.driver` is still calling the `hardening.driver`.

The second problem is that the `JASS_SCRIPTS` variable is incorrectly set to `minimize-Sun_ONE-WS.fin` instead of `minimize-firewall.fin`.

The following is the incorrect script.

CODE EXAMPLE 7-6 Sample of Incorrect Script

```
#!/bin/sh
DIR="`/bin/dirname $0`"
export DIR
. ${DIR}/driver.init
. ${DIR}/config.driver
JASS_SCRIPTS="minimize-Sun_ONE-WS.fin"
. ${DIR}/driver.run
. ${DIR}/hardening.driver
```

It should be as follows.

CODE EXAMPLE 7-7 Sample of Correct Script

```
#!/bin/sh
DIR="`/bin/dirname $0`"
export DIR
. ${DIR}/driver.init
. ${DIR}/config.driver
JASS_SCRIPTS="
minimize-firewall.fin"
. ${DIR}/driver.run
. ${DIR}/xsp-firewall-hardening.driver
```

Customizing the Hardening Configuration

Now we are ready to customize and fine-tune the hardening configuration of the proposed firewall. The scripts we started with are based on the hardening.driver. This basis means that the system is turned into a "warm-brick," that is, all of its services are disabled.

Because Solaris 8 OE does not include a Secure Shell client, we need to make some modifications to allow for remote, network-based administration of the firewalls. For the firewall in this case scenario, the requirements specify that FTP services must remain enabled and a Secure Shell client must be installed for remote administration. Restrict both of these services to the private management network only, therefore not enabling listening on any other network interfaces. For information about restricting these services, refer to the Sun BluePrint OnLine article titled "Solaris Operating Environment Security: Updated for Solaris 9 Operating Environment."

In addition to leaving these two services enabled, we leave RPC services enabled so that we can use the Solstice DiskSuite (SDS) graphical user interface (GUI) to configure SDS for disk mirroring. If the SDS GUI is not going to be used, then the RPC services are not needed. In the context of this example, the GUI is required and therefore RPC services are left enabled. Note that installation and configuration of SDS is beyond the scope of this book.

The final modification required for this client is that a customized syslog.conf is crafted that uses xSP's centralized SYSLOG server. This customized syslog.conf file must be installed on each of the firewall systems.

These modifications require changes to a variety of Solaris Security Toolkit configuration options. Each of the required modifications is detailed in the following sections.

"Enable FTP Service" on page 120

"Install Secure Shell Software" on page 121

"Enable RPC Service" on page 122

"Customize the syslog.conf File" on page 123

Enable FTP Service

For the firewall in this case scenario, leave the FTP services enabled.

To Enable FTP Service

1. **To leave FTP enabled, modify the default behavior of the** update-inetd-conf.fin **file by setting the** JASS_SVCS_DISABLE **and** JASS_SVCS_ENABLE **variables.**

   To disable all standard Solaris OE services except for FTP, the best method for our case scenario is to define JASS_SVCS_ENABLE to be "ftp" while ensuring that JASS_SVCS_DISABLE is left with its default value obtained from the finish.init script. (Refer to Chapter 13.)

2. **To implement the change as recommended (through the environment variables), add an entry similar to the following to** xsp-firewall-secure.driver **before the call to** xsp-firewall-hardening.driver.

   ```
   JASS_SVCS_ENABLE="ftp"
   ```

3. **Ensure that FTP is available only on xSP's management network by implementing it through the firewall software.**

   One of the other requirements stated was that FTP should be available only on xSP's management network. On Solaris 8 OE, you can implement this requirement either through incorporating TCP Wrappers onto the system or through the firewall software itself. In this case scenario, we implement it through the firewall software.

Install Secure Shell Software

Because Solaris 8 OE does not include a Secure Shell client, install a Secure Shell client for remote administration.

You can configure the Solaris Security Toolkit software to install the OpenSSH tool. Use the `install-openssh.fin` script, which is listed in the `config.driver` file used by `xsp-firewall-secure.driver`.

To Install Secure Shell

1. **Copy the default** `config.driver` **to** `xsp-firewall-config.driver`**.**

2. **In the copy of the file, uncomment the entry for** `install-openssh.fin`**.**

3. **Modify the entry in** `xsp-firewall-secure.driver` **that calls** `config.driver` **to call** `xsp-firewall-config.driver` **instead.**

4. **Obtain the latest version of OpenSSH.**

   As with patches and OE releases, use the most recent version of OpenSSH. Refer to the OpenSSH web pages for the latest release information:

   `http://www.openssh.org`

5. **Compile the latest OpenSSH package, name it appropriately, and install it in the** `Packages` **directory.**

   For more information about this package, refer to the Sun BluePrint OnLine article titled "Configuring OpenSSH for the Solaris Operating Environment."

6. **Update the** `install-openssh.fin` **script to reflect the correct OpenSSH package name.**

   Modifications to the `install-openssh.fin` script might be required. This script defines the package name of the OpenSSH package to be formatted similar to the following.

   ```
   OBSDssh-3.5p1-sparc-sun4u-5.8.pkg
   ```

   Where the package name follows the version number (`3.5p1`), the architecture (`sparc`), the version of the architecture (`sun4u`), the OE for which the package was compiled (`5.8`), and a `pkg` suffix.

7. **Ensure that SSH is only available on xSP's management network by implementing it through the firewall software.**

   One of the other requirements stated was that Secure Shell should be available only on xSP's management network. With Solaris 8 OE, you can implement this requirement either through incorporating TCP Wrappers onto the system or through the firewall software itself. In this case scenario, we implement it through the firewall software. Note that this requirement could also be implemented by modifying the Secure Shell server's configuration.

Enable RPC Service

Leave RPC services enabled so that you can use SDS for disk mirroring, which requires RPC.

This modification is relatively straightforward because a specific finish script, `disable-rpc.fin`, is available to disable RPC services during a Solaris Security Toolkit run.

Note – Remotely accessing RPC services on a system should be explicitly denied by the system's firewall configuration.

To Enable RPC

Comment out the entry for `disable-rpc.fin` **in the** `xsp-firewall-hardening.driver`.

Our normal recommendation on disabling scripts from drivers is to comment them out instead of removing them. However, care must be taken when commenting out entries in the JASS_SCRIPTS definition, because only certain combinations of comment values are accepted.

The following is the comment, contained in the `driver.funcs` script, on what the Solaris Security Toolkit software accepts as comment indicators in the JASS_SCRIPTS definition.

```
Very rudimentary comment handler. This code will only
recognize comments where a single '#' is placed before the
file name (separated by whitespace or not). It then will only
skip the very next argument.
```

Customize the `syslog.conf` File

The final modification required for this client is that a customized `syslog.conf` is crafted that uses xSP's centralized SYSLOG server. This customized `syslog.conf` file must be installed on each of the firewall systems.

To Customize the `syslog.conf` File

1. **Copy the xSP standard** `syslog.conf` **file, rename it** `syslog.conf.jordan`, **then place it in the** `Files/etc` **directory.**

   The Solaris Security Toolkit software supports several different modes of copying files. The most appropriate option for this configuration is to append the system's host name as a suffix to the file so that the `syslog.conf` file is only copied to `jordan`, because it has unique firewall-specific modifications. In this case, the client is called `jordan`, so the actual filename used in `Files/etc` is `syslog.conf.jordan`. It is important to note that the `JASS_FILES` definition must not have this suffix appended. For more information about suffixes, refer to Chapter 13, "`JASS_FILES`" on page 306.

2. **If the xSP standard** `syslog.conf` **file is not available, create a custom** `syslog.conf` **file as follows:**

   a. **Copy the** `syslog.conf` **file included with the Solaris Security Toolkit software, then rename it** `syslog.conf.jordan`, **and place it in the** `Files/etc` **directory.**

   b. **Modify the** `syslog.conf.jordan` **to conform to the xSP standard for** SYSLOG.

3. **Verify that the** `/etc/syslog.conf` **file is listed in the** `JASS_FILES` **definition of the** `xsp-firewall-hardening.driver`.

By default, the modified JASS_FILE definition in xsp-firewall-hardening.driver appears as follows.

CODE EXAMPLE 7-8   Sample Output of Modified xsp-firewall-hardening.driver

```
JASS_FILES="
                    /etc/dt/config/Xaccess
                    /etc/init.d/inetsvc
                    /etc/init.d/nddconfig
                    /etc/init.d/set-tmp-permissions
                    /etc/issue
                    /etc/motd
                    /etc/notrouter
                    /etc/rc2.d/S00set-tmp-permissions
                    /etc/rc2.d/S07set-tmp-permissions
                    /etc/rc2.d/S70nddconfig
                    /etc/syslog.conf
    "
```

At this point, all of the required modifications have been made. The installation of the OE, minimization, and hardening are customized for a specific application and fully automated. The only processes not fully automated are the configuration and installation of the firewall software and Solstice DiskSuite. Although it is possible to perform these configurations by using JumpStart technology, it is beyond the scope of this book. Refer to the Sun BluePrint book *JumpStart™ Technology: Effective Use in the Solaris™ Operating Environment*.

Installing the Client

After making all of the modifications to the drivers, install the client as described in this section.

To Install the Client

1. **After all of the required modifications are made to the drivers, install the client using the JumpStart infrastructure.**

   This task is done using the following command from the client's ok prompt.

   ```
   ok> boot net - install
   ```

2. **If any errors are encountered, fix them and reinstall the client's OE.**

Testing for Quality Assurance

The final task in the process involves verifying that the applications and services offered by the system are functioning correctly. Also, this task verifies that the security profile successfully implemented the required modifications.

It is important that this task be done thoroughly and soon after the reboot of the now hardened and minimized platform, to ensure that any anomalies or problems are detected and corrected rapidly. This process is divided into two tasks: verifying profile installation and verifying application and service functionality.

To Verify Profile Installation

To verify that the Solaris Security Toolkit software installed the security profile correctly and without error, review and evaluate the following.

1. **Review the installation log file.**

   This file is installed in `JASS_REPOSITORY/jass-install-log.txt`.

Note – This log file can be used as a reference to understand exactly what the Solaris Security Toolkit software did to the system. For each run on a system, there is a new log file stored in a directory based on the start time of the run. These files, and any other files in the `JASS_REPOSITORY` directory, must never be modified directly.

---

2. **Use the audit option to assess the security configuration of the system.**

   For detailed information about the audit option, refer to Chapter 6. For this scenario, we use the following command from the directory into which the Solaris Security Toolkit software was installed on the client.

   CODE EXAMPLE 7-9   Assessing a Security Configuration

   ```
   # ./jass-execute -a xsp-firewall-secure.driver
   [NOTE] Executing driver, xsp-firewall-secure.driver
   ================================================================
   xsp-firewall-secure.driver: Driver started.
   ================================================================


   ================================================================
   JASS Version:    4.0
   [...]
   ```

   If the Solaris Security Toolkit verification run encounters any inconsistencies, they are noted. A summary at the end of the run reports on the total number of inconsistencies found. The entire output of the run is in the `JASS_REPOSITORY` directory.

To Verify Application and Service Functionality

The verification process for applications and services typically involves the execution of a well-defined test and acceptance plan. This plan is used to exercise the various components of a system or application to determine that they are in an available and working order. While using this type of plan is strongly recommended, it may not always be available. If such a plan is not available, test the system in a reasonable way based on how it is used. The goal of this effort is to ensure that the hardening process in no way affected the ability of applications or services to perform their functions.

1. **If you discover that an application or service malfunctions after the system is hardened, use the techniques described in Chapter 2 to determine the problem.**

   For example, we highly recommend using the `truss` command. This command can often be used to determine at what point an application is having difficulty. Once this is known, the problem can be targeted and traced back to the change made by the Solaris Security Toolkit software.

Note – Based on the collective experience of many who have deployed the Solaris Security Toolkit software, the majority of problems can be avoided using the approach in this book.

---

2. **In a similar fashion, test the Checkpoint Firewall-1 NG software, trace any issues back to Solaris Security Toolkit software modifications, and correct the issues.**

3. **If the final list of packages requires modification, modify the profile, reinstall the system, and repeat the testing.**

PART **II**   Reference

The chapters in this Part contain reference information for understanding and using the internals of the Solaris Security Toolkit software.

This Part contains the following chapters:

Chapter 8 "Using Framework Functions"

Chapter 9 "Using File Templates"

Chapter 10 "Using Drivers"

Chapter 11 "Using Finish Scripts"

Chapter 12 "Using Audit Scripts"

Chapter 13 "Using Environment Variables"

Using Framework Functions

This chapter provides reference information for using, adding, modifying, and removing framework functions. Framework functions provide flexibility for you to change the behavior of the Solaris Security Toolkit software without modifying source code.

Use framework functions to limit the amount of coding that is needed to develop new finish and audit scripts, and to keep common functionality consistent. For example, by using the common logging functions, you can configure the reporting mechanism without needing to develop or alter any additional source code. Similarly, by using this modular code for common functions, bugs and enhancements can be more systematically addressed.

In addition, framework functions support the undo option. For example, using the framework function `backup_file` in place of a `cp` or `mv` command allows that operation to be reversed during an undo run.

This chapter contains the following topics:

Customizing Framework Functions

The Solaris Security Toolkit software is based on a modular framework that you can combine in various ways to suit your organization's needs. Sometimes, however, the standard features provided by the Solaris Security Toolkit software may not meet your site's needs. You can supplement the standard features by customizing framework functions to enhance and extend the functionality provided by the Solaris Security Toolkit software. The framework functions configure how the Solaris Security Toolkit software runs, define the functions that it uses, and initialize environment variables.

In most cases, you can easily copy standard framework function files and scripts, then customize the functionality for your use. For example, using the user.run file, you can add, modify, replace, or extend the standard framework functions. The user.run file is similar in purpose to the user.init file, except that you use the user.init file to add or modify environment variables.

In some cases, you may need to develop new framework functions. In this case, use similar framework functions as a guide or template for coding, and be sure to follow the recommendations provided in this book. Development should only be undertaken by users who are familiar with the Solaris Security Toolkit software's design and implementation.

Caution – Take extreme care when developing your own framework functions. Incorrect programming may compromise the Solaris Security Toolkit software's ability to properly implement or undo changes or to audit a system's configuration. Furthermore, changes made to the software could adversely impact the target platform on which the software is run.

The following provides an example where Solaris Security Toolkit functionality is extended by customizing the standard framework. In this example, the mount_filesystems function is replaced to enable the developer to mount additional file systems during a JumpStart installation. The mount_filesystems function is copied directly from the driver.funcs script into the user.run file. The modifications to it are in line numbers 8 and 9.

CODE EXAMPLE 8-1 Extending Functionality by Customizing the Framework

```
1    mount_filesystems()

2    {

3        if [ "${JASS_STANDALONE}" = "0" ]; then

4            mount_fs ${JASS_PACKAGE_MOUNT} ${JASS_ROOT_DIR} \

5                ${JASS_PACKAGE_DIR}

6            mount_fs ${JASS_PATCH_MOUNT} ${JASS_ROOT_DIR} \

7                ${JASS_PATCH_DIR}

8            mount_fs 192.168.0.1:/apps01/oracle \

9                ${JASS_ROOT_DIR}/tmp/apps-oracle

10       fi

11   }
```

For the sake of simplicity, the variable used to mount the new file system is not converted to Solaris Security Toolkit environment variables. To aid in portability and flexibility, we generally recommend that you abstract the actual values using environment variables. This approach allows changes to be made consistently, because the software is deployed into environments with different requirements, such as production, quality assurance, and development.

Note – You could implement the same functionality within a finish script that uses this mount point, so that the mounting, use, and unmounting of the file system is self-contained within the script. However, it may be more effective and efficient to mount the file system using mount_filesystems when a single file system is used by more than one script.

Caution – A disadvantage to modifying mount_filesystems is that when you install updates of the Solaris Security Toolkit software, you might need to modify the mount_filesystems again.

Using Common Log Functions

These functions control all logging and reporting functions and are located in the Drivers directory in a file called common_log.funcs. The logging and reporting functions are used in all of the Solaris Security Toolkit software's operational modes; therefore, they are considered common functions. For example, common functions such as logWarning and logError are in this file.

This section describes the following common log functions.

logBanner

This function displays banner messages. These messages typically precede driver, finish, or audit script run output. Also, banner messages are used at the start and end of a run and are only displayed if the software's logging verbosity is at least 3. For more information on verbosity levels, refer to Chapter 13.

Banner messages take two forms. If you pass an empty string to this function, then a single line separator is displayed. This line is often used to force a "break" in the displayed output. If you enter a single string value, then the output is displayed between a pair of single line separators. For example, the following code is an example of a banner message.

CODE EXAMPLE 8-2   Sample Banner Message

```
================================================================

JASS Version:   4.0

Node name:      imbulu

Host ID:        8085816e

Host address:   192.168.0.1

MAC address:    8085816e

OS version:     5.9

Date:           Wed Jan  1 22:27:15 EST 2003

================================================================
```

You can control banner messages through the JASS_LOG_BANNER environment variable. For more information on this environment variable, refer to Chapter 13.

logDebug

This function displays debugging messages. This function accepts a single string argument to be displayed as a debugging message. By default, no debugging messages are displayed by the Solaris Security Toolkit software. This functionality is for future use and for you to add debugging log messages to your code. Debugging messages are only displayed if the verbosity is at least 4. For more information about verbosity levels, refer to Chapter 13.

logError

This function displays error messages. This function accepts a single string value that is displayed as an error message. Error messages are those that contain the string [ERR].

Example usage:

```
logError "getScore: Score value is not defined."
```

Example output:

```
[ERR ] getScore: Score value is not defined.
```

You can control error messages through the JASS_LOG_ERROR environment variable. For more information on this environment variable, refer to Chapter 13.

logFailure

This function displays failure messages. This function accepts a single string value that is displayed as a failure message. Failure messages are those that contain the string [FAIL].

Example usage:

```
logFailure "Package SUNWatfsr is installed."
```

Example output:

```
[FAIL] Package SUNWatfsr is installed.
```

You can control failure messages through the JASS_LOG_FAILURE environment variable. For more information on this environment variable, refer to Chapter 13.

logFileContentsExist and logFileContentsNotExist

Use these functions to log messages associated with the success or failure of checks. These functions together report on the results of a file content check. These functions are used primarily with the check_fileContentsExist and check_fileContentsNotExist functions, although they can be used independently if necessary.

You can supply the following arguments to this function:

A string value representing the name of the file to test

A string value representing the search pattern

A non-negative integer representing the vulnerability value result

A string value representing related information that you want displayed for users after a PASS or FAIL message (optional)

Example usage:

```
logFileContentsExist /etc/default/inetinit "TCP_STRONG_ISS=2" 0
```

Example output:

```
[PASS] File /etc/default/inetinit has content matching
TCP_STRONG_ISS=2.
```

These functions display either success or failure messages. You can control these messages through the JASS_LOG_FAILURE and JASS_LOG_SUCCESS environment variables. For more information on these environment variables, refer to Chapter 13.

logFileExists and logFileNotExists

Use these functions to log messages associated with the success or failure of a check. These functions together report on the results of a file check. These functions are primarily used with the check_fileExists and check_fileNotExists functions, although they can be used independently if necessary.

You can supply the following arguments to this function:

A string value representing the name of the file to test

A non-negative integer representing the vulnerability value result

If this argument is passed a null string value, then this function reports the result in the form of a notice using the logNotice function. Otherwise, it reports the result as a failure using the logFailure function.

A string value representing related information that you want displayed for users after a PASS, FAIL, or NOTE message (optional)

Example usage:

```
logFileExists /etc/issue
```

Example output:

```
[NOTE] File /etc/issue was found.
```

These functions display either success or failure messages. You can control these messages through the JASS_LOG_FAILURE and JASS_LOG_SUCCESS environment variables. For more information on these environment variables, refer to Chapter 13.

logFileGroupMatch and logFileGroupNoMatch

Use these functions to log messages associated with the success or failure of a check. These functions together report on the results of a file group membership check. These functions are used primarily with the check_fileGroupMatch and check_fileGroupNoMatch functions, although they can be used independently if necessary.

You can supply the following arguments to this function:

A string value representing the name of the file to test

A string value representing the group to check

A non-negative integer representing the vulnerability value result

A string value representing related information that you want displayed for users after a PASS or FAIL message (optional)

Example usage:

```
logFileGroupMatch /etc/motd sys 0
```

Example output:

```
[PASS] File /etc/motd has group sys.
```

These functions display either success or failure messages. You can control these messages through the JASS_LOG_FAILURE and JASS_LOG_SUCCESS environment variables. For more information on these environment variables, refer to Chapter 13.

logFileModeMatch and logFileModeNoMatch

Use these functions to log messages associated with the success or failure of a check. These functions together report on the results of a file permissions check. These functions are used primarily with the check_fileModeMatch and check_fileModeNoMatch functions, although they can be used independently if necessary.

You can supply the following arguments to this function:

A string value representing the name of the file to test

A string value representing the permissions to check

A non-negative integer representing the vulnerability value result

A string value representing related information that you want displayed for users after a PASS or FAIL message (optional)

Example usage:

```
logFileModeMatch /etc/motd 0644 0
```

Example output:

```
[PASS] File /etc/motd has mode 0644.
```

These functions display either success or failure messages. You can control these messages through the JASS_LOG_FAILURE and JASS_LOG_SUCCESS environment variables. For more information on these environment variables, refer to Chapter 13.

logFileNotFound

This function is used by the software to display file not found messages. This function is used throughout the Solaris Security Toolkit code in both hardening and audit runs to provide a standard message when a designated file was not found on the system.

You can supply the following arguments to this function:

A string value representing the name of the file to test

A non-negative integer representing the vulnerability value result

If this argument is passed a null string value, then this function reports the result in the form of a notice using the logNotice function. Otherwise, it reports the result as a failure using the logFailure function.

A string value representing related information that you want displayed for users after a FAIL or NOTE message (optional)

Example usage:

```
logFileNotFound /etc/motd
```

Example output:

```
[NOTE] File /etc/issue was not found.
```

You can control notice and failure messages through the JASS_LOG_NOTICE and JASS_LOG_FAILURE environment variables, respectively. For more information on this environment variable, refer to Chapter 13.

logFileOwnerMatch and logFileOwnerNoMatch

Use these functions to log the messages associated with the success or failure of a check. These functions report on the results of a file ownership check. These functions are used primarily with the check_fileOwnerMatch and check_fileOwnerNoMatch functions, although they can be used independently if necessary.

You can supply the following arguments to this function:

A string value representing the name of the file to test

A string value representing the ownership to check

A non-negative integer representing the vulnerability value result

A string value representing related information that you want displayed for users after a PASS or FAIL message (optional)

Example usage:

```
logFileOwnerMatch /etc/motd root 0
```

Example output:

```
[PASS] File /etc/motd has owner root.
```

These functions display either success or failure messages. You can control these messages through the JASS_LOG_FAILURE and JASS_LOG_SUCCESS environment variables. For more information on these environment variables, refer to Chapter 13.

logFileTypeMatch and logFileTypeNoMatch

Use these functions to log the messages associated with the success or failure of a check. These functions report on the results of a file type check. These functions are used primarily with the check_fileTypeMatch and check_fileTypeNoMatch functions, although they can be used independently if necessary.

You can supply the following arguments to this function:

A string value representing the name of the file to test

A string value representing the file type to check

The following types are detected by the software:

b	Block special file
c	Character special file
d	Directory
D	Door
f	Regular file
l	Symbolic link
p	Named pipe (fifo)
s	Socket

A non-negative integer representing the vulnerability value result

A string value representing related information that you want displayed for users after a PASS or FAIL message (optional)

Example usage:

```
logFileTypeMatch /etc/motd f 0
```

Example output:

```
[PASS] File /etc/motd is a regular file.
```

These functions display either success or failure messages. You can control these messages through the JASS_LOG_FAILURE and JASS_LOG_SUCCESS environment variables. For more information on these environment variables, refer to Chapter 13.

logFinding

This function displays audit finding messages. This function accepts a single string argument to be displayed as a message. The input for this function is processed by the `printPrettyPath` function prior to display. In addition, if the verbosity level is less than 3, then optional tags are prepended to the message. The following are the optional tags that you can prepend by this function:

Time Stamp – If the `JASS_DISPLAY_TIMESTAMP` environment variable is 1, then the timestamp as defined by the `JASS_TIMESTAMP` environment variable prepends to the finding message.

Target Host Name – If the `JASS_DISPLAY_HOSTNAME` environment variable is 1, then the target's host name as defined by the `JASS_HOSTNAME` environment variable prepends to the finding message.

Current Script Name – If the `JASS_DISPLAY_SCRIPTNAME` environment variable is 1, then the name of the current audit script prepends to the finding message.

Note – If the finding occurs outside of an audit script, such as within the flow of the `driver.run` script, then the name of the current driver is used.

You can use all three output tags collectively or independently. The order of the position in the resulting output line is as they are listed. For more information on this function and verbosity levels, refer to Chapter 13.

Example usage:

```
logFinding "/etc/motd"
```

Example output:

```
test-script /etc/motd
```

logFormattedMessage

Use this function to generate formatted audit script headers that display information such as the script name, purpose, and rationale for the check. This function accepts a single string value and formats the message that is passed to the function.

These messages are reformatted as follows:

- Maximum width of 75 characters
- Prepended with the string " # " (pound symbol with a space before and after it)
- Duplicate slashes in path names are removed

Formatted messages are displayed only when the verbosity level is at least 3. For more information on this function and verbosity levels, refer to Chapter 13.

Example usage:

```
logFormattedMessage "Check system controller secure shell
configuration."
```

Example output:

```
# Check system controller secure shell configuration.
```

logInvalidDisableMode

Use this function to display an error message when the JASS_DISABLE_MODE environment variable is set to an invalid value. This utility function reports on the state of the JASS_DISABLE_MODE environment variable. This function takes no arguments and generates the following output:

```
[ERR ] The JASS_DISABLE_MODE parameter has an invalid value. The
[ERR ] value must either be 'script' or 'conf', but the current value
[ERR ] is [...].
```

For more information on this environment variable, refer to Chapter 13.

logInvalidOSRevision

Use this function when either the check_os_revision or
check_os_min_revision functions fail their checks. This utility function reports
when a function is being called on a version of the Solaris OE for which it does not
apply. For example, use this function when there is an attempt to use a Solaris 8 OE
script with the Solaris 2.6 OE.

Example usage:

```
logInvalidOSRevision "5.9"
```

Example output:

```
[NOTE] This script is only applicable for Solaris version
5.9.
```

To specify multiple versions, enter a hyphen (-) between versions, for example,
"5.6-5.8."

This function displays notice messages. You can control messages through the
JASS_LOG_NOTICE environment variable. For more information on this
environment variable, refer to Chapter 13.

logMessage

Use this function to display any message that you want to display to users. Use this
function for messages that do not have any tags associated with them. Similar to the
logFormattedMessage function, this function displays an unformatted message.
This function accepts a single string value that is displayed as is, with no
modification.

Unformatted messages are only displayed if the verbosity level is at least 3. For more
information onthis function and verbosity levels, refer to Chapter 13.

Example usage:

```
logMessage "Verify system controller static ARP configuration."
```

Example output:

```
Verify system controller static ARP configuration.
```

logNotice

Use this function to display notice messages. This function accepts a single string value that is displayed as a notice message. Notice messages are those that contain the string [NOTE].

Example usage:

```
logNotice "Service ${svc} does not exist in ${INETD}."
```

Example output:

```
[NOTE] Service telnet does not exist in /etc/inetd.conf.
```

You can control notice messages through the JASS_LOG_NOTICE environment variable. For more information on this environment variable, refer to Chapter 13.

logPackageExists and logPackageNotExists

Use these functions to log the messages associated with the success or failure of a check. These functions report on the results of a check that determines if a software package is installed. These functions are used primarily with the check_packageExists and check_packageNotExists functions, although they can be used independently if necessary.

You can supply the following arguments to this function:

A string value representing the name of the software package to test

A non-negative integer representing the vulnerability value result

A string value representing related information that you want displayed for users after a PASS or FAIL message (optional)

Example usage:

```
logPackageExists SUNWcsr 0
```

Example output:

```
[PASS] Package SUNWcsr is installed.
```

These functions display either success or failure messages. You can control these messages through the JASS_LOG_FAILURE and JASS_LOG_SUCCESS environment variables. For more information on these environment variables, refer to Chapter 13.

logPatchExists and logPatchNotExists

Use these functions to log the messages associated with the success or failure of a check. These functions report on the results of a check that determines if a software patch is installed. These functions are used primarily with the check_patchExists and check_patchNotExists functions, although they can be used independently if necessary.

You can supply the following arguments to this function:

A string value representing the patch identifier (number) to test

A non-negative integer representing the vulnerability value result

A string value representing related information that you want displayed for users after a PASS or FAIL message (optional)

Example usage:

```
logPatchExists 123456-01 0
```

Example output:

```
[PASS] Patch ID 123456-01 or higher is installed.
```

These functions display either success or failure messages. You can control these messages through the JASS_LOG_FAILURE and JASS_LOG_SUCCESS environment variables. For more information on these environment variables, refer to Chapter 13.

logProcessArgsMatch and logProcessArgsNoMatch

Use these functions to log the messages associated with the success or failure of a check. These functions report on the results of a check for run-time process arguments. These functions are used primarily with the check_processArgsMatch and check_processArgsNoMatch functions, although they can be used independently if necessary.

You can supply the following arguments to this function:

A string value representing the name of the process to test

A string value representing the argument search pattern

A non-negative integer representing the vulnerability value result

A string value representing related information that you want displayed for users after a PASS or FAIL message (optional)

Example usage:

```
logProcessArgsMatch inetd "-t" 0
```

Example output:

```
[PASS] Process inetd found with argument -t.
```

These functions display either success or failure messages. You can control these messages through the JASS_LOG_FAILURE and JASS_LOG_SUCCESS environment variables. For more information on these environment variables, refer to Chapter 13.

logProcessExists and logProcessNotExists

Use these functions to log the messages associated with the success or failure of a check. These functions report on the results of a check for a process. These functions are used primarily with the `check_processExists` and `check_processNotExists` functions, although they can be used independently if necessary.

You can supply the following arguments to this function:

A string value representing the name of the process to test

A non-negative integer representing the vulnerability value result

A string value representing related information that you want displayed for users after a PASS or FAIL message (optional)

Example usage:

```
logProcessExists nfsd 0
```

Example output:

```
[PASS] Process nfsd was found.
```

These functions display either success or failure messages. You can control these messages through the `JASS_LOG_FAILURE` and `JASS_LOG_SUCCESS` environment variables. For more information on these environment variables, refer to Chapter 13.

logProcessNotFound

Use this function to log a FAIL message for any process that is not found. This function displays "process not found" messages. This function provides a standard message when a designated process cannot be found on a system.

You can supply the following arguments to this function:

A string value representing the name of the process to test

A string value representing related information that you want displayed for users after a PASS or FAIL message (optional)

Example usage:

```
logProcessNotFound inetd
```

Example output:

```
[FAIL] Process inetd was not found.
```

You can control these messages through the `JASS_LOG_FAILURE` environment variable. For more information on these environment variables, refer to Chapter 13.

`logServiceConfigExists` and `logServiceConfigNotExists`

Use these functions to log the messages associated with the success or failure of a check. These functions report on the results of a check that determines if a configuration file exists. These functions are used primarily with the `check_serviceConfigExists` and `check_serviceConfigNotExists` functions, although they can be used independently if necessary.

You can supply the following arguments to this function:

A string value representing the name of the service configuration file to test

A non-negative integer representing the vulnerability value result

A string value representing related information that you want displayed for users after a `PASS` or `FAIL` message (optional)

Example usage:

```
logServiceConfigExists /etc/apache/httpd.conf 0
```

Example output:

```
[PASS] Service Config File /etc/apache/httpd.conf was found.
```

These functions display either success or failure messages. You can control these messages through the `JASS_LOG_FAILURE` and `JASS_LOG_SUCCESS` environment variables. For more information on these environment variables, refer to Chapter 13.

logStartScriptExists and logStartScriptNotExists

Use these functions to log the messages associated with the success or failure of a check. These functions report on the results of a check that determines if a run-control start script exists. These functions are used primarily with the `check_startScriptExists` and `check_startScriptNotExists` functions, although they can be used independently if necessary.

You can supply the following arguments to this function:

A string value representing the name of the start script to test

A non-negative integer representing the vulnerability value result

A string value representing related information that you want displayed for users after a PASS or FAIL message (optional)

Example usage:

```
logStartScriptExists /etc/rc3.d/S89sshd 0
```

Example output:

```
[PASS] Start Script /etc/rc3.d/S89sshd was found.
```

These functions display either success or failure messages. You can control these messages through the `JASS_LOG_FAILURE` and `JASS_LOG_SUCCESS` environment variables. For more information on these environment variables, refer to Chapter 13.

logStopScriptExists and logStopScriptNotExists

Use these functions to log the messages associated with the success or failure of a check. These functions report on the results of a check that determines if a run-control stop script exists. These functions are used primarily with the `check_stopScriptExists` and `check_stopScriptNotExists` functions, although they can be used independently if necessary.

You can supply the following arguments to this function:

A string value representing the name of the stop script to test

A non-negative integer representing the vulnerability value result

A string value representing related information that you want displayed for users after a PASS or FAIL message (optional)

Example usage:

```
logStopScriptExists /etc/rc2.d/K03sshd 0
```

Example output:

```
[PASS] Stop Script /etc/rc2.d/K03sshd was found.
```

These functions display either success or failure messages. You can control these messages through the JASS_LOG_FAILURE and JASS_LOG_SUCCESS environment variables. For more information on these environment variables, refer to Chapter 13.

logSuccess

Use this function to display success messages. This function accepts a single string value that is displayed as an audit success message. Success messages are those that contain the string " [PASS]."

Example usage:

```
logSuccess "Package SUNWsshdr is installed."
```

Example output:

```
[PASS] Package SUNWsshdr is installed.
```

You can control success messages through the JASS_LOG_SUCCESS environment variable. For more information on this environment variable, refer to Chapter 13.

logWarning

Use this function to display warning messages. This function accepts a single sting value that is displayed as a warning message. Warning messages are those that contain the string " [WARN]."

Example usage:

```
logWarning "User ${acct} is not listed in ${JASS_PASSWD}."
```

Example output:

```
[WARN] User abc is not listed in /etc/passwd.
```

You can control warning messages through the JASS_LOG_WARNING environment variable. For more information on this environment variable, refer to Chapter 13.

Using Common Miscellaneous Functions

These functions are for common miscellaneous functions that are used within several areas of the Solaris Security Toolkit software and are not specific to functionality provided by other framework functions (files ending with a .func suffix). These functions are in the Drivers directory in a file called common_misc.funcs. Common utility functions such as isNumeric and printPretty are in this file.

This section describes the common miscellaneous functions.

isNumeric

Use this function to determine if input arguments are positive numbers. It is used throughout the software by helper functions whenever input must be validated to ensure that it consists of a single, positive integer. This function accepts a single string argument and determines if the value is a positive integer. If the value is a positive integer, this function displays a value of 0, otherwise it displays a value of 1.

invalidVulnVal

Use this function to determine if input arguments are positive numbers. This function accepts a single string argument and determines if the value is a positive integer. It logs an error message for each failure. This function is necessary to determine where there may be invalid arguments supplied to a function as a vulnerability value. In all other aspects, this function behaves like its isNumeric counterpart. This function applies only to audit operations.

checkLogStatus

Use this function to determine if a given input string is set to LOG. This function accepts a single string argument and determines whether the calling function should log its results. If the string evaluated is the string LOG, then this function echoes a value of 1, indicating that the calling function should log its results. If the input string contains any other value, this function echoes a value of 0, indicating that no output is logged by the calling function. This function applies only to audit operations.

adjustScore

Use this function to adjust the score outside of the methods provided by the functions defined in the audit_public.funcs file. This function accepts a positive integer argument representing the value that is added to the current score for an audit script. For example, there might be times when only the audit script can determine a failure. In those cases, use this function to adjust the score, accounting for the failure. If one is not suppled, it logs an error message and does not adjust the score. This function applies only to audit runs.

printPretty

Use this function to format printed output so that it is easier to read. This function accepts an unformatted input string and processes it. The resulting string is wrapped at 72 characters with each line of output indented by three characters.

printPrettyPath

Use this function to format path names. This function accepts as input an unformatted path name. This function strips any redundant forward slashes from the input string, then displays the result. If the string is empty, then the keyword "<No Value>" is displayed in its place.

Using Driver Functions

These functions are for driver functionality. These functions are in the driver.funcs file, located in the Drivers directory. Functions such as add_pkg and copy_a_file are in this file.

When customizing or creating scripts, use the following functions to perform standard operations.

add_patch

Use this function to add Solaris OE patches to the system. By default, this function expects that the patches installed are located in the JASS_PATCH_DIR directory. TABLE 8-1 lists the options for this function.

TABLE 8-1 Options for add_patch Finish Script Function

-o <options>	Options to be passed on
-M <patchdir>	The fully qualified path to the source directory
<patchlist>	List of patches or name of file containing a list of patches to apply

Example usage:

```
add_patch 123456-01
```

```
add_patch -M ${JASS_PATCH_DIR}/OtherPatches patch_list.txt
```

add_pkg

Use this function to add Solaris OE packages to the system. By default, this function expects that the packages are located in the JASS_PACKAGE_DIR directory. These packages are in one of the standard Sun formats, spooled directories or package stream files. This function automatically adds the necessary manifest entries to permit this operation to be reversed during an undo run. During an undo run, packages added using this function are removed from the system. TABLE 8-2 lists the options for this function.

TABLE 8-2 Options for add_pkg Function

-a <ask_file>	The pkgadd ask file name. By default, the pkgadd ask file, noask_pkgadd, is used if no other file is specified.
-d <src_loc>	The fully qualified path to the source package (streams or directory) to be installed
-o <options>	The pkgadd command options
<package>	The package to be installed

Example usage:

```
add_pkg ABCtest
```

```
add_pkg -d ${JASS_ROOT_DIR}/${JASS_PACKAGE_DIR}/SUNWjass.pkg \
SUNWjass
```

add_to_manifest

Use this function to manually insert entries into a manifest file during hardening runs without needing to call one of the helper functions. This approach is most often done when a command must be executed for the undo operation to complete. We recommend that you use this option with care, to protect the integrity of the system and the Solaris Security Toolkit's repository.

Caution – Exercise extreme caution when using the X manifest option. The commands specified by this operation are executed during an undo run of the Solaris Security Toolkit as the root user. Failure to do so may result in data loss or could render a target system unstable. For example, an X manifest entry of rm -rf/ would delete the system's root partition during an undo run.

The add_to_manifest command uses the following syntax:

```
add_to_manifest <operation> <src> <dst> <args>
```

This command puts an entry in the JASS_RUN_MANIFEST file in JASS_REPOSITORY/jass-manifest.txt, critical to the ability to undo the changes made by a finish script.

Note – Not all of the operations used by the Solaris Security Toolkit support each of these arguments. Also, the meaning of the options for src, dst, and args can differ based on the operation selected.

The operations supported by the `add_to_manifest` function are listed in TABLE 8-3. This table includes a sample resulting manifest entry after each option.

TABLE 8-3　add_to_manifest Options and Sample Manifest Entries

Option	Description

C	Indicates a file was copied. In this case, the `src` and `dst` parameters represent the original and copied file names, respectively. No other arguments are used.
	`install-templates.fin /etc/syslog.conf /etc/ \`
	`syslog.conf.JASS.20020823230626`

D	Indicates a directory was created. In this case, the `src` parameter represents the name of the newly created directory. No other arguments are used. `disable-lp.fin            /var/spool/cron/crontabs.JASS`

J	Indicates a new file was created on the system. This operation is used only when the file specified by the `src` parameter does not exist on the system. During an undo run, files tagged with this operation code are removed. This operation uses both the `src` and `dst` parameters to represent the original name of the file and its saved file name (which must include the `JASS_SUFFIX`).
	`disable-power-mgmt.fin /noautoshutdown  \`
	`/noautoshutdown.JASS.20020823230629`

M	Indicates a file was moved. In this case, the `src` and `dst` parameters represent the original and moved file names, respectively. No other arguments are used.
	`disable-ldap-client.fin /etc/rcS.d/K41ldap.client \`
	`/etc/rcS.d/_K41ldap.client.JASS.20020823230628`

R	Indicates a file was removed from the system. In this case, only the `src` parameter represents the name of the file that was removed. Files marked with this operation code cannot be restored using the Solaris Security Toolkit undo command.

S	Indicates a symbolic link was created. In this case, the `src` and `dst` parameters represent the source and target file names, respectively. During an undo run, the symbolic links for files tagged with this operation are removed from the system.
	`install-templates.fin ../init.d/nddconfig      /etc/rc2.d/ \`
	`S70nddconfig`

X	Indicates a command was defined that should be run when the Solaris Security Toolkit processes a manifest entry that has this operation code. A special operation, this one is most often used to execute complex commands that go beyond the standard operations. For example, in the `install-fix-modes.fin` finish script, the following manifest entry is added to instruct the software to undo changes made by the Fix Modes program: `/opt/FixModes/fix-modes -u` This command instructs the software to run the `fix-modes` program with the `-u` option. Note that all commands processed by this operation code should be specified using an absolute path to the program.

backup_file

Use this function to back up an existing file system object. This function backs up the original file using a standard naming convention. The convention appends JASS_SUFFIX to the original file name. This function automatically adds the necessary manifest entries to permit this operation to be reversed during an undo run.

The JASS_SAVE_BACKUP variable specifies if the Solaris Security Toolkit software saves or does not save backup copies of files modified during a run. If this environment variable is set to 0, then this function does not save backup files on the system. If files are not saved, then the run cannot be reversed by using the undo command.

Example usage:

```
backup_file /etc/motd
```

check_os_min_version

Use this function to detect functionality that exists in multiple releases of the Solaris OS. This function takes only one argument, indicating the minimal OS release version. If the actual release of the OS on the target platform is greater than or equal to the argument, then the function returns 0, otherwise this function returns 1. If an error is encountered, then this function returns 255.

For example, this function can be used as follows.

CODE EXAMPLE 8-3 Detecting Functionality That Exists in Multiple OS Releases

```
if check_os_min_revision 5.6 ; then
    if [ "${JASS_KILL_SCRIPT_DISABLE}" = "1" ]; then
        disable_rc_file ${JASS_ROOT_DIR}/etc/rcS.d K10dtlogin
        disable_rc_file ${JASS_ROOT_DIR}/etc/rc0.d K10dtlogin
        disable_rc_file ${JASS_ROOT_DIR}/etc/rc1.d K10dtlogin
    fi
    disable_rc_file ${JASS_ROOT_DIR}/etc/rc2.d S99dtlogin
else
    logInvalidOSRevision "5.6 and later"
fi
```

In this example, the Common Desktop Environment (CDE) was not included in the Solaris OE until version 2.6, and this script checks to ensure that the version is at least 5.6, before attempting to disable the run-control scripts listed.

check_os_revision

Use this function to check for a specific OS revision or range of values. This function can take either one or two arguments. If one argument is supplied, then the script returns 0 only if the target operating system revision is the same as the argument, otherwise it returns 1.

Similarly, if two arguments are provided, the target operating system revision must be between the two values inclusively for the result to be 0. In either case, if an error is encountered, this function returns a value of 255.

For example, this function can be used as follows.

CODE EXAMPLE 8-4 Checking for a Specific OS Revision or Range

```
if check_os_revision 5.5.1 5.8; then
    if [ "${JASS_DISABLE_MODE}" = "conf" ]; then
        disable_conf_file ${JASS_ROOT_DIR}/etc asppp.cf
    elif [ "${JASS_DISABLE_MODE}" = "script" ]; then
        if [ "${JASS_KILL_SCRIPT_DISABLE}" = "1" ]; then
            disable_rc_file ${JASS_ROOT_DIR}/etc/rcS.d K50asppp
            disable_rc_file ${JASS_ROOT_DIR}/etc/rc0.d K47asppp
            disable_rc_file ${JASS_ROOT_DIR}/etc/rc0.d K50asppp
            disable_rc_file ${JASS_ROOT_DIR}/etc/rc1.d K47asppp
            disable_rc_file ${JASS_ROOT_DIR}/etc/rc1.d K50asppp
        fi
        disable_rc_file ${JASS_ROOT_DIR}/etc/rc2.d S47asppp
    fi
else
    logInvalidOSRevision "5.5.1-5.8"
fi
```

In this example, the script disables only its scripts or configuration files, based on the value of JASS_DISABLE_MODE, when the target OS revision is or falls between Solaris OE versions 2.5.1 and 8 inclusively.

copy_a_dir

Use this function to recursively copy the contents of a directory. This function takes two arguments: a source directory name and a destination directory name. This function copies the contents of the source directory to the directory specified by the destination parameter. This function creates the new directory if it does not already exist. This function automatically adds the necessary manifest entries to permit this operation to be reversed during an undo run.

Example usage:

```
copy_a_dir /tmp/test1 /tmp/test2
```

copy_a_file

Use this function to copy exactly one regular file. This function takes two arguments: a source file name and a destination file name. This function copies the contents of the source file to the file name specified by the destination parameter. This function automatically adds the necessary manifest entries to permit this operation to be reversed during an undo run.

Example usage:

```
copy_a_file /tmp/test-file-a /tmp/test-file-b
```

copy_a_symlink

Use this function to copy a symbolic link to the target platform. This function takes two arguments: a source link name and a destination file name. This function creates a new symbolic link based on the source link specified using the new file name passed as the destination parameter. This function automatically adds the necessary manifest entries to permit this operation to be reversed during an undo run.

Example usage:

```
copy_a_symlink /tmp/test-link-a /tmp/test-link-b
```

copy_files

Use this function to copy a set of file system objects from the `JASS_HOME_DIR/Files` directory tree to a target system. This function uses the appropriate copy functions listed previously to ensure that the changes made can be reversed during an undo run. This function is capable of copying regular files, directories, and symbolic links.

Example usage:

```
copy_files /etc/init.d/nddconfig
```

```
copy_files "/etc/init.d/nddconfig /etc/motd /etc/issue"
```

This function extends capability by permitting the selective copy of objects based on tags appended to their file names.

The files that are copied by this function are selected by the following criteria:

`/some/fully/qualified/path/file`

In this option, the software copies the file to a target system, unless one of the previous options matches a file by the same name.

For example: `/etc/issue`

`/some/fully/qualified/path/file.${HOST}`

In this option, the software copies the object only if the name of the target platform matches the tag specified by `${HOST}`. This host environment variable uses the same naming format as the `JASS_HOSTNAME` environment variable.

For example: `/etc/issure.jordan`

`/some/fully/qualified/path/file+${OS}`

In this option, the software only copies the object if the OS revision of the target platform matches the tag specified by `${OS}`. The OS parameter uses the same naming format as the `JASS_OS_REVISION` environment variable. So, a file to be used only on the Solaris 8 OE is denoted as "`filename+5.8`".

For example: `/etc/issue+5.10`

Note – When the file length/size is zero, the file is not copied to the system.

The order of precedence used to match a file is listed. For example, if a host-specific and general file both exist, the host-specific file is used if the name of a target system matches the host name defined by the host-specific file.

Note – The copy_files function silently ignores any objects listed that are not found in the JASS_HOME_DIR/Files directory tree.

create_a_file

Use this function to create an empty file on a target system. This function uses a combination of the touch, chown, and chmod commands to create an empty file with a specific owner, group, and set of permissions.

Note – This function does not adjust permissions or ownerships on a file that exists.

This function creates a file with specific permissions. For example "create_a_file -o guppy:staff -m 750 /usr/local/testing" would create the file testing in the /usr/local directory, owned by guppy and group of staff, with permissions 750. This function accepts the options listed in TABLE 8-4.

TABLE 8-4   create_a_file Command Options

Option	Valid Input
[-o user[:group]]	Follows syntax of chown(1) and accepts user and user:group
[-m perms]	Follows syntax of chmod(1) and accepts perms
/some/fully/ qualified/path/file	The fully qualified path to the file

Example usage:

```
create_a_file /usr/local/testing
```

```
create_a_file -o root /usr/local/testing
```

```
create_a_file -o root:sys /usr/local/testing
```

```
create_a_file -o root -m 0750 /usr/local/testing
```

create_file_timestamp

Use this function to create a unique time-stamp value for a given file and for all file backup operations. This function is useful for creating a backup of an already backed-up file when a unique suffix value is needed. The time-stamp value created is in the same format as JASS_TIMESTAMP. The resulting time-stamp value created by this function is stored in the JASS_SUFFIX environment variable. For more information, refer to Chapter 13, "This variable creates the JASS_REPOSITORY directory, /var/opt/SUNWjass/run/JASS_TIMESTAMP. As noted previously, this directory contains the logs and manifest information for each run of the Solaris Security Toolkit software. This variable contains the timestamp associated with the start of a run, and its value is maintained for the entire run. As a result, its value is unique for each run. This unique value allows information for each run to be clearly separated from all others, based on the time that the run was started. By default, this variable is set to date '+%EY%m%d%OH%OM%S'. This command creates a timestamp of the form YYYYMMDDHHMMSS. For example, a run started at 1:30 p.m. on April 1, 2003 would be represented by the value 20030401013000." on page 319.

Example usage:

```
create_file_timestamp /usr/local/testing
```

disable_conf_file

Use this function to disable service configuration files. This function accepts two string values representing the directory name in which the file is located and the service configuration file name. This function disables the service configuration file by prepending a prefix of "_" (underscore) to the file name, thereby preventing its execution.

Example usage:

```
disable_conf_file /etc/dfs dfstab
```

This example renames a file from /etc/dfs/dfstab to /etc/dfs/_dfstab.JASS.<timestamp>. This function automatically adds the necessary manifest entries to permit this operation to be reversed during an undo run.

disable_file

Use this function to disable files that cannot be stored in their original directory. For example, the /var/spool/cron/crontabs directory contains individual user crontab files. If a disabled or backed-up copy of a crontab file were stored in the crontabs directory, then the cron service would indicate an error, because there would be no user name that matched the names of the disabled or backed-up files.

To address this issue, this function creates a mirror directory with a .JASS suffix within which to store any of the disabled files. For example, if the file to be disabled is located in the /var/spool/cron/crontabs directory, this function creates a /var/spool/cron/crontabs.JASS directory in which the disabled file is moved.

The file to be disabled, as with the other disable functions, has a suffix of .JASS.<timestamp>. The difference with this function is that the disabled file is not stored in the same directory as the original file.

Example usage:

```
disable_file /var/spool/cron/crontabs/uucp
```

In this example, the file /var/spool/cron/crontabs/uucp is moved to the /var/spool/cron/crontabs.JASS directory and renamed as uucp.JASS.<timestamp>. This function automatically adds the necessary manifest entries to permit this operation to be reversed during an undo run.

disable_rc_file

Use this function to disable the execution of a run-control file. This function accepts two string values representing the directory name in which the script is located and the run-control script name. This function disables the script by prepending a prefix of "_" (underscore) to the file name, thereby preventing its execution by run-control framework. To be executed, a script name must begin with either an "S" or a "K" depending on its purpose as a start or kill run-control script. In addition, a suffix of .JASS.<timestamp> is appended to the disabled file.

Example usage:

```
disable_rc_file /etc/rc2.d S71rpc
```

This example renames a file from /etc/rc2.d/S71rpc to /etc/rc2.d/_S71rpc.JASS.<timestamp>. This function automatically adds the necessary manifest entries to permit this operation to be reversed during an undo run.

is_patch_applied and is_patch_not_applied

Use these functions to determine if a patch is or is not applied to a system. These functions accept a single string value representing the patch number to check.

This value can be specified in one of two ways:

You can specify the patch number as in "123456." These functions display a value of 0 if the patch is installed on a target system. If the patch is not installed, they display a value of 1.

Example usage:

```
is_patch_applied 123456
```

You can specify the patch number and revision number as in "123456-03." These functions display a value of 0 if the patch is on the system and has at a minimum the same revision as specified. If the patch is not on the system, a value of 1 is displayed. If the patch is installed, however, and its revision is not at least the value specified, then these functions display a value of 2.

Example usage:

```
is_patch_applied 123456-02
```

mkdir_dashp

Use this function to create a new directory on a target system. This function accepts a single string value representing the name of the directory to create. This function uses the -p option to mkdir so that no error is reported if the target directory exists. This function automatically adds the necessary manifest entries to permit this operation to be reversed during an undo run.

Example usage:

```
mkdir_dashp /usr/local
```

move_a_file

Use this function to move a file from one name to another. This function requires two entries: a source file name and a destination file name. This function moves, or renames, the source file to the file name specified by the destination parameter. This function automatically adds the necessary manifest entries to permit this operation to be reversed during an undo run.

Example usage:

```
move_a_file /tmp/test-file-a /tmp/test-file-b
```

rm_pkg

Use this function to remove Solaris OE packages from a system. The operations performed by this function are final and cannot be reversed during an undo run. The options for this function are listed in TABLE 8-5.

TABLE 8-5   rm_pkg Function Options

-a <ask_file>	The pkgrm ask file name. By default, the pkgrm ask file, noask_pkgrm, is used if no other file is specified.
-o <options>	The pkgrm command options
<package>	The package to be removed

Example usage:

```
rm_pkg SUNWadmr
```

Using Audit Functions

Two types of audit functions are in the software: private and public. The functions defined in the `audit_private.funcs` file are private and not for public use. Never use the private scripts defined in this file. Only use the public scripts defined in the `audit_public.funcs` file.

The public functions define audit functions used in audit scripts, which are located in `JASS_AUDIT_DIR`. Functions defined in this file are public and can be freely used in both standard and custom audit scripts. Note that in many cases, the functions defined in this file are stubs that call functions defined in the `audit_private.funcs` file. These stubs were implemented to allow users to code their scripts to these public interfaces without needing to care if the underlying code will be modified or enhanced in newer releases.

Use these functions as part of audit scripts to assess components of the system's stored and run-time configurations. The following functions are public interfaces to the Solaris Security Toolkit software's audit framework.

When customizing or creating audit scripts, use the following functions to perform standard operations.

check_fileContentsExist and check_fileContentsNotExist

Use these functions to determine if a designated file has content matching a supplied search string. These functions search a designated file to match its content with a search string. The search string can be in the form of a regular expression. These functions display a 0 for success, 1 for failure, and 255 for error condition.

You can supply the following arguments to this function:

A string value representing the name of the file(s) to test.

A string value representing the search pattern.

A non-negative integer representing the vulnerability value to be used if the audit check fails.

A string value representing the logging status of the function. If this value is equivalent to the string value LOG, then the results are logged automatically by either the log_FileContentsExist or the log_FileContentsNotExist functions. If any other string keyword is supplied, logging is not automatic, and the calling program code has to log any status messages.

A string value representing related information that you want displayed for users after a PASS or FAIL message (optional). This information is simply passed to the logging function if the environment variable is set to "LOG."

Example usage:

```
check_fileContentsExist /etc/default/inetinit \
"TCP_STRONG_ISS=2" 1 LOG
```

check_fileExists and check_fileNotExists

Use these functions to determine if a file exists on a target system. These functions display a status of 0 for success, 1 for failure, and 255 for any error condition.

You can supply the following arguments to this function:

A string value representing the name of the file(s) to test.

A non-negative integer representing the vulnerability value to be used if the audit check fails.

A string value representing the logging status of the function. If this value is equivalent to the string value LOG, then the results of this function are logged automatically. If any other string keyword is supplied, logging is not automatic and the calling program code has to log any status messages.

A string value representing related information that you want displayed for users after a PASS or FAIL message (optional). This information is simply passed to the logging function if the environment variable is set to LOG.

Example usage:

```
check_fileExists /etc/inet/inetd.conf 1 LOG
```

check_fileGroupMatch and check_fileGroupNoMatch

Use these functions to determine if a file belongs to a group on a target system. These functions display a status of 0 for success, 1 for failure, and 255 for any error condition.

You can supply the following arguments to this function:

A string value representing the name of the file(s) to test.

A string value representing the group to check. The group value can be a name or a group identifier (ID). If a group name is numeric and does not appear in a name service table, it is taken as a group ID.

A non-negative integer representing the vulnerability value to be used if the audit check fails.

A string value representing the logging status of the function. If this value is equivalent to the string value LOG, then the results of this function are logged automatically. If any other string keyword is supplied, logging is not automatic, and the calling program code has to log any status messages.

A string value representing related information that you want displayed for users after a PASS or FAIL message (optional). This information is simply passed to the logging function if the environment variable is set to LOG.

Example usage:

```
check_fileGroupMatch /etc/passwd sys 1 LOG

check_fileGroupMatch /etc/passwd 3 1 LOG
```

check_fileModeMatch and check_fileModeNoMatch

Use these functions to determine if a file has the permissions specified on a target system. These functions display a status of 0 for success, 1 for failure, and 255 for any error condition.

You can supply the following arguments to this function:

A string value representing the name of the file(s) to test.

A string value representing the mode or permissions to check. The permissions value can be either a symbolic or octal value. This function accepts the same values for this environment variable as does the find(1)command's perm option.

A non-negative integer representing the vulnerability value to be used if the audit check fails.

A string value representing the logging status of the function. If this value is equivalent to the string value LOG, then the results of this function are logged automatically. If any other string keyword is supplied, logging is not automatic, and the calling program code has to log any status messages.

A string value representing related information that you want displayed for users after a PASS or FAIL message (optional). This information is simply passed to the logging function if the environment variable is set to LOG.

Example usage:

```
check_fileModeMatch /etc/passwd "0444" 1 LOG

check_fileModeMatch /etc/passwd "ugo=r" 1 LOG
```

check_fileOwnerMatch and check_fileOwnerNoMatch

Use these functions to determine if a file belongs to a specific user on a target system. These functions display a status of 0 for success, 1 for failure, and 255 for any error condition.

You can supply the following arguments to this function:

A string value representing the name of the file(s) to test.

A string value representing the user to check. The user value can be either a name or a user identifier.

A non-negative integer representing the vulnerability value to use if the audit check fails.

A string value representing the logging status of the function. If this value is equivalent to the string value LOG, then the results of this function are logged automatically. If any other string keyword is supplied for this argument, logging is not automatic, and the calling program code has to log any status messages.

A string value representing related information that you want displayed for users after a PASS or FAIL message (optional). This information is simply passed to the logging function if the above environment variable is set to LOG.

Example usage:

```
check_fileOwnerMatch /etc/passwd root 1 LOG
check_fileOwnerMatch /etc/passwd 0 1 LOG
```

check_fileTemplate

Use this function to determine if a file template defined by the Solaris Security Toolkit software matches its counterpart installed on a target system. For example, if you were to use this function to check the file template /etc/motd, this function would compare the contents of JASS_FILES_DIR/etc/motd with /etc/motd to determine if they were the same. If they were identical, this function would display 0 for success, 1 for failure, or 255 for any error condition. If you specify more than one file, they all must pass to get a display code of 0.

You can supply the following arguments to this function:

A string value representing the name or a list of files separated by spaces (for example, a b c) to test.

A non-negative integer representing the vulnerability value to be used if the check fails.

A string value representing the logging status of the function. If this value is equivalent to the string value LOG, then the results of this function are logged automatically. If any other string keyword is supplied, logging is not automatic, and the calling program code has to log any status messages.

A string value representing related information that you want displayed for users after a PASS or FAIL message (optional). This information is simply passed to the logging function if the environment variable is set to LOG.

Example usage:

```
check_fileTemplate /etc/motd 1 LOG
```

check_fileTypeMatch and check_fileTypeNoMatch

Use these functions to determine if a file system object is a specific object type on a target system. These functions display a 0 for success, 1 for failure, and 255 for any error condition.

You can supply the following arguments to this function:

A string value representing the name of the file(s) to test.

A string value representing the file type to check. For more information on available types, refer to "logFileTypeMatch and logFileTypeNoMatch" on page 143.

TABLE 8-6 lists the types detected by the software:

TABLE 8-6   File Types Detected by Using the `check_fileTemplate` Function

b	Block special file
c	Character special file
d	Directory
D	Door
f	Regular file
l	Symbolic link
p	Named pipe (fifo)
s	Socket

A non-negative integer representing the vulnerability value to be used if the check fails.

A string value representing the logging status of the function. If this value is equivalent to the string value LOG, then the results of this function are logged automatically. If any other string keyword is supplied, logging is not automatic, and the calling program code has to log any status messages.

A string value representing related information that you want displayed for users after a PASS or FAIL message (optional). This information is simply passed to the logging function if the environment variable is set to LOG.

Example usage:

```
check_fileTypeMatch /etc/passwd f 1 LOG
check_fileTypeMatch /etc d 1 LOG
```

check_minimized

Use this function when a package check should only be performed on a minimized platform. This function is similar to the check_packagesNotExist function, except that its behavior is controlled by the JASS_CHECK_MINIMIZED environment variable. If a target system is not minimized, then the JASS_CHECK_MINIMIZED environment variable should be set to 0. In this case, this function does not perform any of its checks and simply displays a value of 0 with a notice indicating that a check was not run. Otherwise, this function behaves exactly as the check_packageNotExists function and displays a 0 for success, 1 for failure, and 255 for any error condition.

You can supply the following arguments to this function:

A string value representing the name of the package(s) to test.

A non-negative integer representing the vulnerability value to be used if the check fails.

A string value representing the logging status of the function. If this value is equivalent to the string value LOG, then the results of this function are logged automatically. If any other string keyword is supplied, logging is not automatic, and the calling program code has to log any status messages.

A string value representing related information that you want displayed for users after a PASS or FAIL message (optional). This information is simply passed to the logging function if the above environment variable is set to LOG.

Example usage:

```
check_minimized SUNWatfsu 1 LOG
```

check_packageExists and check_packageNotExists

Use these functions to determine if a software package is installed on a target system. These functions display a 0 for success, 1 for failure, and 255 for any error condition.

You can supply the following arguments to this function:

A string value representing the name of the package(s) to test.

A non-negative integer representing the vulnerability value to be used if the audit check fails.

A string value representing the logging status of the function. If this value is equivalent to the string value LOG, then the results of this function are logged automatically. If any other string keyword is supplied, logging is not automatic, and the calling program code has to log any status messages.

A string value representing related information that you want displayed for users after a PASS or FAIL message (optional). This information is simply passed to the logging function if the environment variable is set to LOG.

Example usage:

```
check_packageExists SUNWsshdu 1 LOG
```

check_patchExists and check_patchNotExists

Use these functions to determine if a software patch is installed on a target system. These functions display a 0 for success, 1 for failure, and 255 for any error condition.

You can supply the following arguments to this function:

A string value representing the name of the patch(es) to test.

A non-negative integer representing the vulnerability value to be used if the check fails.

A string value representing the logging status of the function. If this value is equivalent to the string value LOG, then the results of this function are logged automatically. If any other string keyword is supplied, logging is not automatic, and the calling program code has to log any status messages.

A string value representing related information that you want displayed for users after a PASS or FAIL message (optional). This information is simply passed to the logging function if the environment variable is set to LOG.

Example usage:

```
check_patchExists 123456 1 LOG

check_patchExists 123456-01 1 LOG
```

Note – You can specify a patch revision. If you do, then any installed revision must be equal to or greater than the revision specified. If you do not specify a revision, then this function indicates success if any version of the patch is installed.

---

check_processArgsMatch and check_processArgsNoMatch

Use these functions to determine if a process is running on the system with specific run-time arguments. These functions display a 0 for success, 1 for failure, and 255 for any error condition.

You can supply the following arguments to this function:

A string value representing the name of the process(s) to test.

A string value representing the run-time arguments to check.

A non-negative integer representing the vulnerability value to be used if the check fails.

A string value representing the logging status of the function. If this value is equivalent to the string value LOG, then the results of this function are logged automatically. If any other string keyword is supplied, logging is not automatic, and the calling program code has to log any status messages.

A string value representing related information that you want displayed for users after a PASS or FAIL message (optional). This information is simply passed to the logging function if the above environment variable is set to LOG.

Example usage:

```
check_processArgsMatch /usr/sbin/syslogd "-t" 1 LOG
```

check_processExists and check_processNotExists

Use these functions to determine if a process is running on a target system. These functions display a 0 for success, 1 for failure, and 255 for any error condition.

You can supply the following arguments to this function:

A string value representing the name of the process(es) to test.

A non-negative integer representing the vulnerability value to be used if the check fails.

A string value representing the logging status of the function. If this value is equivalent to the string value LOG, then the results of this function are logged automatically. If any other string keyword is supplied, logging is not automatic, and the calling program code has to log any status messages.

A string value representing related information that you want displayed for users after a PASS or FAIL message (optional). This information is simply passed to the logging function if the above environment variable is set to LOG.

Example usage:

```
check_processExists sshd 1 LOG
```

check_serviceConfigExists and check_serviceConfigNotExists

Use these functions to determine if a service configuration file exists on a target system. These functions display a 0 for success, 1 for failure, and 255 for any error condition.

You can supply the following arguments to this function:

A string value representing the name of the service configuration file(s) to test.

A non-negative integer representing the vulnerability value to be used if the check fails.

A string value representing the logging status of the function. If this value is equivalent to the string value LOG, then the results of this function are logged automatically. If any other string keyword is supplied, logging is not automatic, and the calling program code has to log any status messages.

A string value representing related information that you want displayed for users after a PASS or FAIL message (optional). This information is simply passed to the logging function if the above environment variable is set to LOG.

Example usage:

```
check_serviceConfigExists /etc/ssh/sshd_config 1 LOG
```

check_startScriptExists and check_startScriptNotExists

Use these functions to determine if a run-control start script exists on a target system. These functions display a 0 for success, 1 for failure, and 255 for any error condition.

You can supply the following arguments to this function:

A string value representing the name of the run-control start script(s) to test.

A non-negative integer representing the vulnerability value to be used if the check fails.

A string value representing the logging status of the function. If this value is equivalent to the string value LOG, then the results of this function are logged automatically. If any other string keyword is supplied, logging is not automatic, and the calling program code has to log any status messages.

A string value representing related information that you want displayed for users after a PASS or FAIL message (optional). This information is simply passed to the logging function if the above environment variable is set to LOG.

Example usage:

```
check_startScriptExists /etc/rc3.d/S89sshd 1 LOG
```

`check_stopScriptExists` and `check_stopScriptNotExists`

Use these functions to determine if a run-control stop script exists on a target system. These functions display a 0 for success, 1 for failure, and 255 for any error condition.

You can supply the following arguments to this function:

A string value representing the name of the run-control stop script(s) to test.

A non-negative integer representing the vulnerability value to be used if the check fails.

A string value representing the logging status of the function. If this value is equivalent to the string value LOG, then the results of this function are logged automatically. If any other string keyword is supplied, logging is not automatic, and the calling program code has to log any status messages.

A string value representing related information that you want displayed for users after a PASS or FAIL message (optional). This information is simply passed to the logging function if the above environment variable is set to LOG.

Example usage:

```
check_stopScriptExists /etc/rc2.d/K03sshd 1 LOG
```

`finish_check`

Use this function to signal that a check script has completed all of its processing and that a score for the script must be computed. This function is typically the last entry in a check script. If you want to display a message indicating a script's termination, then pass a single string argument to this function.

Example usage:

```
finish_check
```

```
finish_check "End of script"
```

start_audit

Use this function to call an audit script. This function is typically the first instruction in an audit script, not including comments or variable declaration. This function defines the name of the script, displays the banners, and resets the score to 0.

You can supply the following arguments to this function:

A string value representing the name of the audit script.

A string value representing a description of the audit script. This description can be multiple lines and is formatted using the `logFormattedMessage` function.

A string value representing related information that you want displayed for users after a PASS or FAIL message (optional). This information is formatted using the `logFormattedMessage` function.

Example usage:

```
start_audit disable-apache.aud "Apache" "Description of Check"
```

Example output:

```
#-----------------------------------------------------------------
# Apache
#
# Description of Check
#-----------------------------------------------------------------
```

## CHAPTER 9

Using File Templates

This chapter provides reference information about how to use, modify, and customize the file templates included in the Solaris Security Toolkit software. Also, this chapter describes how drivers process functions and other information stored in file templates.

Note – The files in the Files directory are for JumpStart installations. For more information, refer to Chapter 1.

This chapter contains the following topics:

Customizing File Templates

File templates are an integral part of the Solaris Security Toolkit software. These files provide a mechanism for you to customize and distribute scripts easily through environment variables, OE version numbers, and client host names. You can leverage the contents of the Files directory in combination with finish scripts to isolate related changes, depending on the design of your security profile (driver).

This section provides instructions and recommendations for customizing file templates, including instructions for creating new files in the Files directory.

For information about customizing drivers, finish scripts, and audit scripts, refer to the following chapters:

To customize drivers, refer to Chapter 10.

To customize finish scripts, refer to Chapter 11.

To customize audit scripts, refer to Chapter 12.

Note – Consider submitting a request for enhancement if you think that your customized files could benefit a wider audience. The Solaris Security Toolkit development team is always looking for ways to improve the software to benefit users.

To Customize a File Template

Use the following steps to customize file templates (files from here on) so that your custom versions are available and not overwritten when newer versions of software are released and installed on your systems.

1. **Copy the files and any related files that you want to customize.**

2. **Rename the copies with names that identify the files as custom files.**

   For recommendations, refer to Chapter 1, "Configuring and Customizing the Solaris Security Toolkit Software" on page 15.

3. **If applicable, modify your custom drivers to call the uniquely named files appropriately.**

The following code sample shows how we modify the `JASS_FILES` environment variable to customize which files are copied to a particular host.

CODE EXAMPLE 9-1   Modifying Driver Sample `abccorp-starfire_ssp-hardening.driver`

```
JASS_FILES="
[...]
        /etc/init.d/nddconfig
        /etc/rc2.d/S70nddconfig
[...]
"
```

In this case, a customized hardening driver called `abccorp-starfire_ssp-hardening.driver` uses a custom `nddconfig` file. Instead of modifying the `nddconfig` original file, which could be overwritten with the next Solaris Security Toolkit release, create a custom `nddconfig` script by appending the host name of the destination system to the file name in the Files directory. For example:

CODE EXAMPLE 9-2   Creating a Custom `nddconfig` Script

```
# pwd
/opt/jass-n.n
# find Files -name "*nddconfig*"
Files/etc/init.d/nddconfig
Files/etc/init.d/nddconfig.ssp-db-serv
Files/etc/rc2.d/S70nddconfig -> ../init.d/nddconfig
```

Note – Be advised that in some cases a script name cannot be changed because a specific name is required by the software. In these cases, use a suffix, as described in this chapter. Or, create a finish script that makes the copies and renames the files as appropriate. If you use this latter option, make sure that the copy and rename operations are compatible with reversing the changes through an undo run. For more information about customizing files, drivers, and scripts so that changes can be reversed, refer to Chapter 4.

Understanding Rules for How Files Are Copied

Files are copied automatically by the software from the JASS_HOME_DIR/Files directory based on the way you define the JASS_FILES and JASS_FILE_<OS version> environment variables. For information about these environment variables, refer to Chapter 13.

The Solaris Security Toolkit software differentiates between multiple files in the JASS_HOME_DIR/Files directory and the definitions in the JASS_FILES and JASS_FILE_<OS version> environment variables.

The files that are copied by the copy_files function are selected by the following criteria:

    /some/fully/qualified/path/file.${HOST}

In this option, the software copies the object only if the name of the target platform matches the value specified by ${HOST}. This host environment variable uses the same naming format as the JASS_HOSTNAME environment variable.

For example: /etc/issue.jordan

    /some/fully/qualified/path/file+${OS}

In this option, the software only copies the object if the OS revision of the target platform matches the value specified by ${OS}. The OS parameter uses the same naming format as the JASS_OS_REVISION environment variable. So, a file to be used only on the Solaris 8 OE is denoted as "filename+5.8".

For example: /etc/issue+5.9

    /some/fully/qualified/path/file

In this option, the software copies the file to a target system, unless one of the previous options matches a file by the same name.

For example: /etc/issue

Note – When the file length/size is zero, the file is not copied to the system.

The order of precedence used to match a file is listed. For example, if a host-specific and general file both exist, the host-specific file is used if the name of a target system matches the host name defined by the host-specific file.

Using Configuration Files

You can configure the Solaris Security Toolkit software by editing configuration files that reference environment variables. This feature allows you to use the Solaris Security Toolkit software drivers in different environments, without modifying finish or audit scripts directly.

All Solaris Security Toolkit environment variables are maintained in a set of configuration files. These configuration files are imported by drivers, which make the variables available to finish and audit scripts as they are called by the drivers.

The Solaris Security Toolkit software has three primary configuration files, all of which are stored in the Drivers directory:

```
driver.init
finish.init
user.init.SAMPLE
```

driver.init

This file contains environment variables that define aspects of the Solaris Security Toolkit software framework and overall operation.

Note – Do not alter the `driver.init` file, because it is overwritten when you upgrade to subsequent versions of the Solaris Security Toolkit software.

Core environment variables such as `JASS_VERSION` and `JASS_ROOT_DIR` are in the `driver.init` script.

This script loads the `user.init` script, thereby incorporating any user variables or environment variable overrides. Also, this script loads the contents of the `finish.init` file to set any finish script variables that might not have been defined. This script serves as the public interface used by drivers to load all of the variables used by the Solaris Security Toolkit software. None of the other initialization functions are supposed to be directly accessed by any of the driver, finish, or audit scripts.

This file contains the following environment variables:

- JASS_AUDIT_DIR
- JASS_DISABLE_MODE
- JASS_FILES_DIR
- JASS_FINISH_DIR
- JASS_HOME_DIR
- JASS_HOSTNAME
- JASS_ISA_CAPABILITY
- JASS_MODE
- JASS_OS_REVISION
- JASS_OS_TYPE
- JASS_PACKAGE_DIR
- JASS_PATCH_DIR
- JASS_PKG
- JASS_REPOSITORY

- JASS_ROOT_DIR
- JASS_RUN_AUDIT_LOG
- JASS_RUN_CHECKSUM
- JASS_RUN_INSTALL_LOG
- JASS_RUN_MANIFEST
- JASS_RUN_SCRIPT_LIST
- JASS_RUN_UNDO_LOG
- JASS_RUN_VERSION
- JASS_SAVE_BACKUP
- JASS_STANDALONE
- JASS_SUFFIX
- JASS_TIMESTAMP
- JASS_USER_DIR
- JASS_VERSION

Each of these environment variables is described in Chapter 13.

finish.init

This file contains environment variables that define the behavior of the individual finish scripts. The two factors that contribute to how a system is hardened are as follows:

The driver selected contains the list of finish scripts to execute and files to install.

The finish.init file defines how the executed finish scripts act.

Note – Do not alter the finish.init file, because it is overwritten when you upgrade to subsequent versions of the Solaris Security Toolkit software.

This file contains the following environment variables:

- `JASS_ACCT_DISABLE`
- `JASS_ACCT_REMOVE`
- `JASS_AGING_MAXWEEKS`
- `JASS_AGING_MINWEEKS`
- `JASS_AGING_WARNWEEKS`
- `JASS_AT_ALLOW`
- `JASS_AT_DENY`
- `JASS_BANNER_FTPD`
- `JASS_BANNER_TELNETD`
- `JASS_CPR_MGT_USER`
- `JASS_CRON_ALLOW`
- `JASS_CRON_DENY`
- `JASS_CRON_LOG_SIZE`
- `JASS_FIXMODES_DIR`
- `JASS_FIXMODES_OPTIONS`
- `JASS_FTPD_UMASK`
- `JASS_FTPUSERS`
- `JASS_KILL_SCRIPT_DISABLE`
- `JASS_LOGIN_RETRIES`
- `JASS_MD5_DIR`
- `JASS_PASSWD`
- `JASS_PASS_LENGTH`
- `JASS_POWER_MGT_USER`
- `JASS_REC_PATCH_OPTIONS`
- `JASS_RHOSTS_FILE`
- `JASS_ROOT_GROUP`
- `JASS_ROOT_PASSWORD`
- `JASS_SADMIND_OPTIONS`
- `JASS_SENDMAIL_MODE`
- `JASS_SGID_FILE`
- `JASS_SHELLS`
- `JASS_SHELL_DISABLE`
- `JASS_SUID_FILE`
- `JASS_SUSPEND_PERMS`
- `JASS_SVCS_DISABLE`
- `JASS_SVCS_ENABLE`
- `JASS_TMPFS_SIZE`
- `JASS_UMASK`
- `JASS_UNOWNED_FILE`
- `JASS_WRITEABLE_FILE`

Each of these environment variables is described in Chapter 13.

`user.init.SAMPLE`

This file is for adding user-defined variables. You can override variables defined in the `driver.init` and `finish.init` files by defining the variables in the `user.init` file. This feature allows administrators to customize the Solaris Security Toolkit software to suit their site needs and requirements.

A user.init.SAMPLE is included to provide suggestions on what must be defined for the software to function properly. Copy and modify the copy of user.init.SAMPLE to fit your environment, then rename the file user.init. Because a user.init file is not included with the software, you can create and customize it without concern for it getting overwritten by software upgrades.

This file contains the following environment variables:

- JASS_PACKAGE_MOUNT
- JASS_PATCH_MOUNT

Each of these environment variables is described in Chapter 13.

The user.init file provides default values for the JASS_PACKAGE_MOUNT and JASS_PATCH_MOUNT environment variables. These variables can be modified to reference your JumpStart server and directory paths.

Make any modifications to the JASS_SVCS_ENABLE and JASS_SVCS_DISABLE variables and other environment variables through the user.init file. However, because variables might already be used in specific drivers, care must be taken when modifying the behavior of the Solaris Security Toolkit software.

For example, the suncluster3x-secure.driver uses JASS_SVCS_ENABLE to leave certain services enabled in the /etc/inetd.conf file. If you want other services enabled, then create and customize a version of the suncluster3x driver file, comment out the definition of JASS_SVCS_ENABLE, and add a new JASS_SVCS_ENABLE definition to the user.init file.

By default, only the following environment variables need to be verified when moving the JumpStart environment from one site to another:

```
JASS_PACKAGE_MOUNT
JASS_PATCH_MOUNT
```

The user.init.SAMPLE file defines default values for these two variables to be <JumpStart server IP address>/jumpstart/Packages and <JumpStart server IP address>/jumpstart/Patches, respectively. These are the recommendations made in Chapter 5 and in the Sun BluePrints book *JumpStart™ Technology: Effective Use in the Solaris™ Operating Environment*. If you follow the recommendations made in these other sources, then no changes are required in the user.init.SAMPLE file. Simply copy this file to user.init.

Note – If you remove SUNWjass using the pkgrm command, the user.init and user.run files, if created, are not removed. However, the Files directory and sysidcfg files exist in the current distribution of the Solaris Security Toolkit software, and would, therefore, be removed.

Using File Templates

The software uses the Files directory with the `JASS_FILES` environment variable and the `copy_files` function. This directory stores file templates that are copied to a JumpStart client during a hardening run.

The following file templates are in the Files directory:

```
.cshrc
.profile
etc/default/sendmail
etc/dt/config/Xaccess
etc/hosts.allow
etc/hosts.deny
etc/init.d/inetsvc
etc/init.d/nddconfig
etc/init.d/set-tmp-permissions
etc/init.d/sms_arpconfig
etc/issue
etc/motd
etc/notrouter
etc/rc2.d/S00set-tmp-permissions
etc/rc2.d/S07set-tmp-permissions
etc/rc2.d/S70nddconfig
etc/rc2.d/S73sms_arpconfig
etc/security/audit_class
etc/security/audit_control
etc/security/audit_event
etc/sms_domain_arp
etc/sms_sc_arp
etc/syslog.conf
sbin/noshell
```

The following subsections describe these files.

.cshrc

This configuration file is provided as a sample. It provides some base-level configuration for csh users by setting some common csh variables such as file completion and history. In addition, it sets the kill and erase terminal options, as well as a command line prompt that includes the path to the current working directory. This file is not required for the software to function properly and can be modified or replaced as appropriate for your environment.

By default, this file is copied by the config.driver to the system being hardened.

.profile

This configuration file is provided as a sample. As distributed with the software, this configuration only defines a UMASK, the PATH, and MANPATH for any root sh started shells.

This file is not required for the software to function properly and can be modified or replaced as appropriate for your environment.

By default, this file is copied by the config.driver to the system being hardened.

etc/default/sendmail

With the release of Solaris 8 OE, a sendmail configuration file can be used to run sendmail in queue processing mode only. This file is copied only onto Solaris 8 OE systems being hardened by the disable-sendmail.fin script.

The disable-sendmail.fin script is OE version aware and modifies the behavior of sendmail based on the OE being hardened. For more information, refer to the Sun BluePrint OnLine article titled "Solaris Operating Environment Security: Updated for Solaris 9 OE."

By default, this file is copied by the disable-sendmail.fin to the system being hardened.

etc/dt/config/Xaccess

This file disables all remote access, whether direct or broadcast, to any X server running on the system. Depending on the X support requirements and the environment the Solaris Security Toolkit software is used in, this file might not be appropriate.

By default, this file is copied by the `hardening.driver` to the system being hardened.

etc/hosts.allow and etc/hosts.deny

These two files are installed on Solaris 9 OE systems by the finish script `enable-tcpwrappers.fin`. After installing the `hosts.allow` and `hosts.deny` files, the finish script enables TCP Wrappers by modifying the `/etc/default/inetd` configuration file.

The `hosts.allow` and `hosts.deny` files are samples to customize for your security profile based on local policies, procedures, and requirements. The default configuration of the `hosts.allow` defines permitted Solaris Secure Shell access to be LOCAL, which means that SSH connections are only permitted from the subnet to which the system is connected. The default configuration of the `hosts.deny` file is to deny all connection attempts not permitted in the `hosts.allow`.

By default, this file is copied by the `enable-tcpwrappers.fin` to the system being hardened.

etc/init.d/inetsvc

This file replaces the default /etc/init.d/inetsvc file with a minimized version containing only the commands required for the configuration of network interfaces. The minimized script has only 23 lines, as compared to 257 lines of the Solaris 9 OE version. The minimized inetsvc script is as follows:

CODE EXAMPLE 9-3 Sample Minimized inetsvc Script

```
#!/sbin/sh
'start')
        /usr/sbin/ifconfig -au netmask + broadcast +
        /usr/sbin/inetd -s -t &
        ;;
'stop')
        /usr/bin/pkill -x -u 0 '(in.named|inetd)'
        ;;
*)
        echo "Usage: $0 { start | stop }"
        exit 1
        ;;
esac
```

Although this script is used successfully by a variety of Sun customers, it has no support for the DHCP or BIND servers. Therefore, this file should be used only in environments that use static IP assignment.

By default, this file is copied by the hardening.driver to the system being hardened.

etc/init.d/nddconfig

This file copies over the nddconfig startup script required to implement network settings, which improve security. For information about configuring network settings for security, refer to the Sun BluePrints OnLine article titled "Solaris Operating Environment Network Settings for Security: Updated for the Solaris 9 Operating Environment."

By default, this file is copied by the hardening.driver to the system being hardened.

etc/init.d/set-tmp-permissions

This file sets the correct permissions on the /tmp and /var/tmp directories when a system is rebooted. If an inconsistency is found, it is displayed to standard output and logged via SYSLOG. This file is installed in /etc/rc2.d twice to permit this check to be performed both before and after the mountall command is run from S01MOUNTFSYS. This check helps ensure that both the mount point and the mounted file system have the correct permissions and ownership.

By default, this file is copied by the hardening.driver to the system being hardened.

etc/init.d/sms_arpconfig

This file, in combination with the /etc/rc2.d/S73sms_arpconfig, /etc/sms_domain_arp, and /etc/sms_sc_arp is for use on Sun Fire 12K and 15K systems to implement static Address Resolution Protocol (ARP) on the internal IP-based management network for additional security. For information about how to use these capabilities, refer to the Sun BluePrint OnLine articles titled "Securing the Sun Fire 12K and 15K System Controllers" and "Securing the Sun Fire 12K and 15K Domains."

By default, this file is copied by the s15k-static-arp.fin to the system being hardened.

etc/issue and /etc/motd

These files are based on US government recommendations and provide legal notice that user activities could be monitored. If an organization has specific legal banners, they can be installed into these files.

These files are provided as default templates. Have your legal counsel provide and/or review notices that apply to your organization.

By default, this file is copied by the hardening.driver to the system being hardened.

etc/notrouter

This file disables IP forwarding between interfaces on a system by creating an `/etc/notrouter` file. The client no longer functions as a router, regardless of the number of network interfaces.

By default, this file is copied by the `hardening.driver` to the system being hardened.

etc/rc2.d/S00set-tmp-permissions and etc/rc2.d/S07set-tmp-permissions

These files set the correct permissions on the `/tmp` and `/var/tmp` directories when a system is rebooted. If an inconsistency is found, it is displayed to standard output and logged via SYSLOG. These scripts are installed into `/etc/rc2.d` twice to permit this check to be performed both before and after the `mountall` command is run from `S01MOUNTFSYS`. This check helps ensure that both the mount point and the mounted file system have the correct permissions and ownership.

By default, these files are copied by the `hardening.driver` to the system being hardened.

Note – These files are symbolic links to `/etc/init.d/set-tmp-permissions`.

---

etc/rc2.d/S70nddconfig

This file copies over the `S70nddconfig` startup script required to implement network settings, which improve security. Refer to the Sun BluePrints OnLine article titled "Solaris Operating Environment Network Settings for Security: Updated for Solaris 9 Operating Environment."

By default, this file is copied by the `hardening.driver` to the system being hardened.

Note – This file is a symbolic link to `/etc/init.d/nddconfig`.

---

etc/rc2.d/S73sms_arpconfig

This file in conjunction with the /etc/init.d/sms_arpconfig, /etc/sms_domain_arp, and /etc/sms_sc_arp files is for use on Sun Fire 12K and 15K systems to implement static Address Resolution Protocol (ARP) on the internal IP-based management network for additional security. For information about how to use these capabilities, refer to the Sun BluePrint OnLine articles titled "Securing the Sun Fire 12K and 15K System Controllers" and "Securing the Sun Fire 12K and 15K Domains."

By default, this file is copied by the s15k-static-arp.fin to the system being hardened.

Note – This file is a symbolic link to /etc/init.d/sms_arpconfig.

---

etc/security/audit_class, etc/security/audit_control, and etc/security/audit_event

These are configuration files for the Solaris OE auditing subsystem, also referred to as the Solaris Basic Security Module, released in February 2001. If you add these three files to a Solaris 8 OE system, it configures the auditing subsystem.

These files are only installed by the Solaris Security Toolkit software on Solaris 8 OE systems. For more information, refer to the Sun BluePrints OnLine article titled "Auditing in the Solaris 8 Operating Environment."

By default, these files are copied by the enable-bsm.fin to the system being hardened.

etc/sms_domain_arp and /etc/sms_sc_arp

These files in combination with the /etc/init.d/sms_arpconfig and /etc/S70sms_arpconfig files are for use on Sun Fire 12K and 15K systems to implement static Address Resolution Protocol (ARP) on the internal IP-based management network for additional security. For information about how to use these capabilities, refer to the Sun BluePrint OnLine articles titled "Securing the Sun Fire 12K and 15K System Controllers" and "Securing the Sun Fire 12K and 15K Domains."

By default, these files are copied by the s15k-static-arp.fin to the system being hardened.

etc/syslog.conf

This file performs additional logging. It serves as a placeholder for organizations to add their own centralized log server (or servers) so that proactive log analysis can be done.

By default, this file is copied by the `hardening.driver` to the system being hardened.

sbin/noshell

This file tracks access attempts to any accounts that are locked using this file. Log messages are forwarded to `syslog` using the `auth` facility at the `crit` severity (`authcrit`) level. The log messages are of the format:

```
Unauthorized access attempt on ${HNAME} by ${UNAME}
```

Where *HNAME* is host name and *UNAME* is user name.

By default, this file is copied by the `disable-system-accounts.fin` to the system being hardened.

## CHAPTER 10

Using Drivers

This chapter provides reference information about using, adding, modifying, and removing drivers. This chapter describes the drivers used by the Solaris Security Toolkit software to harden, minimize, and audit Solaris OE systems. A series of drivers and related files make up a security profile.

The default driver (secure.driver) in the Solaris Security Toolkit software disables all services, including network services, not required for the OS to function. This action may not be appropriate for your environment. Evaluate which security modifications are required for your system, then make adjustments by using the information in this chapter and related chapters.

This chapter contains the following topics:

"Understanding Driver Functions and Processes" on page 204

"Customizing Drivers" on page 208

"Using Standard Drivers" on page 212

"Using Product-Specific Drivers" on page 217

Understanding Driver Functions and Processes

The core processing for hardening and audit runs are defined by the functions in the `driver.run` script. During these operations, the driver in use calls the `driver.run` script after the security profile is configured. That is, after the `driver.init` file is called and the `JASS_FILES` and `JASS_SCRIPTS` environment variables are defined, the driver calls the `driver.run` script functions. This script processes each of the entries contained in the `JASS_FILES` and `JASS_SCRIPTS` environment variables in both the hardening and audit operations.

The high-level processing flow of this script is as follows:

Load functionality (`.funcs`) files

Perform basic checks

Load user functionality overrides

Mount file systems to JumpStart client (JumpStart mode only)

Copy or audit files specified by the `JASS_FILES` environment variable (optional)

Execute scripts specified by the `JASS_SCRIPTS` environment variable (optional)

Compute total score for the run (audit operation only)

Unmount file systems from JumpStart client (JumpStart mode only)

Each of these functions are described in detail in the following subsections.

Load Functionality Files

The first task of the `driver.run` script is to load the functionality files. Loading these files at this stage allows the `driver.run` script to take advantage of the functionality in each of the files. Also, any scripts that are executed can take advantage of the common functions. The functionality files loaded during this task are the following:

```
common_misc.funcs
common_log.funcs
driver.funcs
audit_public.funcs
```

Perform Basic Checks

The Solaris Security Toolkit software checks to determine if core environment variables are set. This check ensures that the software is properly executed. If any of the checks fail, the software reports an error and exits. The software checks to ensure the following:

The JASS_OS_REVISION environment variable is defined. If this environment variable was not defined, it is possible that either the driver.init script was not called or the environment variable was improperly modified.

For JumpStart mode, the JASS_PACKAGE_MOUNT environment variable is defined. If this environment variable is not properly defined, then the software might not be able to locate the Packages directory during a JumpStart installation.

For JumpStart mode, the JASS_PATCH_MOUNT environment variable is defined. If this environment variable is not properly defined, then the software might not be able to locate the Patches directory during a JumpStart installation.

Load User Functionality Overrides

Before continuing to process the current profile, the Solaris Security Toolkit software loads the user.run file, if it exists. This file stores all site or organization-specific functions, including those that override any Solaris Security Toolkit software default functions. By default, this file does not exist and must be manually created by the user if this functionality is needed.

This capability allows you to extend or enhance the functionality of the software by implementing new functions or customizing existing ones to better suit your environment. This file is similar to the user.init, except that this file is for functions, whereas the user.init file is for environment variables.

Mount File Systems to JumpStart Client

In JumpStart mode, the driver.run script calls an internal subroutine called mount_filesystems. This routine mounts the following directories onto the JumpStart client:

JASS_PACKAGE_MOUNT, which is mounted onto JASS_PACKAGE_DIR

JASS_PATCH_MOUNT, which is mounted onto JASS_PATCH_DIR

If other file system mount points are required, use the user.run script to implement them. This routine is JumpStart mode specific and is not executed during standalone mode runs.

> **Note –** If using a local, bootable CD-ROM for JumpStart installation, modify this functionality to access the directories from the local media. No changes are necessary if accessing the Patches and Packages directory from a remote server using NFS.

Copy or Audit Files

After the software establishes its foundation by loading common functions, initializing environment variables, and mounting file systems (if needed), it is ready to begin its work. Whether performing a hardening or audit operation, the software assembles a complete list of file templates to be copied to or verified on a target system. The software does this task by concatenating the entries found in the `JASS_FILES` global environment variable with entries found in the `JASS_FILES_x_x` OS version environment variable (for example, `JASS_FILES_5_8` for Solaris 8 OE). Note that both the global and OS environment variables are optional, and either or none can be defined. The combined list is stored in the `JASS_FILES` environment variable. For more information about this variable, refer to Chapter 13, "JASS_FILES" on page 306.

If the resulting list has at least one entry, the software prepends the `JASS_SCRIPTS` list with a special finish script called `install-templates.fin`. In hardening runs, this script takes the contents of the resulting list and copies it to a target system before other finish scripts are run. In audit runs, the `install-templates.aud` script verifies that the files were successfully copied to a target system.

Execute Scripts

The software executes the scripts defined by the `JASS_SCRIPTS` environment variable. Whether performing a hardening or audit operation, the software assembles a complete list of file templates to be copied to or verified on a target system. The software does this task by concatenating the entries found in the `JASS_SCRIPTS` global environment variable with entries found in the `JASS_SCRIPTS_x_x` OS version environment variable (for example, `JASS_SCRIPTS_5_8` for Solaris 8 OE). Note that both the global and OS environment variables are optional, and either or none can be defined. The combined list is stored in the `JASS_SCRIPTS` environment variable. For more information about this variable, refer to Chapter 13, "This variable specifies a list of finish scripts to execute on a target system when you want to use a specific driver. For each entry, make sure you provide a corresponding finish script with the same name located in the `JASS_FINISH_DIR` directory." on page 317.

In hardening runs, each finish script is executed in turn. The finish scripts are stored in the `JASS_FINISH_DIR` directory.

In audit runs, some additional processing must be done first. Before a script defined by JASS_SCRIPTS executes, it must first be transformed from its finish script name to its audit script counterpart. The Solaris Security Toolkit software automatically changes the file name extension from .fin to .aud. In addition, the software expects the audit script to be in the JASS_AUDIT_DIR. After this alteration is made, the software executes each audit script in turn.

The output of the scripts is processed in one or more of the following ways:

Logged to the file specified by the jass-execute -o option. If a file is not specified, the output is directed to standard output. This option is only available in standalone mode.

Logged into the /var/sadm/system/logs/finish.log file on the JumpStart client during JumpStart installations. The /var/sadm/system/logs/finish.log is the standard log file used by any JumpStart command run on the client. This option is only available in JumpStart mode.

Logged to the file JASS_REPOSITORY/<timestamp>/jass-install-log.txt or jass-audit-log.txt. The timestamp is a fully qualified time parameter of the form YYYYMMDDHHMMSS. This value is constant for each run of the Solaris Security Toolkit software and represents the time at which the run was started. For example, a run started at 1:30 p.m. on April 1, 2003 would be represented by the value 20030401013000. These log files are generated during every run. In hardening runs, the software creates the jass-install-log.txt file. In audit runs, the software creates the jass-audit-log.txt file. Do not modify the contents of these files.

Calculate Total Score for the Run

In audit runs, after all of operations are completed for a driver, the software calculates the driver's total score. This score denotes the status of the driver and is part of the grand total if multiple drivers are called. If only one driver is used, then this total and the grand total are the same value. The score is zero if all of the checks passed. If any checks fail, the score is a number representing how many checks or subchecks fail.

Unmount File Systems From JumpStart Client

When operating in JumpStart mode, after all operations are completed for a driver, the software unmounts those file systems mounted during the process "Mount File Systems to JumpStart Client" on page 205. This functionality typically marks the end of a JumpStart client's installation. At this point, control returns to the calling driver. The driver can either exit and end the run or it can call other drivers and start new processing.

Customizing Drivers

Modifying the Solaris Security Toolkit drivers is one of the tasks done most often because each organization's policies, standards, and application requirements differ, even if only slightly. For this reason, the Solaris Security Toolkit software supports the ability to customize tasks undertaken by a driver.

If your system or application requires some of the services and daemons that are automatically disabled by the Solaris Security Toolkit software, or if you want to enable any of the inactive scripts, do so before executing the Solaris Security Toolkit software.

Similarly, if there are services that must remain enabled, and the Solaris Security Toolkit software automatically disables them, override the defaults before executing the applicable driver in the Solaris Security Toolkit software. We recommend that you review the configuration of the software and make all necessary customization before changing the system's configuration. This approach is more effective than discovering that changes must be reversed and reapplied using a different configuration.

There are two primary ways in which services can be disabled using the Solaris Security Toolkit software. The first way involves modifying drivers to comment out or remove any finish scripts defined by the `JASS_SCRIPTS` parameter that should not be run. This approach is one of the most common ways to customize drivers.

For example, if your environment requires NFS-based services, you can leave them enabled. Comment out the `disable-nfs-server.fin` and `disable-rpc.fin` scripts by prepending a # sign before them in your local copy of the `hardening.driver`. Alternatively, you can remove them entirely from the file. As a general rule, it is recommended that any entries that are commented out or removed should be documented in the file header, including information such as:

- Name of the script that is disabled
- Name of the person who disabled the script
- Timestamp indicating when the change was made
- Brief description for why this change was necessary

Including this information can be very helpful in maintaining drivers over time, particularly when they must be updated for newer versions of the software.

Note – Never make changes directly to the drivers distributed with the Solaris Security Toolkit software. Always modify local copies of drivers so that the changes made are not impacted by the removing or upgrading of the Solaris Security Toolkit software.

The other method for disabling services is to customize environment variables. This approach is typically done in either the driver or the user.init file. Make changes in the user.init file only if the changes are global in nature and used by all of the drivers. Otherwise, localize the change to just the drivers requiring the change.

For example, to enable or disable services started by the inetd daemon, use the JASS_SVCS_ENABLE and JASS_SVCS_DISABLE environment variables. Refer to Chapter 13 for detailed information about using variables. Also, refer to "Customizing and Assigning Variables" on page 296 in Chapter 13.

To Customize a Driver

Use the following steps to customize a driver so that newer versions of the original files do not overwrite your customized versions. Furthermore, this step should be taken to help ensure that customized files are not accidentally deleted during software upgrades or removal.

1. **Copy the driver and related files that you want to customize.**

   For example, if you want to create a secure.driver specific to your organization, copy the following drivers located in the Drivers directory:

   ```
   secure.driver
   config.driver
   hardening.driver
   ```

   The config.driver and hardening.driver must be copied, because they are called by the secure.driver. This step is unnecessary if the driver you are customizing does not call or use other drivers.

2. **Rename the copies with names that identify the files as custom drivers.**

   For example, using your company's name, your files would look like:

   ```
   abccorp-secure.driver
   abccorp-config.driver
   abccorp-hardening.driver
   ```

   For more information, refer to Chapter 1, "Configuring and Customizing the Solaris Security Toolkit Software" on page 15.

3. **Modify your custom** *prefix*-secure.driver **to call the new related** *prefix*-config.driver **and** *prefix*-hardening.driver **files accordingly.**

   This step is necessary to prevent the new prefix-secure.driver from calling the original config.driver and hardening.driver. This step is not necessary if the drivers being customized do not call or use other drivers.

4. **To copy, add, or remove files from a driver, modify the** `JASS_FILES` **environment variable.**

For detailed information about this variable, refer to Chapter 13.

The following code example is taken from the `Drivers/config.driver` file. This security profile performs basic configuration tasks on a platform. We use this security profile as an example because it provides clear samples of how both file templates and finish scripts are used.

In this example, this driver is configured to copy the `/.cshrc` and `/.profile` files from the `JASS_HOME_DIR/Files/` directory onto the target platform when the `driver.run` function is called.

```
JASS_FILES="
/.cshrc
/.profile
"
```

a. **To change the contents of either of these files, modify the copies of the files located in the** `JASS_HOME_DIR/Files/` **directory.**

b. **If you only need to add or remove file templates, simply adjust the** `JASS_FILES` **variable accordingly.**

c. **If you want to define the Solaris OE version, append the major and minor operating system version to the end of the** `JASS_FILES` **variable, separated by underscores.**

The Solaris Security Toolkit software supports operating system-version specific file lists. These file lists are added to the contents of the general file list only when the Solaris Security Toolkit software is run on a defined version of the Solaris OE.

5. **To add or remove scripts from a driver, modify the** `JASS_SCRIPTS` **variable.**

For detailed information about this variable, refer to Chapter 13.

6. **To call other drivers, create a nested or hierarchical security profile.**

This technique is often useful when attempting to enforce standards across the majority of platforms while still providing for platform or application-specific differences.

The following code example is taken from the `secure.driver` file. This file is used as a wrapper to call both configuration and hardening drivers that, in this case, implement the actual functionality of the security profile. Although this is often the model used, it should be noted that this need not be the case. In fact, each driver supports the JASS_FILES and JASS_SCRIPTS convention, even if it is not always used (as is the case in this example).

CODE EXAMPLE 10-1 Creating a Nested or Hierarchical Security Profile

```
DIR="`/bin/dirname $0`"
export DIR

. ${DIR}/driver.init
. ${DIR}/config.driver
. ${DIR}//hardening.driver
```

The following example illustrates a slightly more complex configuration where the driver not only calls other foundational drivers, but also implements its own functionality. In this case, this new security profile installs the /etc/named.conf file and runs the configure-dns.fin script after it runs the config.driver and hardening.driver drivers.

CODE EXAMPLE 10-2 Having a Driver Implement Its Own Functionality

```
DIR="`/bin/dirname $0`"
export DIR

. ${DIR}/driver.init
. ${DIR}/config.driver
. ${DIR}//hardening.driver

JASS_FILES="
/etc/named.conf
"

JASS_SCRIPTS="
configure-dns.fin
"

. ${DIR}/driver.run
```

Note – This sample is just an example of how you can nest drivers to provide various levels of functionality and coverage. The /etc/named.conf and configure-dns.fin references are for example purposes only. Those files are not supplied by default with the Solaris Security Toolkit software.

7. **When finished customizing your driver, save it in the Drivers directory.**

8. **Test the driver to ensure that it functions properly.**

Using Standard Drivers

This section describes the following drivers, which are supplied by default in the Drivers directory:

"config.driver" on page 212
"hardening.driver" on page 213
"secure.driver" on page 215
"undo.driver" on page 216

In addition to these standard drivers, product-specific drivers are also included with the Solaris Security Toolkit distribution. For a list of product-specific drivers, refer to "Using Product-Specific Drivers" on page 217.

config.driver

This driver is called by the secure.driver and is responsible for implementing tasks associated with that driver set. By grouping related functions into a single driver, you can create common functions and use them as building blocks to assemble more complex configurations. In the following example, machines with different security requirements can share the same base Solaris OE configuration driver, because similar tasks are separated into their own driver.

This example is taken from the config.driver.

CODE EXAMPLE 10-3 Sample Output of config.driver

```
DIR="`/bin/dirname $0`"
export DIR

. ${DIR}/driver.init

JASS_FILES="
/.cshrc
"

JASS_SCRIPTS="
set-root-password.fin
set-term-type.fin
"

. ${DIR}/driver.run
```

This driver performs several tasks. It calls the `driver.init` to initialize the Solaris Security Toolkit framework and to configure its runtime environment. Then, it sets both the `JASS_FILES` and `JASS_SCRIPTS` environment variables. These variables define the actual configuration changes that are undertaken by this driver. After these variables are set, the `driver.run` script is called. The `driver.run` script completes the installation of the files and executes all configuration-specific scripts.

In the example, the `.cshrc` file contained in `JASS_HOME_DIR/Files` directory is copied to `/.cshrc` and the finish scripts (`set-root-password.fin` and `set-term-type.fin`) are run on the system.

hardening.driver

Most of the security-specific scripts included in the Solaris Security Toolkit software are listed in the `hardening.driver`. This driver builds upon those changes by implementing additional security enhancements that are not included in the `hardening.driver`. This driver, similar to the `config.driver`, defines scripts to be run by the `driver.run` script.

The following scripts are listed in this driver:

```
disable-ab2.fin
disable-apache.fin
disable-asppp.fin
disable-autoinst.fin
disable-automount.fin
disable-dhcpd.fin
disable-directory.fin
disable-dmi.fin
disable-dtlogin.fin
disable-ipv6.fin
disable-kdc.fin
disable-keyserv-uid-nobody.fin
disable-ldap-client.fin
disable-lp.fin
disable-mipagent.fin
disable-nfs-client.fin
disable-nfs-server.fin
disable-nscd-caching.fin
disable-ppp.fin
disable-preserve.fin
disable-power-mgmt.fin
disable-remote-root-login.fin
disable-rhosts.fin
disable-rpc.fin
disable-samba.fin
```

```
disable-sendmail.fin
disable-ssh-root-login.fin
disable-slp.fin
disable-snmp.fin
disable-spc.fin
disable-syslogd-listen.fin
disable-system-accounts.fin
disable-uucp.fin
disable-vold.fin
disable-xserver-listen.fin
disable-wbem.fin
enable-coreadm.fin
enable-ftpaccess.fin
enable-ftp-syslog.fin
enable-inetd-syslog.fin
enable-priv-nfs-ports.fin
enable-process-accounting.fin
enable-rfc1948.fin
enable-stack-protection.fin
install-at-allow.fin
install-ftpusers.fin
install-loginlog.fin
install-newaliases.fin
install-sadmind-options.fin
install-security-mode.fin
install-shells.fin
install-sulog.fin
remove-unneeded-accounts.fin
set-banner-dtlogin.fin
set-banner-ftpd.fin
set-banner-sendmail.fin
set-banner-sshd.fin
set-banner-telnetd.fin
set-ftpd-umask.fin
set-login-retries.fin
set-power-restrictions.fin
set-root-group.fin
set-rmmount-nosuid.fin
set-sys-suspend-restrictions.fin
set-system-umask.fin
set-tmpfs-limit.fin
set-user-password-reqs.fin
set-user-umask.fin
update-at-deny.fin
update-cron-allow.fin
update-cron-deny.fin
update-cron-log-size.fin
```

```
update-inetd-conf.fin
install-md5.fin
install-fix-modes.fin
```

Note – By default, all changes made by the finish scripts provided are reversable, except for changes made by the `install-strong-permissions.fin` script. The changes made by this script must be manually reversed in the event that the changes are no longer wanted.

In addition, the following scripts are listed in the `hardening.driver`, but are commented out by default:

```
disable-keyboard-abort.fin
disable-picld.fin
enable-tcpwrappers.fin
enable-bsm.fin
install-strong-permissions.fin
```

For descriptions of these scripts, refer to Chapter 11.

secure.driver

The `secure.driver` is the default driver used in the `rules` file for client installation. This driver is a ready-to-use driver that implements *all* the hardening functionality in the Solaris Security Toolkit software. This driver performs the initialization tasks required, then calls the `config.driver` and `hardening.driver` drivers to configure the system and perform all the hardening tasks.

The following are the contents of the `secure.driver`.

CODE EXAMPLE 10-4 `secure.driver` Contents

```
DIR="`/bin/dirname $0`"
export DIR

. ${DIR}/driver.init

. ${DIR}/config.driver

. ${DIR}/hardening.driver
```

undo.driver

This driver provides the undo functionality during an undo run. This driver is called when you invoke the `jass-execute` command with the `-u` option. This driver is quite straightforward and contains the following.

CODE EXAMPLE 10-5 `undo.driver` Contents

```
DIR="`/bin/dirname $0`"
export DIR

. ${DIR}/driver.init

. ${DIR}/undo.run
```

When called by `./jass-execute -u`, this driver initializes itself much the same way as any other driver by calling `driver.init`, then passing control to a different driver, `undo.driver` in this case.

Caution – Never call or modify this driver directly.

Using Product-Specific Drivers

This section lists product-specific drivers, which are used to harden specific Sun products or configurations. These drivers are included with the Solaris Security Toolkit in the Drivers directory. TABLE 10-1 lists product specific drivers.

New drivers are released periodically to harden new and updated Sun products. Newer versions of the Solaris Security Toolkit software may offer new and revised drivers.

TABLE 10-1   Product-Specific Drivers

Product	Driver Name
Desktop systems	`desktop-secure.driver`
Sun™ ONE (formerly iPlanet™) Web Servers	`install-Sun_ONE-WS.driver`
JumpStart technology	`jumpstart-secure.driver`
Sun™ Cluster 3.x Software	`suncluster3x-secure.driver`
Sun Fire™ Midframe System Controller	`sunfire_mf_msp-secure.driver`
Sun Enterprise™ 10000 System Service Processors	`starfire_ssp-secure.driver`
Sun Fire 12K and 15K Domains	`sunfire_15k_domain-secure.driver`
Sun Fire 12K and 15K System Controllers	`sunfire_15k_sc-secure.driver`

Note – Although each of the drivers listed have the form *name*`-secure.driver`, note that each product-specific driver includes three drivers: `name-secure.driver`, `name-config.driver` and `name-hardening.driver`. Only the `name-secure.driver` is listed for the sake of brevity. The name and function of the scripts follow the convention listed.

desktop-secure.driver

This driver is provided as an example, based on the `secure.driver`, to highlight what changes may be necessary to secure a desktop system. This script is a guide; therefore, you may need to customize it, depending on your environment. The differences between this and the `secure.driver` are as follows:

The following `inetd` services are not disabled: Telnet, FTP, `dtspc` (CDE subprocess control service), `rstatd` (Kernel statistics server) and `rpc.smserverd` (used for volume management in Solaris 9).

The following file templates are not used: `/etc/dt/config/Xaccess`, and `/etc/syslog.conf`

The following finish scripts are not used: `disable-dtlogin.fin`, `disable-automount.fin`, `disable-lp.fin`, `disable-nfs-client.fin`, `disable-rpc.fin`, `disable-vold.fin`, and `disable-xserver-listen.fin`

install-Sun_ONE-WS.driver

Applicable only to JumpStart mode, this driver calls the `minimize-Sun_ONE-WS.fin` script so that the Solaris Security Toolkit software can install the Sun ONE Web Server software. The script removes all Solaris OE packages not required to successfully install and run the Sun ONE Web Server (formerly iPlanet Web Server) software. In addition, this driver calls the `hardening.driver` mentioned previously, to harden the platform after it is minimized.

The following are the contents of the `install-Sun_ONE-WS.driver`.

CODE EXAMPLE 10-6 `install-Sun_ONE-WS.driver` Contents

```
DIR="`/bin/dirname $0`"
export DIR

. ${DIR}/driver.init

. ${DIR}/config.driver

JASS_SCRIPTS="
minimize-Sun_ONE-WS.fin
install-Sun_ONE-WS.fin
"
. ${DIR}/driver.run

. ${DIR}/hardening.driver
```

If you build a JumpStart client using this driver, then you must include this driver in the `rules` file list. This driver performs all the actions specified by the `config.driver` and `hardening.driver`, in addition to the functionality in the `minimize-Sun_ONE-WS.fin` and `install-Sun_ONE-WS.fin` scripts.

For more information about this driver, refer to the Sun BluePrints OnLine article titled "Minimizing the Solaris Operating Environment."

jumpstart-secure.driver

This driver is provided as an example, based on the `secure.driver`, to highlight what changes may be necessary to secure a JumpStart server. This driver is a guide, and you may need to customize it, depending on your environment. The differences between this and the `secure.driver` are as follows:

The tftp `inetd` (Trivial FTP) service is not disabled

The following finish scripts are not used: `disable-nfs-server.fin` and `disable-rpc.fin`.

suncluster3x-secure.driver

This driver provides a baseline configuration for hardening Sun Plex (Sun Cluster 3.0 and newer) software releases. You can modify the driver to remove Solaris OE functionality being disabled; however, do not alter enabled services that are required for the Sun Cluster software to work properly. For more information, refer to the Sun BluePrint OnLine article titled "Securing the Sun Cluster 3.x Software."

sunfire_mf_msp-secure.driver

This driver is for hardening the midframe service processor (MSP) when building secured Sun Fire midframe environments. This driver automates and simplifies building a secure MSP, but one that still has all of the required services enabled. For more information, refer to the Sun BluePrint OnLine article titled "Securing the Sun Fire Midframe System Controller."

starfire_ssp-secure.driver

This driver is for creating supported and hardened Sun Enterprise 10000 system service processors (SSP). It is strongly recommended that the SSPs always be hardened, due to their ability to impact the reliability, availability, and serviceability of Sun Enterprise 10000 systems. For more information, refer to the Sun BluePrint OnLine article titled "Securing the Sun Enterprise 10000 System Service Processors."

sunfire_15k_domain-secure.driver

This driver provides a baseline for developing hardened Sun Fire 12K and 15K domains. The configuration implemented by this driver disables all services not required by the Sun Fire 12K and 15K, while enabling optional Solaris OE security features disabled in default configurations. For more information, refer to the Sun BluePrint OnLine article titled "Securing Sun Fire 12K and 15K Domains."

sunfire_15k_sc-secure.driver

This driver is the only supported mechanism by which Sun Fire 12K and 15K system controllers can be secured. All services not required by the SC are disabled by this driver. If some of the disabled services are required, you can modify the driver to not disable them. For more information, refer to the Sun BluePrint OnLine article titled "Securing the Sun Fire 12K and 15K System Controllers."

## CHAPTER 11

Using Finish Scripts

This chapter provides reference information about using, adding, modifying, and removing finish scripts. This chapter describes the scripts used by the Solaris Security Toolkit software to harden and minimize Solaris OE systems.

The default scripts in the Solaris Security Toolkit software disable all services, including network services, not required for the OS to function. This action might not be appropriate for your environment. Evaluate which security modifications are required for your system, then make adjustments by using the information in this chapter.

This chapter contains the following topics:

Customizing Finish Scripts

Finish scripts serve as the heart of the Solaris Security Toolkit software. These scripts collectively implement the majority of security modifications. The finish scripts isolate related changes into single files that can be combined and grouped in any number of ways, depending on the design of the security profile (driver).

This section provides instructions and recommendations for customizing existing finish scripts and creating new finish scripts. Also, it provides guidelines for using finish script functions.

Customize Existing Finish Scripts

Just as with Solaris Security Toolkit drivers, you can customize finish scripts. We recommend that you exercise great care when modifying scripts that are supplied with the Solaris Security Toolkit software. Always modify a copy of the finish script and not the original script directly. Failure to do so may result in a loss of changes upon Solaris Security Toolkit software upgrade or removal. Also, wherever possible, try to minimize and document the modifications made to scripts.

We recommend that you customize finish scripts by using environment variables. The behavior of most finish scripts can be tailored using this technique, thereby eliminating the need to modify the script. If this is not possible, then you might find it necessary to modify the code.

For a list of all environment variables and guidelines for defining them, refer to Chapter 13.

Note – Consider submitting a bug report or request for enhancement if you think that the change could benefit a wider audience. The Solaris Security Toolkit development team is always looking for ways to improve the software to better support its users.

When you install the Solaris Security Toolkit software on a JumpStart server, the finish scripts run from a memory resident mini-root running on the JumpStart client. The mini-root contains almost all of the Solaris OE functions. If you create finish scripts, it is sometimes necessary to execute commands using the chroot command, because the client disk is mounted on /a. This limitation is not present during a standalone mode Solaris Security Toolkit software installation.

To Customize a Script

Use the following steps to customize a finish script so that new versions of the original files do not overwrite your customized versions. Furthermore, these files are not removed if the software is removed using the `pkgrm` command.

1. **Copy the script and the related files that you want to customize.**

2. **Rename the copies with names that identify the files as custom scripts and files.**

   For naming guidelines, refer to Chapter 1, "Configuring and Customizing the Solaris Security Toolkit Software" on page 15.

3. **Modify your custom script and files accordingly.**

   The following code example shows how to automate software installation using `install-openssh.fin`. In this example, the code expects the version of OpenSSH to be "2.5.2p2," however, the current version of OpenSSH is "3.5p1." Obviously, the version to install varies depending on when the software is installed. This script can also be altered to support a commercial version of the Secure Shell product.

CODE EXAMPLE 11-1 Sample `install-openssh.fin` Script

```
#!/bin/sh

# NOTE: This script is not intended to be used for Solaris 9+.
  logMessage "Installing OpenSSH software.\n"

if check_os_revision 5.5.1 5.8 ; then
    OPENSSH_VERSION="2.5.2p2"
    OPENSSH_NAME="OBSDssh"
    OPENSSH_PKG_SRC="${OPENSSH_NAME}-${OPENSSH_VERSION}-`uname -p`
`uname -m`-`uname -r`.pkg"
    OPENSSH_PKG_DIR="${JASS_ROOT_DIR}/${JASS_PACKAGE_DIR}"

    # Install the OpenSSH package onto the client


    if [ "${JASS_STANDALONE}" = "1" ]; then
       logNotice "This script cannot be used in standalone mode due
to the potential for overwriting the local OBSHssh installation."
    else
logMessage "Installing ${OPENSSH_NAME} from ${OPENSSH_PKG_DIR}/
${OPENSSH_PKG_SRC}"
       if [ -f ${OPENSSH_PKG_DIR}/${OPENSSH_PKG_SRC} ]; then
          add_pkg -d ${OPENSSH_PKG_DIR}/${OPENSSH_PKG_SRC}
${OPENSSH_NAME} add_to_manifest X "pkgrm ${OPENSSH_NAME}"
       else
          logFileNotFound "${OPENSSH_NAME}"
[...]
```

In this case, the only way to adjust this script to support a different version of OpenSSH is to modify it directly. After completing the changes, be sure to change the security profile that uses this script, to account for its new name.

Note – As noted previously, this method of modifying a script directly should rarely be necessary, because most of the Solaris Security Toolkit software's functionality can be customized through variables.

Prevent `kill` Scripts From Being Disabled

Finish scripts that begin with the keyword `disable` are typically responsible for disabling services. Many of these scripts modify shell scripts that are located in the run-control directories (`/etc/rc*.d`). In most cases, run-control scripts are of two flavors: `start` and `kill` scripts. As their name implies, `start` scripts start services and `kill` scripts stop services. The `start` scripts begin with the capital letter "S" and `kill` scripts begin with the capital letter "K."

`Kill` scripts are most often used to prepare a system for shut down or reboot. These scripts shut down services in a logical order so that changes are not lost and the system state is maintained. Typically, both `start` and `kill` scripts are hard links to files in the `/etc/init.d` directory, although this is not always the case.

The default action of the Solaris Security Toolkit software is to disable both `start` and `kill` scripts. This behavior can be altered using the `JASS_KILL_SCRIPT_DISABLE` environment variable. By default, this variable is set to 1, instructing the Solaris Security Toolkit software to disable both start and kill scripts.

There are times when this action is not preferred. For example, `kill` scripts are often used to stop services that were manually started by an administrator. If these scripts are disabled by the Solaris Security Toolkit software, then these services may not be stopped properly or in the correct sequence. To prevent `kill` scripts from being disabled, simply set the `JASS_KILL_SCRIPT_DISABLE` environment variable to 0 in the `user.init` file or in the relevant driver.

Create New Finish Scripts

You can create new finish scripts and integrate them into your deployment of the Solaris Security Toolkit software. Because finish scripts must be developed in Bourne shell, it is relatively easy to add new functionality. For those who are less experienced in UNIX® shell scripting, examine existing finish scripts that perform similar functions to gain an understanding of how to accomplish a given task and to understand the correct sequence of actions.

Consider the following conventions when developing new finish scripts. Understanding these conventions ensures that the scripts are functional in standalone mode, JumpStart mode, and undo operations.

Whenever adding new finish scripts, be sure to consider adding a companion audit script. Audit scripts are used to determine the state of changes made on an existing system. For more information, refer to Chapter 12.

1. Ensure that the finish script understands the relative root directory. The scripts must not be configured to rely on the fact that the "/" directory is the actual root directory of the system. Incorrect configuration prevents the script from working in JumpStart mode when the target's actual root directory is "/a." This convention is easily implemented using the JASS_ROOT_DIR environment variable. For more information about this and other environment variables, refer to Chapter 13.

   In some cases, the program used in a finish script might not support a relocated root directory. In these cases, it might be necessary to use the chroot(1M) command to force the command to run within a relative root directory, such as that described previously. For example, the usermod(1M) command does not allow the user to specify an alternate root directory. In this case, it is necessary to use the chroot(1M) command as follows.

   ```
   chroot ${JASS_ROOT_DIR} /usr/sbin/usermod ...arguments...
   ```

   The Solaris Security Toolkit software automatically detects the location of the platform's real root directory and assigns that value to the JASS_ROOT_DIR variable. We recommend that you use this variable in place of hard-coding a specific path for the root file system. For example, in place of using /etc/inet/inetd.conf within the finish script, use JASS_ROOT_DIR/etc/inet/inetd.conf.

2. Where possible, use the Solaris Security Toolkit software's framework when creating new directories, copying files, or backing up existing files. Using the framework functions ensures that the changes made by a new script are consistent with those done elsewhere, and that they can be safely undone. For a list of framework functions, refer to Chapter 8.

   Examples of framework functions that are compatible with undo are as follows:

   ```
   disable_rc_file
   disable_conf_file
   backup_file
   create_a_file
   ```

3. Wherever possible, attempt to use standard, supportable ways to configure or tune a system. For example, programs like usermod(1M) are preferred over directly modifying the /etc/passwd file. This preference is necessary to make the software as flexible as possible and to make the resulting finish scripts as OS version independent as possible. Also, complicated or obscure ways of configuring a system could actually be harder to debug or maintain over the life of a script. For an example of methods on supportable ways in which changes can be made, refer to the Sun BluePrint OnLine article titled "Solaris Operating Environment Security: Updated for Solaris Operating Environment 9."

4. Make sure that new finish scripts are OS version aware. If a particular function is not needed on a version of the OS, then do not attempt to use it. This approach helps to make the software backward compatible with existing releases and more likely to support future releases. Furthermore, by making finish scripts OS version aware, the number of warning and error messages can be dramatically reduced. The Solaris Security Toolkit software's finish directory contains example scripts that are aware of the OS on which they are being used and that only make changes when necessary. Some sample scripts that use this capability are as follows:

   ```
   enable-rfc1948.fin
   install-ftpusers.fin
   ```

   To make this process simpler for software developers, the framework includes the following two functions:

   ```
   check_os_min_revision
   check_os_revision
   ```

   For detailed information about these functions, refer to Chapter 8.

5. A final consideration when developing or customizing finish scripts is that the Solaris Security Toolkit software could be run more than once on a single platform. The finish scripts must be able to detect whether a change actually needs to be made.

For example, the enable-rfc1948.fin script checks to see if the /etc/default/inetinit script already has the setting TCP_STRONG_ISS=2. If this setting is present, there is no need to back up files or make other changes.

CODE EXAMPLE 11-2 Sample enable-rfc1948.fin Script

```
if [ `grep -c "TCP_STRONG_ISS=2" ${INETINIT}` = 0 ]; then
# The following command will remove any exiting TCP_STRONG_ISS
# value and then insert a new one where TCP_STRONG_ISS is set
# to 2.  This value corresponds to enabling RFC 1948
# unique-per-connection ID sequence number generation.
logMessage "\nSetting 'TCP_STRONG_ISS' to '2' in ${INETINIT}.\n"
backup_file ${INETINIT}
cat ${INETINIT}.${JASS_SUFFIX} |\
sed '/TCP_STRONG_ISS=/d' > ${INETINIT}
echo "TCP_STRONG_ISS=2" >> ${INETINIT}
fi
```

This technique not only reduces the number of unnecessary backup files, but it helps prevent errors and confusion resulting from multiple, redundant changes made in the same files. Also, by implementing this functionality, you are well on your way toward developing the code necessary to implement the finish script's companion audit script.

Using Standard Finish Scripts

Finish scripts perform system modifications and updates during hardening runs. These scripts are not used in any other runs or operations of the software.

The `finish.init` handles all finish script configuration variables. You can override the default variables by modifying the `user.init` file. This file is heavily commented to explain each variable, its impact, and its use in finish scripts. Additionally, refer to Chapter 13 for a description of each variable.

Using variables found in the `finish.init` script, you can customize most of the finish scripts to suit your organization's security policy and requirements. You can customize nearly every aspect of the Solaris Security Toolkit software through variables, without needing to alter the source code. The use of this script is strongly recommended so as to minimize migration issues with new Solaris Security Toolkit software releases.

This section describes the standard finish scripts, which are in the Finish directory. Each of the scripts in the Finish directory is organized into the following categories:

Disable
Enable
Install
Minimize
Print
Remove
Set
Update

In addition to these standard finish scripts, we provide product-specific finish scripts. For a list of product-specific finish scripts, refer to "Using Product-Specific Finish Scripts" on page 259.

Disable Finish Scripts

The following disable finish scripts are described in this section:

disable-ab2.fin

This script prevents the AnswerBook2 (ab2) server from starting. The ab2 server software is distributed on the Documentation CD in the Solaris OE Server pack. This script applies only to systems running the Solaris OE versions 2.5.1 through 8, because the ab2 software is no longer used in the Solaris OE versions 9 and newer.

disable-apache.fin

This script prevents the Apache Web Server, shipped with Solaris OE versions 8 and newer, from starting. This script disables only the Apache services included in the Solaris OE Distribution package. This script does not impact other Apache distributions installed on the system. For more information on this service, refer to the apache(1M) manual page.

disable-asppp.fin

This script disables the asynchronous point-to-point (ASPPP) service from starting. This service implements the functionality described in RFC 1331, The Point-to-Point Protocol (PPP) for the Transmission of Multi-protocol Datagrams over Point-to-Point Links. This script applies only to Solaris OE versions 2.5.1 through 8. For the Solaris 9 OE, this service has been replaced with the PPP service and is disabled using the disable-ppp.fin finish script. For more information on this functionality, refer to the aspppd(1M) manual page.

disable-autoinst.fin

This script prevents a system from being re-installed, by disabling the run-control scripts associated with automatic configuration. These scripts are used only if the /etc/.UNCONFIGURED or /AUTOINSTALL files are created. After initial installation and configuration, there is generally little reason for these scripts to remain available.

Note – Do not use the `disable-autoinst.fin` script if there might be a need to use the functionality provided by the `sys-unconfig`(1M) program to restore a system's configuration to an as-manufactured state.

These startup scripts are never used in a JumpStart environment and should be disabled to help prevent an intruder from reconfiguring the system.

disable-automount.fin

This script disables the NFS automount service. The automount service answers file system mount and unmount requests from the `autofs` file system. When this script is used, the NFS automount service is disabled and all forms of automount maps are affected. For more information on this functionality, refer to the `automountd`(1M) manual page.

Note – Because this service relies on the RPC port mapper, if `disable-automount.fin` is not used, then the `disable-rpc.fin` script should not be used either.

disable-dhcp.fin

This script disables the DHCP Server included in Solaris OE versions 8 and 9. For more information on this server, refer to the `dhcpd`(1M) manual page.

disable-directory.fin

This script prevents the Sun ONE Directory Server (bundled with the Solaris 9 OE) from starting. Note that this script is for use only with the Sun ONE Directory Server. This script does not affect either the unbundled product or the Sun ONE Directory Server software provided with other Solaris OE versions. By default, the Solaris Security Toolkit software disables only the services supplied with the Solaris OE. For more information on this server, refer to the `directoryserver`(1M) manual page.

disable-dmi.fin

This script prevents the Desktop Management Interface (DMI) from starting. This script applies only to systems running Solaris OE versions 2.6 or newer. For more information on this service, refer to the `dmispd`(1M) and `snmpXdmid`(1M) manual pages.

disable-dtlogin.fin

This script prevents any windowing environment from being started at boot time, for example, the Common Desktop Environment (CDE) service. However, this script does not prevent a windowing environment from being started at a later time (for example, after a system is booted). This script applies only to systems running the Solaris OE version 2.6 or newer. For more information on this service, refer to the `dtlogin`(1X) and `dtconfig`(1) manual pages.

Note – Because this service relies on the RPC port mapper, if `disable-rpc.fin` is used, then the `disable-dtlogin.fin` script should not be used.

---

disable-ipv6.fin

This script disables the use of IPv6 on specific network interfaces by removing the the associated host name files in `/etc/hostname6.*`. Also, this mechanism prevents the `in.ndpd` service from running. This script applies only to systems running the Solaris OE versions 8 and newer. This script should not be used if IPv6 functionality is required on the system.

disable-kdc.fin

This script prevents the Kerberos Key Distribution (KDC) service from starting. Note that if `JASS_DISABLE_MODE` is set to `conf`, the `kdc.conf` file is disabled, thus impacting the ability to act as a Kerberos client. This script should not be used in that manner if the system must act as a Kerberos client. This script applies only to systems running the Solaris OE version 9. For more information on this service, refer to the `krb5kdc`(1M) and `kdc.conf`(4) manual pages.

disable-keyboard-abort.fin

This script configures the system ignore keyboard abort sequences. Typically, when a keyboard abort sequence is initiated, the operating system is suspended and the console enters the OpenBoot™ PROM monitor or debugger. Using this script prevents the system from being suspended. For more information on this capability, refer to the kbd(1) manual page. This script is used only in the Solaris 2.6 OE and newer versions.

Note – Some systems feature key switches with a secure position. On these systems, setting the key switch to the secure position overrides any software default set with this command.

---

disable-keyserv-uid-nobody.fin

This script disables the nobody UID access to secure RPC. In Solaris 9 OE, access is disabled by setting the ENABLE_NOBODY_KEYS variable in the /etc/init.d/rpc to NO. For versions earlier than Solaris 9 OE, access is disabled by adding the -d option to the keyserv command in the /etc/init.d/rpc run-control file. For more information on this service, refer to the keyserv(1M) manual page.

disable-ldap-client.fin

This script prevents the Lightweight Directory Access Protocol (LDAP) client daemons from starting on the system. This service provides the directory lookup capability for the system. If the system is acting as an LDAP client or requires the directory lookup capability, then this script should not be used. This script applies to Solaris 8 OE and newer. For more information on this service, refer to the ldap_cachemgr(1M) and ldapclient(1M) manual pages.

disable-lp.fin

This script prevents the line printer (lp) service from starting. Note that in addition to disabling the service, this script removes the lp user's access to the cron subsystem by adding lp to the /etc/cron.d/cron.deny file, and removing all lp commands in the /var/spool/cron/crontabs directory.

This functionality is distinct from the update-cron-deny.fin script, because the lp packages might or might not be installed on a system. In addition, the lp subsystem may be necessary, while the functions removed by the cron-deny-update.fin script are not.

disable-mipagent.fin

This script prevents the mobile IP (MIP) agents from starting. This service implements the MIP home agent and foreign agent functionality described in RFC 2002, IP Mobility Support. This script applies only to Solaris OE versions 8 and newer. For more information on this service, refer to the mipagent(1M) manual page.

disable-nfs-client.fin

This script prevents the Networked File System (NFS) client service from starting. Also, this disables the network status monitor (statd) and lock manager (lockd) daemons. Note that an administrator can still mount remote file systems onto the system, even if this script is used. Those file systems, however, do not take advantage of the status monitor or lock manager daemons. For more information on this service, refer to the statd(1M) and lockd(1M) manual pages.

Note – If this service is required, then this script should not be used. Further, because this service relies on the RPC service, the disable-rpc.fin script should not be used.

---

disable-nfs-server.fin

This script prevents the NFS service from starting. Also, this script disables the daemons that provide support for NFS logging, mounting, access checks, and client service. Do not use this script if the system must share its file systems with remote clients. For more information on this service, refer to the nfsd(1M), mountd(1M) and dfstab(4) manual pages.

Note – If this service is required, then this script should not be used. Further, because this service relies on the RPC service, the disable-rpc.fin script should also not be used.

---

disable-nscd-caching.fin

This script disables caching for `passwd`, `group`, `hosts`, and `ipnodes` entries by the name service cache daemon (NSCD). For the Solaris 8 OE, patch 110386 version 02 or newer must be applied to fix a bug in the role-based access control (RBAC) facility, otherwise the Solaris Security Toolkit software generates an error message.

The NSCD daemon provides caching for name service requests. It exists to provide a performance boost to pending requests and reduce name service network traffic. The `nscd` maintains cache entries for databases such as `passwd`, `group`, and `hosts`. It does not cache the shadow password file, for security reasons. All name service requests made through system library calls are routed to `nscd`. With the addition of IPv6 and RBAC in Solaris 8 OE, the `nscd` caching capability was expanded to address additional name service databases.

Because caching name service data makes spoofing attacks easier, it is recommended that the configuration of `nscd` be modified to cache as little data as possible. This task is accomplished by setting the positive `ttl` to zero in the `/etc/nscd.conf` file for the name service requests deemed vulnerable to spoofing attacks. In particular, the configuration should be modified so that `passwd`, `group`, and Solaris 8 and 9 OE RBAC information has a positive and negative `ttl` of zero.

Note – There may be a performance impact on systems that use name services intensively.

The `nscd -g` option can be used to view the current `nscd` configuration on a server and is a helpful resource when tuning `nscd`.

Disabling `nscd` entirely is not recommended, because applications make name service calls directly, which exposes various bugs in applications and name service backends.

disable-picld.fin

This script prevents the Platform Information and Control Library (PICL) service from starting. Disabling this service could impact the ability of the system to monitor environmental conditions and should, therefore, be used with care. This script applies only to systems running the Solaris OE versions 2.6 and newer. For more information on this service, refer to the `picld(1M)` manual page.

disable-power-mgmt.fin

This script prevents the power management service from starting. (This service allows the system to power down monitors, spin down disks, and even power off the system itself.) Using this script disables the power management functionality. Additionally, a noautoshutdown file is created to prevent a system administrator from being asked about the state of power management during an automated JumpStart mode installation. This script applies only to systems running the Solaris OE versions 2.6 and newer. For more information on this service, refer to the powerd(1M), pmconfig(1M), and power.conf(4) manual pages.

disable-ppp.fin

This script prevents the Point-to-Point Protocol (PPP) service from starting. This service was introduced in the Solaris 8 OE (7/01) and supplements the older Asynchronous PPP (ASPPP) service. This service provides a method for transmitting datagrams over serial point-to-point links. This script applies only to systems running the Solaris OE versions 8 and newer. For more information on this service, refer to the pppd(1M) and pppoed(1M) manual pages.

disable-preserve.fin

This script prevents the moving of saved files (that were previously edited) to /usr/preserve when a system is rebooted. These files are typically created by editors that were abruptly terminated due to a system crash or loss of a session. These files are normally located in /var/tmp with names beginning with "Ex."

disable-remote-root-login.fin

This script changes the CONSOLE variable in the /etc/default/login file to prevent direct remote root logins. Although this was the default behavior for the Solaris OE since the final update of 2.5.1, it is included to ensure that this setting has not been altered. Note that this setting has no impact on programs, such as Secure Shell, that can be configured to not use the /bin/login program to grant access to a system. For more information on this capability, refer to the login(1) manual page.

disable-rhosts.fin

This script disables `rhosts` authentication for `rlogin` and `rsh` by modifying the Pluggable Authentication Module (PAM) configuration in `/etc/pam.conf`.

The `disable-rlogin-rhosts.fin` finish script was renamed `disable-rhosts.fin` to be more indicative of its actions. In addition, both `rsh` and `rlogin` entries are commented out in the `/etc/pam.conf` file to ensure that `rhosts` authentication is not enabled for either service.

This script applies only to Solaris OE versions 2.6 and newer. For more information on this capability, refer to the `in.rshd`(1M), `in.rlogind`(1M) and `pam.conf`(4) manual pages.

disable-rpc.fin

This script prevents the remote procedure call (RPC) service from starting. Note that disabling this service impacts bundled services such as NFS and CDE, and unbundled services such as Sun Cluster. Also, some third-party software packages expect that this service is available. Before disabling this service, verify that no services or tools require RPC services. For more information on this service, refer to the `rpcbind`(1M) manual page.

Note – The RPC port mapper function should not be disabled if any of the following services are used on the system: automount, NFS, NIS, NIS+, CDE, and volume management (Solaris 9 OE only).

---

disable-samba.fin

This script prevents the Samba file and print sharing service from starting. This script disables only the Samba services included in the Solaris OE distribution. This script does not impact other Samba distributions installed on the system. For more information on this service, refer to the `smbd`(1M), `nmbd`(1M), and `smb.conf`(4) manual pages.

disable-sendmail.fin

This script disables the `sendmail` daemon startup and shutdown scripts, and adds an entry to the `cron` subsystem, which executes `sendmail` once an hour for Solaris OE versions 2.5.1, 2.6, and 7.

For Solaris 8 OE, the `/etc/default/sendmail` file is installed, which implements similar functionality. This method of purging outgoing mail is more secure than having the daemon run continually.

Solaris 9 OE implements another `sendmail` option in which the daemon only listens on the loopback interface. For more information, refer to the Sun BluePrint OnLine article titled "Solaris Operating Environment Security: Updated for Solaris Operating Environment 9."

Note – The Solaris Security Toolkit software modifications only prevent a Solaris OE system from receiving email. Outgoing email is still processed normally.

---

disable-slp.fin

This script prevents the Service Location Protocol (SLP) service from starting. This service provides common server functionality for the SLP versions 1 and 2, as defined by the IETF in RFC 2165 and RFC 2608. SLP provides a scalable framework for the discovery and selection of network services. This script applies only to systems running the Solaris OE versions 2.6 and newer. For more information on this service, refer to the `slpd(1M)` manual page.

disable-snmp.fin

This script prevents the Simple Network Management Protocol (SNMP) service from starting. This script does not prevent third-party SNMP agents from functioning on the system. This script only affects the SNMP agent provided in the Solaris OE. This script applies only to systems running the Solaris OE versions 2.6 and newer. For more information on this service, refer to the snmpdx(1M) and `mibiisa(1M)` manual pages.

disable-spc.fin

This script disables all SunSoft™ Print Client (SPC) startup scripts. This script applies only to systems running the Solaris OE versions 2.6 and newer.

disable-ssh-root-login.fin

This script configures the Secure Shell service distributed in the Solaris 9 OE to restrict remote access to the root account. By default, remote root access is denied using the version of Secure Shell shipped with the Solaris 9 OE. This script verifies that functionality, thereby implementing a mechanism similar to that of the `disable-remote-root-login.fin` script. The script sets the `PermitRootLogin` parameter in `/etc/ssh/sshd_config` to no. For more information on this capability, refer to the sshd_config(4) manual page.

disable-syslogd-listen.fin

This script prevents the SYSLOG service from accepting remote log messages. For Solaris OE versions prior to Solaris 9 OE, this scripts adds the `-t` option to the `syslogd` command line. For Solaris 9 OE, this script sets the `LOG_FROM_REMOTE` variable to NO in the `/etc/default/syslogd` file. Note that this script prevents the daemon from listening on UDP port 514. This script is useful for systems that use SYSLOG services and do not need to receive SYSLOG messages from remote systems.

Note – This script should not be used on SYSLOG servers.

---

disable-system-accounts.fin

This script disables unused system accounts and enables logging of access attempts. Access attempt logging is implemented by creating a new shell as specified by `JASS_SHELL_DISABLE` variable. Specific unused system accounts (other than `root`) are disabled by this script.

The list of accounts that should be disabled on the system are explicitly enumerated in the `JASS_ACCT_DISABLE` variable.

disable-uucp.fin

This script disables the UNIX-to-UNIX Copy (UUCP) startup script. In addition, the nuucp system account is removed with the uucp crontab entries in the `/var/spool/cron/crontabs` directory. For more information on this service, refer to the uucp(1C) and uucico(1M) manual pages.

disable-vold.fin

This script prevents the volume management (VOLD) daemon from starting. The VOLD daemon creates and maintains a file system image rooted at /vol, by default, that contains symbolic names for diskettes, CD-ROMs, and other removable media devices. For more information on this service, refer to the vold(1M) manual page.

Note – Do not use this script if the automatic mounting and unmounting of removable media (such as diskettes and CD-ROMs) is needed.

Note – In the Solaris 9 OE, if this service is required, then this script should not be used. Further, because this service relies on both the RPC and the rpc.smserverd services, they too should not be disabled. To prevent the RPC service from being disabled, do not use the disable-rpc.fin script. Similarly, to prevent the rpc.smserverd service from being disabled, add 100155 to the JASS_SVCS_ENABLE parameter.

---

disable-wbem.fin

This script prevents the web-based enterprise management (WBEM) service from starting. The WBEM is a set of management and Internet-related technologies that unify management of enterprise computing environments. Developed by the Distributed Management Task Force (DMTF), the WBEM enables organizations to deliver an integrated set of standards-based management tools that support and promote World Wide Web technology. Do not use this script if the use of Solaris Management Console (SMC) is needed. This script applies only to systems running the Solaris OE versions 8 and newer. For more information on this service, refer to the wbem(5) manual page.

Note – If this service is required, then do not use this script. Also, because this service relies on the RPC service, the disable-rpc.fin script should not be used .

---

disable-xserver.listen.fin

This script disables the X11 server's ability to listen to and accept requests over TCP on port 6000. This script adds the option -nolisten TCP to the X server configuration line in the /etc/dt/config/Xservers file. If this file does not exist, it is copied from the master location at /usr/dt/config/Xservers. This script is applicable only to the Solaris 9 OE. For more information on this capability, refer to the Xserver(1) manual page.

Enable Finish Scripts

The following enable finish scripts are described in this section:

enable-32bit-kernel.fin

This script sets the `boot-file` variable in the EEPROM of Sun SPARC® systems to the value of `/kernel/unix`. This setting forces the system to boot using a 32-bit kernel. It is useful for products that can run on the Solaris 7 OE or newer, but must run in 32-bit-only mode. This script applies only to `sun4u` systems. This script is included as a convenience for environments using applications that support only 32-bit mode OE.

enable-bsm.fin

This script enables the SunSHIELD™ Solaris Basic Security Module (Solaris BSM) auditing service. Additionally, this script installs a default audit configuration that is described in the Sun BluePrint™ OnLine article titled "Auditing in the Solaris 8 Operating Environment." An `audit_warn` alias is added, if necessary, and assigned to the root account. And, the abort disable code is overridden to permit abort sequences. This setting is most often used in a lights-out data center environment, where physical access to the platform is not always possible. After the system is rebooted, the Solaris BSM subsystem is enabled and auditing begins. For more information on this service, refer to the `bsmconv`(1M) manual page.

enable-coreadm.fin

This script configures the coreadm functionality that is present in Solaris 7 OE and newer. It configures the system to store generated core files under the directory specified by JASS_CORE_DIR. Further, each of the core files are tagged with a specification denoted by the JASS_CORE_PATTERN so that information about the core files can be collected. Typically, the information collected includes the process identifier, effective user identifier, and effective group identifiers of the process, as well as name of the process executable and time the core file was generated. For more information on this capability, refer to the coreadm(1M) manual page.

enable-ftp-syslog.fin

This script forces the in.ftpd daemon to log all File Transfer Protocol (FTP) access attempts through the SYSLOG subsystem. This option is enabled by adding the -l option to the in.ftpd command in the /etc/inetd/inetd.conf file. For more information, refer to the in.ftpd(1M) manual page.

enable-ftpaccess.fin

This script enables the ftpaccess functionality for the FTP service in Solaris 9 OE. This functionality is necessary so that security modifications made by the set-banner-ftp.fin and set-ftpd-umask.fin scripts are used. For example, modifications to set the default greeting, file creation mask, and other parameters documented in ftpaccess(4) manual pages. This script adds the -a argument to the in.ftpd entry in the /etc/inet/inetd.conf file. This script applies only to systems running the Solaris 9 OE.

enable-inetd-syslog.fin

This script configures the Internet services daemon (INETD) to log all incoming TCP connection requests. That is, a log entry occurs via SYSLOG if a connection is made to any TCP service for which the inetd daemon is listening. For Solaris OE versions prior to Solaris 9 OE, this script enables logging by adding the -t option to the inetd command line. In Solaris 9 OE, the script sets the ENABLE_CONNECTION_LOGGING variable in the /etc/default/inetd file to YES.

enable-priv-nfs-ports.fin

This script modifies the `/etc/system` file to enable restricted NFS port access. After setting the variable, only NFS requests originating from ports less than 1024 are accepted.

Note – If the key word value pair is already defined in the `/etc/system` file, the value is rewritten in the file to verify that it is set properly. Otherwise, the keyword value pair is appended to the file.

---

enable-process-accounting.fin

If the required Solaris OE packages (currently `SUNWaccr` and `SUNWaccu`) are installed on the system, this script enables Solaris OE process accounting. For more information on this service, refer to the acct(1M) manual page.

enable-rfc1948.fin

This script creates or modifies the `/etc/default/inetinit` file to enable support of RFC 1948. (This RFC defines unique-per-connection ID sequence number generation.) The script sets the variable `TCP_STRONG_ISS` to 2 in the `/etc/default/inetinit` file. For more information, refer to `http://ietf.org/rfc1948.html`. This script applies only to systems running the Solaris OE versions 2.6 and newer.

enable-stack-protection.fin

For SPARC systems only, this script modifies the `/etc/system` file to enable stack protections and exception logging. These options are enabled by adding the `noexec_user_stack` and `noexec_user_stack_log` to the `/etc/system` file.

If the key word value pairs are already defined in the `/etc/system` file, their values are rewritten in the file to verify that they are set properly. Otherwise, the keyword value pairs are appended to the file. This script applies only to systems running the Solaris OE versions 2.6 and newer. Enabling this feature makes the system noncompliant with the SPARC version 8 Application Binary Interface (ABI), therefore, it is possible that some applications might fail.

Note – After the system is rebooted with these variables set, the system denies attempts to execute the stack directly, and logs any stack execution attempt through SYSLOG. This facility is enabled to protect the system against common buffer overflow attacks.

In Solaris 9 OE and newer versions, many of the core Solaris executables are linked against a map file (`/usr/lib/ld/map.noexstk`). This map file provides functionality similar to the script by making the program's stack non-executable. Using the script is still recommended, however, because its changes are global to the system.

enable-tcpwrappers.fin

This script configures the system to use TCP Wrappers. Included with the Solaris 9 OE, TCP Wrappers allow an administrator to restrict access to TCP services. By default, all services in `/etc/inet/inetd.conf` that are defined as `stream`, `nowait` are protected. This script configures the `/etc/default/inetd` file to set the `ENABLE_TCPWRAPPERS` parameter to YES. Further, this script installs sample `/etc/hosts.allow` and `/etc/hosts.deny` files that control access to services protected by TCP Wrappers.

Note – The sample `hosts.allow` and `hosts.deny` files should be customized prior to their use to ensure that their configuration is appropriate for your organization. File templates are available in `JASS_ROOT_DIR/Files/etc`.

Install Finish Scripts

The following install finish scripts are described in this section:

install-at-allow.fin

This script restricts the at command execution by creating an at.allow file in /etc/cron.d. The file is then populated with the list of users defined in the JASS_AT_ALLOW variable. All users who require at access must be added to the at.allow file. This script should be used with the update-at-deny.fin script to determine access to the at and batch facilities. For more information on this capability, refer to the at(1) manual page.

install-fix-modes.fin

This script both copies the fix-modes software from the JASS_PACKAGE_DIR directory to the client, then executes the program. (The FixModes software was created by Casper Dik; refer to the Preface, "Related Resources" on page xxix.) Use the FixModes software to tighten permissions of a Solaris system.

Note – Although the changes implemented by the FixModes software are integrated into the Solaris 9 OE, the use of FixModes is still recommended because many unbundled and third-party applications benefit from its use.

install-ftpusers.fin

Thisscript creates or modifies the `ftpusers` file that is used to restrict access to the FTP service. This script adds users listed in the `JASS_FTPUSERS` variable to the `ftpusers` file. This script only adds a user to the file if the user's name is not already in the file.

A default `ftpusers` file is included with Solaris OE versions 8 and 9. The path to the file varies. For Solaris OE versions 8 and lower, the file path is `/etc`. For Solaris 9 OE and newer, the path is `/etc/ftpd`. All accounts *not* allowed to use the incoming FTP service should be specified in this file. At a minimum, this should include all system accounts (for example, `bin`, `uucp`, `smtp`, `sys`, and so forth) in addition to the root account. These accounts are often targets of intruders and individuals attempting to gain unauthorized access. Frequently, root access to a server over Telnet is disabled and root FTP access is not. This configuration provides a backdoor for intruders who might modify the system's configuration by uploading modified configuration files.

install-Sun_ONE-WS.fin

This script installs the Sun ONE Web Server software onto the target platform. This script is provided as a sample of how software installation can be automated using JumpStart technology. For additional information, refer to the Sun BluePrint OnLine article titled "Minimizing the Solaris Operating Environment."

install-jass.fin

This script automates the installation of the Solaris Security Toolkit software onto a JumpStart client when the Solaris Security Toolkit software is being run. We recommend this approach so that the Solaris Security Toolkit software is available to be run after patch installations on the client. The installation is performed by installing the Solaris Security Toolkit software package distribution with the Solaris OE command `pkgadd`. This script expects the Solaris Security Toolkit software to be installed in the `JASS_PACKAGE_DIR` directory. The Solaris Security Toolkit software package is installed by default in `/opt/SUNWjass`.

install-loginlog.fin

This script creates the `/var/adm/loginlog` file used by the system to log unsuccessful login attempts. The failed logins are logged after the maximum number of failed logins is exceeded. This number is specified in the `RETRIES` variable, set in the `/etc/default/login` configuration file. See also the `set-login-retries.fin` script. For more information, refer to the `loginlog`(4) manual page.

install-md5.fin

This script automates the installation of the MD5 software. This software is used for creating digital fingerprints of file system objects and is referenced in the Sun BluePrints OnLine article titled "The Solaris Fingerprint Database - A Security Tool for Solaris Software and Files." By default, the MD5 software is installed in the directory specified by the `JASS_MD5_DIR` parameter.

install-newaliases.fin

This script adds the `newaliases` symbolic link to the `/usr/lib/sendmail` program. This link is required in some cases of minimized installations if the `SUNWnisu` package is not installed or is removed. This link is necessary for systems running the Solaris OE versions 2.5.1 through 8, where the `newaliases` was a part of the `SUNWnisu` package.

install-openssh.fin

This script installs the OpenBSD version of OpenSSH into `/opt/OBSDssh`. The distribution for which this script is written is based on the Sun BluePrints OnLine article titled "Configuring OpenSSH for the Solaris Operating Environment." This script does not overwrite host keys if they exist.

Note – Solaris 9 OE includes a version of the Secure Shell software, therefore this script is not used if you install Solaris 9 OE.

The installation is based on having a Solaris OE package stream formatted package called `OBSDssh-3.6p1-sparc-sun4u-5.9.pkg` in the `JASS_PACKAGE_DIR` directory.

install-recommended-patches.fin

This script installs applicable patches from the JASS_HOME_DIR/Patches directory on the JumpStart server. The appropriate Recommended and Security Patch Clusters must be downloaded and extracted to the JASS_HOME_DIR/Patches directory for the script to execute properly.

install-sadmind-options.fin

This script adds the options specified in the JASS_SADMIND_OPTIONS environment variable to the sadmind daemon entry in /etc/inet/inetd.conf. For more information on this service, refer to the sadmind(1M) manual page.

install-security-mode.fin

This script displays the current status of the OpenBoot PROM security mode. This script does not set the EEPROM password directly; it is not possible to script the setting of the EEPROM password during a JumpStart installation. The output of the script provides instructions on how to set the EEPROM password from the command line. This script applies only to systems based on SPARC technology. For more information on this capability, refer to the eeprom(1M) manual page.

install-shells.fin

This script adds the user shells specified in the JASS_SHELLS environment variable to the /etc/shells file. The Solaris OE function getusershell(3C) is the primary user that the /etc/shells file uses to determine valid shells on a system. For more information, refer to the shells(4) manual page. For more information about the JASS_SHELLS environment variable, refer to Chapter 13, "This variable contains a list of shells to add to the JASS_ROOT_DIR/etc/shells file. During hardening runs, the install-shells.fin script adds each shell defined by this variable to the JASS_ROOT_DIR/etc/shells file, if not already present. Similarly, during audit runs, the install-shells.aud script determines if each shell defined by this variable is listed in the shells file." on page 330.

Note – This script only adds a shell to the /etc/shells file if the shell exists on the system, is executable, and is not in the file.

---

install-strong-permissions.fin

This script changes a variety of permissions and ownerships to enhance security by restricting group and user access on a system.

Caution – Exercise care when using this script, because its changes cannot be undone automatically by the Solaris Security Toolkit software. Always ensure that the permissions set by this script are appropriate for your environment and applications.

---

install-sulog.fin

This script creates the /var/adm/sulog file, which enables logging of all su attempts. For more information on this capability, refer to the sulog(4) manual page.

install-templates.fin

This special purpose script should not be called directly by any driver. This script is automatically called by the driver.run program if the JASS_FILES parameter or any of its OS specific values is not empty. This script automates the copying of file templates onto a target system. This functionality was originally in the driver.run script, but was separated to better support the verification of file templates. If needed, based on the contents of the JASS_FILES parameter, this script is the first finish script to run.

Minimize Finish Script

The minimize-Sun_ONE-WS.fin script is provided as an example of how the Solaris OE minimization procedure can be implemented. In this case, this script is used to minimize a system that is used as a web server running the Sun ONE Web Server software.

Print Finish Scripts

The following print finish scripts are described in this section:

print-jass-environment.fin

This script prints out all the environment variables used in the Solaris Security Toolkit software. This script is provided for diagnostic purposes and is often called at the beginning of a driver so that the state of the environment variables can be recorded prior to their use.

print-jumpstart-environment.fin

This script prints out all the environment variables used by a JumpStart installation. This script is provided for diagnostic purposes to aid in debugging problems encountered during a JumpStart installation.

print-rhosts.fin

This script lists all the .rhosts and hosts.equiv files contained in any directory under the JASS_ROOT_DIR directory. The results are displayed on standard output unless the JASS_RHOSTS_FILE variable is defined. If this variable is defined, then all of the results are written to that file.

print-sgid-files.fin

This script prints all files in any directory under the JASS_ROOT_DIR directory with set group ID permissions. The results are displayed on standard output unless the JASS_SGID_FILE variable is defined. If this variable is defined, all of the results are written to that file.

print-suid-files.fin

This script prints all files in any directory under the JASS_ROOT_DIR directory with set user ID permissions. The results are displayed on standard output unless the JASS_SUID_FILE variable is defined. If this variable is defined, all of the results are written to that file.

print-unowned-objects.fin

This script lists all files, directories, and other objects on a system, starting from JASS_ROOT_DIR, that do not have valid users or groups assigned to them. The results are displayed on standard output unless the JASS_UNOWNED_FILE variable is defined.

print-world-writable-objects.fin

This script lists all world-writable objects on a system, starting from JASS_ROOT_DIR. The results are displayed on standard output unless the JASS_WRITEABLE_FILE variable is defined. If this variable is defined, then all of the results are written to that file.

Remove Finish Script

The remove-unneeded-accounts.fin script removes unused Solaris OE accounts from the /etc/passwd and /etc/shadow files using the passmgmt command. This script removes those accounts defined by the JASS_ACCT_REMOVE variable.

Set Finish Scripts

The following set finish scripts are described in this section:

set-banner-dtlogin.fin

This script installs a service banner for the dtlogin service. This banner is presented to a user after successfully authenticating to a system using a graphical interface, such as is provided by the Common Desktop Environment (CDE). This script configures the system to display the contents of a file specified by the file template JASS_ROOT_DIR/etc/dt/config/Xsession.d/0050.warning. By default the contents of the /etc/motd file are displayed. This script applies only to systems running the Solaris OE versions 2.6 and newer.

set-banner-ftpd.fin

This script installs the File Transfer Protocol (FTP) service banner defined by the variable JASS_BANNER_FTPD. For Solaris OE 8 and earlier versions, this banner is defined using the BANNER variable in the /etc/default/ftpd file. For the Solaris OE version 9, this banner is defined using the /etc/ftpd/banner.msg file. For more information, refer to the in.ftpd(1M) or ftpaccess(4) (for Solaris 9 OE) manual pages. This script applies only to systems running the Solaris OE versions 2.6 and newer.

If the install-ftpaccess.fin script is not used, then the change made by this script on a Solaris OE version 9 system does not take effect.

set-banner-telnet.fin

This script installs the Telnet service banner defined by the variable JASS_BANNER_TELNET. This banner is defined using the BANNER variable in the /etc/default/telnetd file. For more information, refer to the in.telnetd(1M) manual page. This script applies only to systems running the Solaris OE versions 2.6 and newer.

set-banner-sendmail.fin

This script installs the Sendmail service banner defined by the variable JASS_BANNER_SENDMAIL. This banner is defined using the SmtpGreetingMessage or De parameter in the /etc/mail/sendmail.cf file. For the Solaris 7 OE and newer, the SmtpGreetingMessage parameter is used. For earlier releases, the De parameter is used to implement this functionality. For more information, refer to the sendmail(1M) manual page.

set-banner-sshd.fin

This script installs the Secure Shell service banner by configuring the Secure Shell service to display the contents of /etc/issue to the user prior to authenticating to the system. This task is accomplished by setting the Banner parameter to /etc/issue in the /etc/ssh/sshd_config file. For more information on this functionality, refer to the sshd_config(4) manual page. This script is used only for systems running the Solaris 9 OE.

set-ftpd-umask.fin

This script sets the default file creation mask for the FTP service. In versions prior to Solaris 9 OE, the script sets the default file creation mask by adding a UMASK value, defined by the JASS_FTPD_UMASK variable, to the /etc/default/ftpd file. For Solaris 9 OE, the script sets the defumask parameter defined in the /etc/ftpd/ ftpaccess file. For more information, refer to the in.ftpd(1M) or ftpaccess(4) (for Solaris 9 OE) manual pages. This script applies only to systems running the Solaris OE versions 2.6 and newer.

If the install-ftpaccess.fin script is not used, then the change made by this script on a Solaris OE version 9 system does not take effect.

set-login-retries.fin

This script sets the RETRIES variable in the /etc/default/login file to the value defined by the JASS_LOGIN_RETRIES variable. By reducing the logging threshold, additional information may be gained. The install-loginlog.fin script enables the logging of failed login attempts. For more information on this capability, refer to the login(1) manual page.

set-power-restrictions.fin

This script alters the configuration of /etc/default/power to restrict user access to power management functions using the JASS_POWER_MGT_USER and JASS_CPR_MGT_USER variables. As a result, access to the system's power management and suspend/resume functionality is controlled. This script applies only to systems running the Solaris OE versions 2.6 and newer. This script works only on software controllable power supplies, for example, power off at PROM prompt.

set-rmmount-nosuid.fin

This script adds two entries to the /etc/rmmount.conf file to disable mounting of Set-UID files. It is important to disable mounting, because someone with access to a system could insert a diskette or CD-ROM and load Set-UID binaries, thereby compromising the system. For more information on this capability, refer to the rmmount.conf(4) manual page.

Note – Solaris OE versions 8 and newer are configured to mount removable media with the nosuid option by default. This script performs the necessary checks regardless of the default settings.

---

set-root-group.fin

This script changes the root user's primary group to JASS_ROOT_GROUP from group indentifier #1 (GID 1, other). This script prevents the root user from sharing a common group with non-privileged users.

set-root-password.fin

This script automates setting the root password by setting the password to an initial value as defined by JASS_ROOT_PASSWORD. The password used in this script should only be used during the installation and must be changed immediately after the JumpStart installation process has successfully completed. By default, the password used by the JASS_ROOT_PASSWORD parameter is t00lk1t.

Note – This script executes only during a JumpStart software installation. It does not execute when the Solaris Security Toolkit software is invoked from the command line.

---

set-sys-suspend-restrictions.fin

This script alters the configuration of /etc/default/sys-suspend to restrict user access to suspend and resume functionality based on the JASS_SUSPEND_PERMS variable. This script applies only to systems running the Solaris OE versions 2.6 and newer. For more information, refer to the sys-suspend(1M) manual page.

set-system-umask.fin

This script ensures that all of the run-control scripts execute with a safe file creation mask based on the setting of JASS_UMASK. This setting is important because using a poorly chosen file creation mask could leave critical files writable by any user.

For versions prior to Solaris 8 OE, this script creates startup scripts at each run level, thereby setting the file creation mask to JASS_UMASK. For Solaris 8 OE versions and newer, the CMASK variable in /etc/default/init is set to JASS_UMASK. For more information on this capability, refer to the init(1M) manual page.

set-term-type.fin

This script sets a default terminal type of `vt100` to avoid issues with systems not recognizing `dtterm`. This script is mainly for use on systems that do not have graphical consoles and are generally accessed over a terminal console or other serial link. This script is provided as a convenience only and does not impact the security of the system.

set-tmpfs-limit.fin

This script installs a limit on the disk space that can be used as part of a `tmpfs` file system. This limit can help prevent memory exhaustion. The usable space is limited by default in this script to the value defined by `JASS_TMPFS_LIMIT`. The `set-tmpfs-limit.fin` script does not run under Solaris OE version 2.5.1, where this functionality is unsupported. For more information on this capability, refer to the `mount_tmpfs`(1M) manual page.

set-user-password-reqs.fin

The changes implemented by this script configure the password policy of a system for the next time that passwords are changed on a system. This profile might need to be further tuned to ensure that applications and operational functions are not adversely impacted by the hardening process.

This script enables more strict password requirements by enabling:

Password aging

Minimum intervals between password changes

Minimum password length

This script accomplishes the requirements by using the values defined by the `JASS_AGING_MINWEEKS`, `JASS_AGING_MAXWEEKS`, `JASS_AGING_WARNWEEKS`, and `JASS_PASSLENGTH` variables to set the appropriate entries in the `/etc/default/passwd` file. This script is especially recommended for systems with nonprivileged user access.

This script modifies only the settings in the `/etc/default/passwd` file. It does not enable password aging for any user. The password aging requirements are implemented for each user upon the next password change. To enable password aging for a user without waiting for a password change event, use the `passwd`(1) command.

set-user-umask.fin

This script sets the default file creation mask (UMASK) to the value defined by
JASS_UMASK for the following user startup files: `/etc/.login`, `/etc/profile`, `/etc/skel/local.cshrc`, `/etc/skel/local.login`, `/etc/skel/local.profile`, and `/etc/default/login`.

Update Finish Scripts

The following update finish scripts are described in this section:

```
update-at-deny.fin
update-cron-allow.fin
update-cron-deny.fin
update-cron-log-size.fin
update-inetd-conf.fin
```

update-at-deny.fin

This script adds the accounts listed in JASS_AT_DENY to the `/etc/cron.d/at.deny` file. This script prevents those users from using `at` and `batch` facilities. This script is used with the `install-at-allow.fin` file to determine access to `at` and `batch` facilities. For more information on this capability, refer to the at(1) manual page.

update-cron-allow.fin

This script adds the accounts listed in JASS_CRON_ALLOW to the `/etc/cron.d/cron.allow` file. This script allows those users to use the `cron` facility. This script is used with the `update-cron-deny.fin` script to determine access to the `cron` facility. For more information on this capability, refer to the crontab(1) manual page.

update-cron-deny.fin

This script adds the accounts listed in JASS_CRON_DENY to the `/etc/cron.d/cron.deny` file. This script prevents those users from accessing the `cron` facility. This script is used with the `update-cron-allow.fin` script to determine access to the `cron` facility. This script does not disable access for the root account user. For more information on this capability, refer to the crontab(1) manual page.

update-cron-log-size.fin

This script adjusts the maximum limit used for storing `cron` log information. For Solaris OE versions prior to Solaris 9 OE, this script adjusts the `LIMIT` variable in the `/etc/cron.d/logchecker` script. For Solaris 9 OE, this script adjusts the `-s` parameter in the `/etc/logadm.conf` file (for the `/var/cron/log` entry).

The size limit used by this script is determined by the `JASS_CRON_LOG_SIZE` environment variable. By default, the limit defined by the Solaris OE is only 0.5 megabytes.

update-inetd-conf.fin

This script disables all services, started from the `inetd`, that are defined by the `JASS_SVCS_DISABLE` variable. This script enables the services listed by the `JASS_SVCS_ENABLE` variable. If the same service is in both variables, the service is enabled. The `JASS_SVCS_ENABLE` variable takes precedence.

All services, including common services such as `in.telnetd`, `in.ftpd`, and `in.rshd`, in the base OS are disabled by default in Solaris OE versions 2.5.1 and newer. The services are disabled after the script inserts a "#" at the start of each line for service entries in the `/etc/inet/inetd.conf` file. Additional services installed by unbundled or third-party software are not disabled.

Using Product-Specific Finish Scripts

This section lists product-specific finish scripts, which are for hardening specific Sun products. These scripts are in the Finish directory. TABLE 11-1 lists product-specific finish scripts.

New finish scripts are released periodically to harden new and updated Sun products. For the latest list of scripts, refer to the Security Web site:

```
http://www.sun.com/security/jass
```

TABLE 11-1 Product-Specific Finish Scripts

Product	Driver Name
Sun Cluster 3.x Software	suncluster3x-set-nsswitch-conf.fin
Sun Fire 12K and 15K Domains	s15k-static-arp.fin
Sun Fire 12K and 15K System Controllers	s15k-exclude-domains.fin s15k-sms-secure-failover.fin s15k-static-arp.fin

suncluster3x-set-nsswitch-conf.fin

This script automates the configuration of a system as a Sun Cluster 3.x node. This script installs the cluster keyword into the /etc/nsswitch.conf file to simplify deploying Sun Cluster 3.x systems. The keyword should be located in the hosts field. This script applies only to Sun Cluster 3.x systems and does not execute on other systems.

For more information, refer to the Sun BluePrints OnLine article titled "Securing Sun Cluster 3.x Software."

s15k-static-arp.fin

This script enables static ARP addresses on the I1 MAN network. The I1 MAN network is a network internal to the SunFire 12K and 15K chassis, which is used for TCP/IP-based communication between the SCs and domains. By using static ARP instead of dynamic ARP, several ARP-based attacks against the SC no longer have any effect. This script applies only to SunFire 12K and 15K SCs and does not execute on other systems.

The following four files are used by the SunFire 12K and 15K optional s15k-static-arp.fin script:

```
/etc/sms_sc_arp
/etc/sms_domain_arp
/etc/rc2.d/S73sms_arpconfig
/etc/init.d/sms_arpconfig
```

For more information, refer to the Sun BluePrints OnLine article titled "Securing the SunFire™ 12K and 15K System Controller" and the article titled "Securing the SunFire™ 12K and 15K Domains."

s15k-exclude-domains.fin

This script disables TCP/IP connectivity between the SC and one or more domains. For more information, refer to the Sun BluePrints OnLine article titled "Securing the SunFire™ 12K and 15K System Controller."

s15k-sms-secure-failover.fin

This script automates enabling the use of Secure Shell by the failover daemon fomd. This script automates much of the Secure Shell configuration, in addition to disabling the use of legacy r* services. This script applies only to SunFire 12K and 15K SCs and does not execute on other systems.

For more information, refer to the Sun BluePrints OnLine article titled "Securing the SunFire™ 12K and 15K System Controller."

## CHAPTER 12

Using Audit Scripts

This chapter provides reference information for using, adding, modifying, and removing audit scripts. Audit scripts provide an easy method for periodically checking the security posture of a system. We recommend that you check your systems regularly to make sure that their security matches your security profile.

The standard audit scripts confirm that modifications controlled by finish scripts were made to the system, and they report any discrepancies occurring since the hardening run. Audit scripts use the same name as their correlating finish script, except they have a different suffix. (Audit scripts use the .aud suffix instead of .fin.)

This chapter contains the following topics:

Customizing Audit Scripts

This section provides instructions and recommendations for customizing existing audit scripts or creating new audit scripts. In addition, guidelines are provided for using audit script functions.

Customize Standard Audit Scripts

Just as with Solaris Security Toolkit drivers and finish scripts, you can customize audit scripts. We recommend that you exercise great care when modifying scripts that are supplied with the Solaris Security Toolkit software. Always modify a copy of the script and not the original directly. Failure to do so may result in a loss of changes during Solaris Security Toolkit software upgrade or removal. Also, wherever possible, make as few changes to the code as possible and document the changes well.

We recommend that you customize audit scripts by using environment variables. The behavior of most scripts can be tailored using this technique, thereby eliminating the need to modify the script directly. If this is not possible, then you may find it necessary to modify the code.

For a list of all environment variables and guidelines for defining them, refer to Chapter 13.

Note – Consider submitting a bug report or request for enhancement if you think that the change could benefit a wider audience. The Solaris Security Toolkit development team is always looking for ways to improve the software to better support its users.

Whenever you customize the standard finish scripts or develop new ones, be sure to take corresponding actions on the related audit scripts.

To Customize An Audit Script

Use the following steps to customize a standard audit script for your system and environment. Use these instructions so that newer versions of the original files do not overwrite your customized versions. Furthermore, these files are not removed if the software is removed using the `pkgrm` command.

1. **Copy the audit script and related files that you want to customize. (Refer to Chapter 6 for information about audit scripts and their related files.)**

2. **Rename the copies with names that identify the files as custom scripts and files.**

   For naming guidelines, refer to Chapter 1, "Configuring and Customizing the Solaris Security Toolkit Software" on page 15.

3. **Modify your custom script and files accordingly.**

   The `finish.init` file provides all audit script configuration variables. You can override the default variables by modifying the `user.init` file. This file is heavily commented to explain each variable, its impact, and its use in audit scripts. For more information about this file and modifying its variables, refer to Chapter 9. Or, if you want the change to be localized rather than to apply to all drivers, modify the driver.

   When you customize audit scripts, it is critical to the accuracy of the audit functionality that both finish and audit scripts can access your customization. This goal is most easily and effectively achieved by modifying environment variables in the `user.init` script instead of modifying other init files or modifying scripts directly.

   The following code example shows how to customize the `install-openssh.aud` script to validate software installation. In this example, these checks ensure that the software package is installed, configured, and set up to run whenever the system reboots.

CODE EXAMPLE 12-1 Sample `install-openssh.aud` Script

```
#
#!/bin/sh
# Copyright (c) 2002 by Sun Microsystems, Inc.
# All rights reserved.
#
#ident  "@(#)install-openssh.aud     1.3     02/12/03       SMI"
#
# ****************************************************************
# Service definition section.
# ****************************************************************
#--------------------------------------------------------------
service="OpenSSH"
servfil="install-openssh.aud"
servhdr_txt="
Rationale for Verification Check:
```

```
#
This script will attempt to determine if the OpenSSH software is
installed, configured and running on the system.  Note that this
script expects the OpenSSH software to be installed in package form
in accordance with the install-openssh.fin Finish script.

Determination of Compliance:

It indicates a failure if the OpenSSH package is not installed,
configured, or running on the system.
"

#----------------------------------------------------------------

servpkg="
   OBSDssh
"

#----------------------------------------------------------------

servsrc="
   ${JASS_ROOT_DIR}/etc/rc3.d/S25openssh.server
"

#----------------------------------------------------------------

servcfg="
   ${JASS_ROOT_DIR}/etc/sshd_config
"

#----------------------------------------------------------------

servcmd="
   /opt/OBSDssh/sbin/sshd
"

#
****************************************************************
# Check processing section.
#
****************************************************************

start_audit "${servfil}" "${service}" "${servhdr_txt}"

logMessage "${JASS_MSG_SOFTWARE_INSTALLED}"

if check_packageExists "${servpkg}" 1 LOG ; then
```

```
#
pkgName="`pkgparam -R ${JASS_ROOT_DIR} ${servpkg} NAME`"
pkgVersion="`pkgparam -R ${JASS_ROOT_DIR} ${servpkg} VERSION`"
pkgBaseDir="`pkgparam -R ${JASS_ROOT_DIR} ${servpkg} BASEDIR`"
pkgContact="`pkgparam -R ${JASS_ROOT_DIR} ${servpkg} EMAIL`"

logNotice "Package has description '${pkgName}'"
logNotice "Package has version '${pkgVersion}'"
logNotice "Package has base directory '${pkgBaseDir}'"
logNotice "Package has contact '${pkgContact}'"

logMessage "\n${JASS_MSG_SOFTWARE_CONFIGURED}"
check_startScriptExists "${servsrc}" 1 LOG
check_serviceConfigExists "${servcfg}" 1 LOG

logMessage "\n${JASS_MSG_SOFTWARE_RUNNING}"
check_processExists "${servcmd}" 1 LOG
fi

finish_audit
```

Create New Audit Scripts

You can create new audit scripts and integrate them into your deployment of the Solaris Security Toolkit software. Because scripts are commonly developed in Bourne shell, it is relatively easy to add new functionality. For those who are less experienced in UNIX shell scripting, examine existing audit scripts that perform similar functions to gain an understanding of how to accomplish a given task and to understand the correct sequence of actions.

The same conventions for developing new finish scripts apply to developing new audit scripts. For these conventions, refer to Chapter 11, "Customizing Finish Scripts" on page 222.

Audit and finish scripts work together. Whenever you add new audit scripts, be sure to consider adding companion finish scripts.

Using Standard Audit Scripts

Audit scripts are the Solaris Security Toolkit software's automated method of validating a security posture by comparing it with a predefined security profile. Use audit scripts to validate that security modifications were made correctly, and to obtain reports on any discrepancies between a system's security posture and your security profile. For detailed information about using audit scripts to validate system security, refer to Chapter 6.

This section describes the standard audit scripts, which are in the Audit directory. Only the functionality performed by the audit scripts is described.

Each of the scripts in the Audit directory is organized into the following categories, which mirror those of the finish scripts in the Finish directory:

Disable
Enable
Install
Minimize
Print
Remove
Set
Update

In addition to these standard audit scripts, we provide product-specific audit scripts. For a list of product-specific audit scripts, refer to "Using Product-Specific Audit Scripts" on page 292.

Disable Audit Scripts

The following disable audit scripts are described in this section:

disable-ab2.aud

This script determines if the AnswerBook 2 service is installed, configured, or running on the system. It indicates a failure if the software is installed, configured to run, or running on the system. This script is necessary only for systems running the Solaris OE versions 2.5.1 through 8, because the AnswerBook 2 software is no longer used in Solaris OE versions 9 and newer.

disable-apache.aud

This script determines if the Apache Web Server is installed, configured, or running on the system. It indicates a failure if the software is installed, configured to run (via a run-control script), or running on the system.

Note that this script checks only for the Apache Web Server that was packaged by Sun and shipped as part of Solaris OE versions 8 and newer.

disable-asppp.aud

This script determines if the ASPPP service is installed, configured, or running on the system. It indicates a failure if the software is installed, configured to run (via a run-control script), or running on the system.

This script applies only to Solaris OE versions 2.5.1 through 8. For Solaris 9 OE, this service was replaced with the Point-to-Point (PPP) service and is verified using the disable-ppp.aud script.

disable-autoinst.aud

This script determines if automated installation functionality is installed or enabled on the system. It indicates a failure if the software is installed or configured to run (via a run-control script).

disable-automount.aud

This script determines if the automount service is installed, configured, or running on the system. It indicates a failure if the software is installed, configured to run (via a run-control script), or running on the system.

Note – If this service is required, then do not use this script. Also, because this service relies on the RPC service, the `disable-rpc.aud` script should not be used.

---

disable-dhcpd.aud

This script determines if the DHCP (server) service is installed, configured, or running on the system. It indicates a failure if the software is installed, configured to run (via a run-control script), or running on the system. This script applies only to the DHCP server included in Solaris OE versions 8 and newer.

disable-directory.aud

This script determines if the Sun ONE Directory (server) service is installed, configured, or running on the system. It indicates a failure if the software is installed, configured to run (via a run-control script), or running on the system. This audit script checks only for the Solaris 9 OE bundled Sun ONE Directory Server. This script does not audit either the unbundled product or the Sun ONE Directory Server software provided with other Solaris OE versions.

disable-dmi.aud

This script determines if the DMI service is installed, configured, or running on the system. It indicates a failure if the software is installed, configured to run (via a run-control script), or running on the system. This script is appropriate only for systems running Solaris OE versions 2.6 or newer.

disable-dtlogin.aud

This script determines if the Common Desktop Environment (CDE) login server, or `dtlogin`, is installed, configured, or running on the system. It indicates a failure if the software is installed, configured to run (via a run-control script), or running on the system. This script is necessary only for systems running the Solaris OE version 2.6 or newer.

Note – If this service is required, then do not use this script. Also, because this service relies on the RPC service, the `disable-rpc.aud` script should not be used.

disable-ipv6.aud

This script checks for the absence of the IPv6 host name files, `/etc/hostname6.*`, that cause IPv6 interfaces to be plumbed. This script checks if the `in.ndpd` service is started. It indicates a failure if any IPv6 interfaces are configured, plumbed, or if the service is running. This script is necessary only for systems running the Solaris OE versions 8 and newer.

disable-kdc.aud

This script determines if the Kerberos Key Distribution (KDC) service is installed, configured, or running on the system. It indicates a failure if the software is installed, configured to run (via a run-control script), or running on the system. If `JASS_DISABLE_MODE` is set to `conf`, the `kdc.conf` file is disabled, thus determining the ability of the system to act as both a Kerberos client and KDC server. Do not use this script in that manner if the system must act as a Kerberos client. This script is necessary only for systems running the Solaris 9 OE.

disable-keyboard-abort.aud

This script determines if the system is configured to ignore keyboard abort sequences. Typically, when a keyboard abort sequence is initiated, the operating system is suspended and the console enters the OpenBoot PROM monitor or debugger. This script determines if the system can be suspended in this way. This script is used only in the Solaris OE versions 2.6 and newer.

Note – Some systems feature key switches with a secure position. On these systems, setting the key switch to the secure position overrides any software default set with the `kdb` command.

disable-keyserv-uid-nobody.aud

This script determines if the `keyserv` service is not configured to prevent the use of default keys for the user `nobody`. This script indicates a failure if the `keyserv` process is not running with the `-d` flag and the `ENABLE_NOBODY_KEYS` parameter is not set to NO (for Solaris OE versions 9 and newer).

disable-ldap-client.aud

This script determines if the Lightweight Directory Access Protocol (LDAP) client service is installed, configured, or running on the system. It indicates a failure if the software is installed, configured to run (via a run-control script), or running on the system. This script applies to Solaris OE versions 8 and newer.

disable-lp.aud

This script determines if the line printer (lp) service is installed, configured, or running on the system. It indicates a failure if the software is installed, configured to run (via a run-control script), or running on the system. This script indicates a failure if the lp user is permitted to use the cron facility or has a crontab file installed.

disable-mipagent.aud

This script determines if the mobile IP (MIP) service is installed, configured, or running on the system. It indicates a failure if the software is installed, configured to run (via a run-control script), or running on the system. This script is necessary only for Solaris OE versions 8 and newer.

disable-nfs-client.aud

This script determines if the Networked File System (NFS) client service is configured or running on the system. It indicates a failure if the software is configured to run or is running on the system.

Note – If this service is required, then do not use this script. Also, because this service relies on the RPC service, the disable-rpc.aud script should not be used.

disable-nfs-server.aud

This script determines if the Networked File System (NFS) server service is configured or running on the system. It indicates a failure if the software is configured to run or is running on the system.

Note – If this service is required, then do not use this script. Also, because this service relies on the RPC service, the disable-rpc.aud script should not be used.

disable-nscd-caching.aud

This script determines if any of the passwd, group, host, or ipnodes services have a positive-time-to-live or negative-time-to-live value that is not set to 0. It indicates a failure if the value is not 0.

disable-picld.aud

This script determines if the Platform Information and Control Library (PICL) service is installed, configured, or running on the system. It indicates a failure if the software is installed, configured to run (via a run-control script), or running on the system. This script is necessary only for systems running the Solaris OE versions 2.6 and newer.

disable-power-mgmt.aud

This script determines if the power management service is installed, configured, or running on the system. It indicates a failure if the software is installed, configured to run (via a run-control script), or running on the system. This script is necessary only for systems running the Solaris OE versions 2.6 and newer.

disable-ppp.aud

This script determines if the Point-to-Point Protocol (PPP) service is installed, configured, or running on the system. It indicates a failure if the software is installed, configured to run (via a run-control script), or running on the system. This service was introduced in Solaris 8 OE (7/01) and supplements the older Asynchronous PPP (ASPPP) service. This script is necessary only for systems running the Solaris OE versions 8 and newer.

disable-preserve.aud

This script determines if the preserve functionality is enabled through its run-control script. If enabled, a failure is indicated.

disable-remote-root-login.aud

This script determines if a root user is permitted to directly log in to or execute commands on a system remotely through programs using /bin/login such as Telnet. It indicates a failure if this is correct.

Note – Other mechanisms to access systems, such as the use of Solaris Secure Shell, that do not use `/bin/login` may still provide direct root access, even if the system passes this test.

disable-rhosts.aud

This script determines if the `rhosts` and `hosts.equiv` functionality is enabled through Pluggable Authentication Module (PAM) configuration in `/etc/pam.conf`. It indicates a failure if this functionality is enabled using the `pam_rhosts_auth.so.1` module in the `/etc/pam.conf` file. This script is necessary only for Solaris OE versions 2.6 and newer.

disable-rpc.aud

This script determines if the Remote Procedure Call (RPC) service is installed, configured, or running on the system. It indicates a failure if the software is installed, configured to run (via a run-control script), or running on the system. In addition, this script indicates a failure for each service registered with the rpcbind port mapper.

Note – The RPC port mapper function should not be disabled if any of the following services are used on the system: automount, NFS, NIS, NIS+, CDE, and volume management (Solaris 9 OE only).

disable-samba.aud

This script determines if the Samba service is installed, configured, or running on the system. It indicates a failure if the software is installed, configured to run (via a run-control script), or running on the system. Only Samba services included in the Solaris OE distribution are verified as being disabled. This script does not impact other Samba distributions installed on the system.

disable-sendmail.aud

By default, the sendmail service is configured to both forward local mail and to receive incoming mail from remote sources. If a system is not intended to be a mail server, then the sendmail service can be configured not to accept incoming messages. This script checks that the sendmail service is configured in such a manner.

This check is performed in a variety of ways depending on the version of the Solaris OE used. For Solaris OE versions 9 and newer, this script checks for the existence of the following in the `/etc/mail/sendmail.cf` file:

```
Name=NoMTA4, Family=inet, Addr=127.0.0.1
```

For Solaris 8 OE, this script checks the `/etc/default/sendmail` file to determine if the MODE parameter is set to "" (nothing). For earlier versions of the Solaris OE, this script determines if the sendmail run-control scripts are disabled and an entry added to the root user's `crontab` file to automate the processing of queued mail.

This script indicates a failure if the sendmail service is not disabled in accordance with the checks unique to the Solaris OE version.

Note – The Solaris Security Toolkit software modifications verify only that a Solaris OE system is not configured to receive email. Outgoing email is still processed normally.

---

disable-slp.aud

This script determines if the Service Location Protocol (SLP) service is installed, configured, or running on the system. It indicates a failure if the software is installed, configured to run (via a run-control script), or running on the system. This script is necessary only for systems running the Solaris OE versions 2.6 and newer.

disable-snmp.aud

This script determines if the Simple Network Management Protocol (SNMP) service is installed, configured, or running on the system. It indicates a failure if the software is installed, configured to run (via a run-control script), or running on the system. This script verifies whether third-party SNMP agents are functioning on the system. It checks only the SNMP agent provided in the Solaris OE versions 2.6 and newer.

disable-spc.aud

This script determines if the SunSoft Print Client (SPC) service is installed, configured, or running on the system. It indicates a failure if the software is installed, configured to run (via a run-control script), or running on the system. This script is necessary only for systems running the Solaris OE versions 2.6 and newer.

disable-ssh-root-login.aud

It indicates a failure if the Solaris Secure Shell service distributed in the Solaris 9 OE does not restrict access to the root account. This script is necessary only for systems running the Solaris OE versions 9 and newer with the Solaris Secure Shell packages installed and enabled.

disable-syslogd-listen.aud

This script determines if the SYSLOG service is configured to accept remote log connections. It indicates a failure if the syslogd process is not running with the -t flag and the LOG_FROM_REMOTE parameter is not set to NO (for the Solaris OE versions 9 and newer).

Note – This script should not be used on SYSLOG servers.

---

disable-system-accounts.aud

For each account name listed in the JASS_ACCT_DISABLE environment variable, this script indicates a failure for each account that is not configured to use the shell defined by the JASS_SHELL_DISABLE variable. Also, this script indicates a failure if the shell program listed in the JASS_SHELL_DISABLE variable does not exist on the system.

Note that this script only checks accounts that are listed in the /etc/passwd file. It does not check for accounts listed in any other naming service (NIS, NIS+ or LDAP).

disable-uucp.aud

This script determines if the UNIX-to-UNIX Copy (UUCP) service is installed, configured, or running on the system. It indicates a failure if the software is installed, configured to run (via a run-control script), or running on the system. Also, it indicates a failure if the nuucp user exists, if in.uucpd exists in /etc/inetd.conf, or if a uucp crontab file is installed.

disable-vold.aud

This script determines if the volume management (VOLD) service is installed, configured, or running on the system. It indicates a failure if the software is installed, configured to run (via a run-control script), or is running on the system.

Note – Do not use this script if automatic mounting and unmounting of removable media (such as diskettes and CD-ROMs) is needed.

disable-wbem.aud

This script determines if the web-based enterprise management (WBEM) service is installed, configured, or running on the system. It indicates a failure if the software is installed, configured to run (via a run-control script), or running on the system. This script is necessary only for systems running the Solaris OE versions 8 and newer.

Note – If this service is required, then do not use this script. Also, because this service relies on the RPC service, the disable-rpc.fin script should not be used either. Do not use this script if you use Solaris Management Console (SMC).

disable-xserver.listen.aud

It indicates a failure if the X11 server is configured to accept client connections using the TCP transport. In addition, it indicates a failure if the X11 server is running in a configuration that permits use of the TCP transport. This script is only applicable to the Solaris 9 OE.

Enable Audit Scripts

The following enable audit scripts are described in this section:

enable-32bit-kernel.aud

This script determines if the system is configured to run in 32-bit mode or is running in 32-bit mode. It indicates a failure if the system is either configured or running in 32-bit mode.

enable-bsm.aud

This script determines if the SunSHIELD Solaris Basic Security Module (Solaris BSM) auditing functionality is enabled and running on the system, if the service is loaded in the /etc/system file, and if the audit_warn alias is defined in /etc/mail/aliases. If one or more of these checks fail, then the script indicates a failure.

enable-coreadm.aud

This script verifies that the system stores generated core files under the directory specified by JASS_CORE_DIR. It indicates a failure if the coreadm functionality present in the Solaris OE versions 7 and newer is not configured. Also, an error condition is generated if core files are not tagged with the specification denoted by JASS_CORE_PATTERN.

enable-ftp-syslog.aud

This script determines if the File Transfer Protocol (FTP) service is not configured to log session and connection information. A failure is indicated if the FTP service logging is not enabled.

enable-ftpaccess.aud

This script determines if the File Transfer Protocol (FTP) service is configured to use the /etc/ftpd/ftpaccess file. This script is necessary only on systems running the Solaris 9 OE. A failure is indicated if FTP is not configured properly.

enable-inetd-syslog.aud

This script determines if the Internet services daemon (inetd) service is configured to log session and connection information. Note that for Solaris OE versions 9 and newer, this script checks that the -t option was added to the inetd command line and that the ENABLE_CONNECTION_LOGGING variable in the /etc/default/ inetd file is set to YES. A failure is indicated if either of these checks fail.

enable-priv-nfs-ports.aud

This script determines if the NFS service is configured to accept only client communication that originates from a port in the privileged range below 1024. A failure is indicated if the NFS service is not configured properly.

enable-process-accounting.aud

This script determines if the processing accounting software is installed, enabled, or running on the system. A failure is indicated if this is not true.

enable-rfc1948.aud

This script determines if the system is configured to use RFC 1948 for its TCP sequence number generation. This script checks both the stored configuration and the actual run-time setting. This script is necessary only on systems running Solaris OE versions 2.6 and newer. A failure is displayed if the system is not configured to use RFC 1948 compliant TCP sequence number generation.

`enable-stack-protection.aud`

This script determines if the `noexec_user_stack` and `noexec_user_stack_log` options are set in the `/etc/system` file to enable stack protections and exception logging. This script is necessary only on systems running the Solaris OE versions 2.6 and newer. If these options are not enabled, a failure is reported.

`enable-tcpwrappers.aud`

This script determines if TCP Wrappers are not installed or configured using the `hosts.allow|deny` templates included with the Solaris Security Toolkit software or enabled by using the `ENABLE_TCPWRAPPERS` variable. This script applies only to Solaris OE versions 9 and newer using the bundled TCP Wrapper packages. A failure is reported the system is not using TCP Wrappers.

Install Audit Scripts

The following install audit scripts are described in this section:

install-at-allow.aud

This script determines if a user name is listed in the JASS_AT_ALLOW variable and does not exist in the /etc/cron.d/at.allow file. The list of user names defined by JASS_AT_ALLOW is, by default, empty. To pass this check, each user name must exist in both the /etc/passwd file and the /etc/cron.d/at.allow file. Furthermore, a user name should not be in the /etc/cron.d/at.deny file. A failure is displayed if a user name is not listed in both files.

install-fix-modes.aud

This script determines if the Fix Modes program was installed and run on the system. It indicates a failure if the software is not installed or has not been run. Further, this script uses Fix Modes in debug mode to determine if any additional file system objects should be adjusted.

install-ftpusers.aud

This script determines if a user name listed in the JASS_FTPUSERS parameter does not exist in the ftpusers file.

install-Sun_ONE-WS.aud

This script determines if the Sun ONE Web Server is installed on the system in accordance with the install-Sun_ONE-WS.fin script. A failure is reported if the software is not installed correctly.

install-jass.aud

This script determines if the Solaris Security Toolkit (SUNWjass) package is installed on the system. A failure is reported if this package is not installed.

install-loginlog.aud

This script checks for the existence and proper ownership and permissions for the /var/adm/loginlog file. It indicates a failure if the file does not exist, has invalid permissions, or is not owned by the root account.

install-md5.aud

This script determines if the MD5 software is installed on the system. A failure is reported if the software is not installed.

install-newaliases.aud

This script checks for the existence of the `/usr/bin/newaliases` program. It indicates a failure if this file does not exist or is not a symbolic link.

install-openssh.aud

This script determines if the OpenSSH package specified by the script is installed and configured. A failure is reported if the package is not installed.

Note – Solaris 9 OE includes a version of the Secure Shell software; therefore, this script is not used if you install Solaris 9 OE.

---

install-recommended-patches.aud

This script determines if the patches listed in the Recommended and Security Patch Cluster file are installed on the system. The patch information is collected from `JASS_HOME_DIR/Patches` directory, based on Solaris OE version of the system being tested. A failure is displayed if one or more of these patches are not installed.

Note that this script indicates success if the version of the patch installed is equal to or greater than the version listed in the patch order file.

install-sadmind-options.aud

This script determines if the `sadmind` service exists in the `/etc/inet/inetd.conf` file. If it does, this script checks to ensure that options are set to those defined by the `JASS_SADMIND_OPTIONS` variable. The default setting is `-S 2`.

install-security-mode.aud

This script checks the status of the EEPROM security mode. It displays a warning if the mode is not command or full. In addition, this script checks the PROM failed login counter and displays a warning if it is not zero.

Note that because the `install-security-mode.fin` script cannot change the security mode of the system, this script only indicates a warning for noncompliance rather than reporting a failure.

install-shells.aud

This script determines if any shell defined by the JASS_SHELLS parameter is not listed in the `shells` file. The list of shells defined by JASS_SHELLS is as follows.

TABLE 12-1   List of `shells` Defined by JASS_SHELLS

/usr/bin/sh	/usr/bin/csh
/usr/bin/ksh	/usr/bin/jsh
/bin/sh	/bin/csh
/bin/ksh	/bin/jsh
/sbin/sh	/sbin/jsh
/bin/bash	/bin/pfcsh
/bin/pfksh	/bin/pfsh
/bin/tcsh	/bin/zsh
/usr/bin/bash	/usr/bin/pfcsh
/usr/bin/pfksh	/usr/bin/pfsh
/usr/bin/tcsh	/usr/bin/zsh

A failure is displayed if any shells listed in JASS_SHELLS are not also listed in the `shells` file.

install-strong-permissions.aud

This script determines if any of the modifications recommended by the `install-strong-permissions.fin` script were not implemented. A failure is displayed if any of these modifications were not made.

install-sulog.aud

This script checks for the proper ownership and permissions of the /var/adm/sulog file. It indicates a failure if the file does not exist, has invalid permissions, or is not owned by the root account.

install-templates.aud

This script determines if the files defined by the `JASS_FILES` variable was successfully copied to the target system. It indicates a failure if either of the two following checks fail: a test to ensure that the source and target file types match (regular file, symbolic link, or directory) and a test to ensure that their contents are the same.

Minimize Audit Script

This script determines if any nonessential packages exist on the system as defined by the minimization finish script, `minimize-Sun_ONE-WS.fin`. A failure is displayed if any of the nonessential packages are present on the system.

Print Audit Scripts

The following print audit scripts are described in this section:

These scripts perform the same functions as the print finish scripts, except that they are customized for audit use.

print-jass-environment.aud

This script displays the variables used by the Solaris Security Toolkit. It does not perform any validation or other checks on the content. The variables and their content are displayed.

print-jumpstart-environment.aud

This script is for JumpStart mode only. It is used to print out JumpStart environment variable settings. This script does not perform any audit checks.

print-rhosts.aud

This script displays a notice for any files found with the name of `.rhosts` or `hosts.equiv`. Further, this script displays the contents of those files for further inspection.

print-sgid-files.aud

This script displays a notice for any files that have the set-gid bit set, and it provides a full (long) listing for further review.

print-suid-files.aud

This script displays a notice for any files that have the set-uid bit set, and it provides a full (long) listing for further review.

print-unowned-objects.aud

This script displays a notice for any files that are not assigned to a valid user and group, and it provides a full (long) listing for further review.

print-world-writable-objects.aud

This script displays a notice for any matching files that are world-writable, and it provides a full (long) listing for further review.

Remove Audit Script

The `remove-unneeded-accounts.aud` script validates that unused Solaris OE accounts, defined by the `JASS_ACCT_REMOVE` variable, were removed from the system.

Set Audit Scripts

The following set audit scripts are described in this section:

set-banner-dtlogin.aud

This script verifies that a service banner for the Common Desktop Environment (CDE) or `dtlogin` service is defined. This script verifies that the system displays the contents of `/etc/motd` by listing it in the file template `JASS_ROOT_DIR/etc/dt/config/Xsession.d/0050.warning`. This script is necessary only for systems running Solaris OE versions 2.6 and newer.

set-banner-ftpd.aud

This script checks that the FTP service banner matches the value defined by the `JASS_BANNER_FTPD` variable. It indicates a failure if the service banner does not match. The value of the variable is `Authorized Use Only`. This script is necessary only for systems running the Solaris OE versions 2.6 and newer.

set-banner-telnet.aud

This script checks that the Telnet service banner matches the value defined by the JASS_BANNER_TELNETD variable. It indicates a failure if the service banner does not match. The value of the variable is Authorized Use Only. This script is necessary only for systems running Solaris OE versions 2.6 and newer.

set-banner-sendmail.aud

This script verifies that the sendmail service is configured to display the service banner as defined by the JASS_BANNER_SENDMAIL environment variable. This banner is displayed to all clients connecting to the sendmail service over the network.

set-banner-sshd.aud

This script verifies that the Secure Shell service banner is displayed by ensuring that the Secure Shell service displays the contents of /etc/issue to the user prior to authenticating access to the system. This script is used only for systems running Solaris 9 OE.

set-ftpd-umask.aud

This script checks that the FTP service banner matches the value defined by the JASS_FTPD_UMASK variable. It indicates a failure if the file creation mask value does not match. The value of variable is 022. This script is necessary only for systems running Solaris OE versions 2.6 and newer.

set-login-retries.aud

This script determines if the login RETRIES parameter is assigned the value defined by the JASS_LOGIN_RETRIES variable. The variable default is set to 3. A failure is displayed if the variable is not set to the default.

set-power-restrictions.aud

This script checks the /etc/default/power file and indicates a failure if the PMCHANGEPERM and CPRCHANGEPERM parameters do not have a hyphen "-" as their values.

This script is necessary only for systems running Solaris OE versions 2.6 and newer.

set-rmmount-nosuid.aud

This script determines if the /etc/rmmount.conf file restricts the mounting of removable UFS or HSFS file systems by enforcing the nosuid parameter. A failure is displayed if this restriction is not defined in the /etc/rmmount.conf file.

Note – Solaris OE versions 8 and newer are configured to mount removable media with the nosuid option by default. This script performs the necessary checks regardless of the default settings.

---

set-root-group.aud

This script determines if the root account's primary group is set to the value defined by the JASS_ROOT_GROUP variable. A failure is displayed if it is not defined properly.

set-root-password.aud

This script checks the password of the root account. It indicates a failure if the value is the same as that of the JASS_ROOT_PASSWORD variable. This check is done to encourage users to change the root password from the value defined by JASS_ROOT_PASSWORD as soon as possible.

set-sys-suspend-restrictions.aud

This script checks the /etc/default/sys-suspend file. It indicates a failure if the PERMS parameter does not have a hyphen "-" as its value. This script is necessary only for systems running Solaris OE versions 2.6 and newer.

set-system-umask.aud

This script determines if the system's default file creation mask is set to the value defined by the JASS_UMASK variable. The default value is set to 022. A failure is displayed if the variable is not properly defined.

`set-term-type.aud`

This script determines if the `/etc/profile` and the `/etc/login` files set the default terminal type to `vt100`. A failure is displayed if the default terminal type is not defined properly. This script is provided as a convenience only, and a failure does not impact the security of a system.

`set-tmpfs-limit.aud`

This script determines if any `tmpfs` file systems are defined in the `/etc/vfstab` file without their size being limited to the `JASS_TMPFS_SIZE` variable, which is set to a default of 512 MBytes. The `set-tmpfs-limit.aud` script does not run under Solaris 2.5.1 OE, where this functionality is unsupported. A failure is reported if the `tmpfs` file system size does not comply with the `JASS_TMPFS_SIZE` value.

`set-user-password-reqs.aud`

This script reviews the password policy settings on the system as defined previously. It indicates an error if the values do not match the following default values defined by the Solaris Security Toolkit:

```
MINWEEKS - "1"

MAXWEEKS - "8"

WARNWEEKS - "1"

PASSLENGTH - "8"
```

The default values are contained in the following environment variables:

```
JASS_AGING_MINWEEKS

JASS_AGING_MAXWEEKS

JASS_AGING_WARNWEEKS

JASS_PASS_LENGTH
```

set-user-umask.aud

This script determines if any of the following files do not set the umask parameter to the value defined by the JASS_UMASK variable. The default value is set 022.

```
/etc/.login
/etc/profile
/etc/skel/local.cshrc
/etc/skel/local.login
/etc/skel/local.profile
/etc/default/login
```

A failure is displayed if these files do not set the umask parameter appropriately.

Update Audit Scripts

The following update audit scripts are described in this section:

update-at-deny.aud

This script determines if a user type is listed in the JASS_AT_DENY variable and is not listed in the /etc/cron.d/at.deny file. The list of user types defined by the JASS_AT_DENY variable is as follows:

```
root
daemon
bin
sys
adm
lp
uucp
smmsp
nobody
noaccess
```

To pass this check, each user type must exist in both the /etc/passwd file and the /etc/cron.d/at.deny file. The user type must not exist in the /etc/cron.d/at.allow file, because it would override the setting (due to precedence). A failure is displayed if any of these checks fail.

update-cron-allow.aud

This script determines if a user ID is listed in the JASS_CRON_ALLOW variable and not in /etc/cron.d/cron.allow file. By default, the value is only the root user. A failure is displayed if this check fails.

update-cron-deny.aud

This script determines if a user ID is listed in the JASS_CRON_DENY variable and not in the /etc/cron.d/cron.deny file. The list of user types defined by the JASS_CRON_DENY variable is as follows:

daemon
bin
sys
adm
lp
uucp
smmsp
nobody
noaccess

To pass this check, each user ID must exist in both the /etc/passwd file and the /etc/cron.d/cron.deny file. Furthermore, the user ID must not exist in the /etc/cron.d/cron.allow file, because it would override this setting (due to precedence). A failure is displayed if any of these checks fail.

update-cron-log-size.aud

This script determines if the cron facility is configured to increase its default size limit for log files. The check method is based on the version of the Solaris OE and the value of the JASS_CRON_LOG_SIZE variable. The size limit defined by the JASS_CRON_LOG_SIZE variable is 20480 KBytes. A failure is displayed if the size limitation is not correct.

update-inetd-conf.aud

This script determines if any of the services listed in the JASS_SVCS_DISABLE variable are disabled in /etc/inetd.conf. This script also checks to ensure that services listed in the JASS_SVCS_ENABLE variable are enabled in the /etc/inetd.conf file. If a service is listed in both variables, then the service is left enabled by the JASS_SVCS_ENABLE variable. A failure is displayed if any of these checks fail.

The JASS_SVCS_DISABLE parameter is populated as shown in TABLE 12-2.

TABLE 12-2 Sample Output of JASS_SVCS_DISABLE

ftp	rquotad	echo	fs	100146	100083
telnet	rusersd	discard	ufsd	100147	100221
name	sprayd	daytime	100232	100150	100235
talk	walld	chargen	100235	100134	100155
uucp	rexd	100087	536870916	100229	uuidgen
smtp	shell	rwalld	kerbd	100230	sun-dr
tftp	login	rstatd	printer	100242	
finger	exec	100068	100234	300326	
systat	comsat	100083	dtspc	100232	
netstat	time	100221	xaudio	100068	

The JASS_SVCS_ENABLE variable is, by default, empty. Some drivers may use it, such as the suncluster3x-secure.driver.

Using Product-Specific Audit Scripts

This section lists product-specific audit scripts for specific Sun products. These scripts are in the Audit directory.

New audit scripts are released periodically for new and updated Sun products. For the latest list of scripts, refer to the Security Web site:

```
http://www.sun.com/security/jass
```

TABLE 12-3   Product-Specific Audit Scripts

Product	Driver Name
Sun Cluster 3.x Software	`suncluster3x-set-nsswitch-conf.aud`
Sun Fire 12K and 15K Domains	`s15k-static-arp.aud`

Sun Fire 12K and 15K System Controllers	`s15k-exclude-domains.aud`
	 `s15k-sms-secure-failover.aud`
	 `s15k-static-arp.aud`

suncluster3x-set-nsswitch-conf.aud

This script determines if the `/etc/nsswitch.conf` file lists the `cluster` keyword as the first source for the host's database. This script applies only to Sun Cluster 3.x systems and should not be executed on other systems. A failure is displayed if this is not true.

For more information, refer to the Sun BluePrints OnLine article titled "Securing Sun Cluster 3.x Software."

s15k-static-arp.aud

For SMS versions 1.2 and newer, this script verifies that the static ARP configuration files are installed. For system controllers (SC), the file is `/etc/sms_sc_arp`. For domains, the file is `/etc/sms_domain_arp`.

This script checks that all existing domains have Ethernet addresses as listed in the SC static ARP startup script and corresponding data file.

For more information, refer to the Sun BluePrints OnLine article titled "Securing the SunFire™ 12K and 15K System Controller" and "Securing the SunFire™ 12K and 15K Domains."

s15k-exclude-domains.aud

For SMS versions 1.2 and newer, this script determines if the `/etc/opt/SUNWSMS/SMS/config/MAN.cf` file exists. If it does, this script checks to ensure that all the domains listed are excluded from the I1 MAN. The script excludes all domains from the I1 MAN. If the site has altered the script to exclude only a subset of the domains, this script issues a warning about each domain that is still part of the I1 MAN.

For more information, refer to the Sun BluePrints OnLine article titled "Securing the SunFire™ 12K and 15K System Controller."

s15k-sms-secure-failover.aud

For SMS versions 1.2 and newer, this script determines if the system controller is configured based on the recommendations in the Sun BluePrints OnLine article titled "Securing the SunFire™ 12K and 15K System Controller." It indicates a failure if any of the services listed in the `SMS_SVCS_DISABLE` variable are enabled in `/etc/inet/inetd.conf`.

## CHAPTER 13

Using Environment Variables

This chapter provides reference information about using environment variables. This chapter describes all of the variables used by the Solaris Security Toolkit software and provides tips and techniques for customizing their values.

This chapter contains the following topics:

Customizing and Assigning Variables

The Solaris Security Toolkit software contains environment variables that provide a simple and easy way to customize and direct the behavior of its drivers and scripts. Because they are simply Bourne shell variables, all of the rules that apply to shell variables apply to Solaris Security Toolkit variables. This section provides information and recommendations for customizing and assigning variables.

Within the Solaris Security Toolkit software, there are four categories of environment variables:

Framework function variables

Finish and audit script variables

JumpStart mode variables

User variables

Note – All of the categories listed can be assigned or customized.

Before customizing variables, it is important that you understand the role of each variable type and its purpose within the Solaris Security Toolkit software. Setting and customizing variables are key to configuring the Solaris Security Toolkit software to suit your system, environment, and security policies. For detailed information about using variables, refer to "Using Environment Variables" on page 302.

In some cases, you might find that customizing the standard variables, drivers, and scripts does not address your specific needs. In these cases, you might want to develop variables, drivers, and scripts for your environment. For more information about developing variables, refer to "Creating Environment Variables" on page 300.

This section contains the following topics:

"Assign Static Variables" on page 297

"Assign Dynamic Variables" on page 297

"Assign Complex Substitution Variables" on page 298

"Assign Global and Profile-Based Variables" on page 300

Assign Static Variables

Static variables are those that are assigned a fixed or static value. This value is set before the Solaris Security Toolkit run is initiated and, unless its value is changed by the external factors, remains constant throughout the run. Also, the value of these variables does not change depending on the context or environment in which the software is run.

Static variables are helpful when a policy setting is not dependent on external factors such as the system's type, network settings, or applications installed. For example, password aging is usually defined by a corporate or divisional policy. Assigning a static variable would apply a setting to all systems and devices within the corporation or division. Because password aging is not dependent on external factors, system administrators usually set it as a static variable.

The following is an example of assigning a static variable.

```
JASS_AGING_MAXWEEKS="8"
JASS_AGING_MINWEEKS="1"
```

In this case, user passwords are configured to expire eight weeks after their most recent change. Furthermore, the second variable, also defined as a static variable, restricts user password changes to one per week maximum.

Assign Dynamic Variables

Dynamic variables are those that generally require greater flexibility and whose values are based on the output of commands or the contents of files. In this way, the variable is more aware of the environment in which it is run and is able to adapt to the environment more effectively. The following is an example of assigning a dynamic variable.

```
JASS_AT_DENY="`awk -F: '{ print $1 }' ${JASS_PASSWD}`"
```

In this case, each of the users defined in the JASS_PASSWD (for example, JASS_ROOT_DIR/etc/passwd) file are added to the variable JASS_AT_DENY. The list of users varies depending on the system on which the Solaris Security Toolkit software is run. In this way, the software is more responsive to its environment. Similar constructions can be made to include all users except for some predefined exceptions. The following example illustrates such a case where every user on the system is added to the JASS_CRON_DENY variable with the exception of the root and ORACLE accounts.

```
JASS_CRON_DENY="`awk -F: '{ print $1 }' ${JASS_PASSWD} |\
   egrep -v '^root|^oracle'`"
```

Assign Complex Substitution Variables

Taking the assigning methods a step further is the notion of complex substitution. Using this technique, more sophisticated values can be assigned to a variable based perhaps on policy, file content, or other mechanisms.

An example of how this is achieved combines assigning both static and dynamic variables. In this example, the JASS_FTPUSERS is assigned a value based both on a static list and the output of the JASS_ROOT_DIR/etc/passwd file.

```
JASS_FTPUSERS="`awk -F: '$1 !~ /^ftp/ { print $1 }' \
${JASS_PASSWD}` guest"
```

In this example, the guest account is always added to the JASS_FTPUSERS variable. In addition, each user listed in JASS_PASSWD whose login name does not begin with the prefix "ftp" is also added to the JASS_FTPUSERS variable. Using combinations of these techniques, almost any configuration can be achieved capable of meeting the needs of most organizations.

Another sophisticated technique is to define a substitution policy based on a shell script or function. For such an example, refer to the declaration of the JASS_SHELLS variable in the Drivers/finish.init file. In this case, the variable assignment is dependent on the version of the OS.

CODE EXAMPLE 13-1   Variable Assignment Based on OS Version

```
#
if [ -z "${JASS_SHELLS}" ]; then
# These shells are by default found in Solaris 2.5.1 to Solaris 7
JASS_SHELLS="
        /usr/bin/sh       /usr/bin/csh      /usr/bin/ksh
        /usr/bin/jsh      /bin/sh           /bin/csh
        /bin/ksh          /bin/jsh          /sbin/sh
```

CODE EXAMPLE 13-1 Variable Assignment Based on OS Version *(Continued)*

```
#
if [ -z "${JASS_SHELLS}" ]; then

     /sbin/jsh"
# This is to handle special cases by OE.
case ${JASS_OS_REVISION} in

     5.8 | 5.9)

          JASS_SHELLS="${JASS_SHELLS}

               /bin/bash        /bin/pfcsh        /bin/pfksh

               /bin/pfsh        /bin/tcsh         /bin/zsh

               /usr/bin/bash    /usr/bin/pfcsh    /usr/bin/pfksh

               /usr/bin/pfsh    /usr/bin/tcsh     /usr/bin/zsh"

     ;;

   esac
fi

export JASS_SHELLS

# This function could be further enhanced, for example, to remove
# those shell entries that do not exist on the system. This
# could be done by adding the following code:
tmpShells="${JASS_SHELLS}"

JASS_SHELLS=""

for shell in ${tmpShells}; do

   if [ -x "${JASS_ROOT_DIR} ${shell}]; then

      JASS_SHELLS="${JASS_SHELLS}/${shell}"

   fi
done
```

This type of functionality can be useful on minimized systems where some of the shells are not available, such as /usr/bin/bash or /usr/bin/tcsh, which exist in the SUNWbash and SUNWtcsh packages respectively. This technique helps to reduce the number of notice and warning messages generated by the software due to improper assignment of variables.

Assign Global and Profile-Based Variables

Global variables can be assigned to override the default values of many of the Solaris Security Toolkit variables. Customize the `user.init` file to define and assign variables for which default values are to be overridden during each Solaris Security Toolkit run. This file is read by the `driver.init` program whenever a software run is initiated.

Also, you can assign profile-based variables to override default values. This override occurs within the profile itself, after the call to the `driver.init` file. Assigning variables within a profile allows variables to be updated, extended, and overridden for specific profiles rather than for all of them. For example, the file `desktop-secure.driver` contains the following profile-based variable override:

```
JASS_SVCS_ENABLE="telnet ftp dtspc rstatd 100155"
```

In this case, the `JASS_SVCS_ENABLE` variable is assigned to include entries for Telnet, FTP, `dtspc`, `rstatd`, and `rpc.smserverd` (100155) services. This assignment instructs the software to leave these services enabled (or to enable them if they were disabled). Normally, the default behavior of the software is to disable those services, per the `JASS_SVCS_DISABLE` variable.

Creating Environment Variables

Although, typically, the standard Solaris Security Toolkit variables provide what you need and can be customized for your system and environment, occasionally, you might need to develop new variables. Often this requirement occurs when you develop your own scripts. You can create new variables and assign them to support your site-specific or custom scripts. Creating new variables enables you to take advantage of the software's framework and modularity.

To quickly and easily build new functionality or implement additional customization, we recommend that you leverage the existing capabilities of the software. Use the standard variables as samples from which to develop new variables. Whenever possible, customize the standard variables rather than develop new ones. By using the software's framework in this way, it is possible to develop and support less-customized code.

Note – The prefix `JASS_` is reserved for use by the Solaris Security Toolkit software developers. This prefix must not be used when creating new variables. Use a prefix unique to your company or organization.

To simplify portability and configuration issues, the environment variables defined in the various .init scripts are used throughout the Solaris Security Toolkit software.

If you require additional variables, add them as environment variables to the user.init and user.run scripts.

To add a new variable, add the variable declaration with its default value and export it in the user.init file. This process provides a global, default value that you can subsequently change as needed by overriding it within a security profile (driver). For example, the following code adds a new variable ABC_TESTING with a default value of "0" to the user.init file.

```
ABC_TESTING="0"

export ABC_TESTING
```

There are times when the value of the variable should only be set if it is currently undefined. This approach is most useful when permitting an administrator to change values from the login shell. To accomplish this task, you would alter the previous code sample as follows.

```
if [ -z "${ABC_TESTING}" ]; then

    ABC_TESTING="0"

fi

export ABC_TESTING
```

Using Environment Variables

This section provides descriptions of all the standard variables defined by the Solaris Security Toolkit software, listed in alphabetical order. Where applicable, recommendations and other helpful information are provided so that you can use these variables more effectively.

Within the software, the four categories of environment variables are as follows:

Framework variables

Finish and audit script variables

JumpStart mode variables

User variables

Each of the variables described in this section is defined in one of the following files, depending on its function within the Solaris Security Toolkit software. (As noted previously, the functions are divided into categories based on their purpose.)

`driver.init` (framework and JumpStart mode variables)

`finish.init` (finish and audit script variables)

`user.init` (user variables and global override variables)

For detailed information about these files, refer to Chapter 9.

To simplify portability and configuration issues, the environment variables defined in the various `.init` scripts are used throughout the Solaris Security Toolkit software.

If you require additional variables, add them as environment variables to the `user.init` and `user.run` scripts. For more information, refer to "Creating Environment Variables" on page 300.

Note – The default environment variable values used by scripts are defined in the `finish.init` script.

This section presents the variables in the following organization:

"Define Framework Variables" on page 303

"Define Script Behavior Variables" on page 321

"Define JumpStart Mode Variables" on page 335

Define Framework Variables

Framework variables are those that are defined and used by the Solaris Security Toolkit software to either maintain configuration state or to provide core variables that are used by the software. These variables are typically global and are in the software framework, its core functions, and scripts.

You can dramatically change the behavior of the software by changing these variables. We recommend that you change them only when absolutely necessary. Also, changes should be made only by experienced administrators who clearly understand the impact of the changes and can resolve any resulting problems.

Note – Not all framework variables can be modified. This limitation was done to promote consistency between Solaris Security Toolkit software deployments and to aid in supporting those configurations.

Caution – Never attempt to directly change any framework variables that cannot otherwise be overridden.

JASS_AUDIT_DIR

The convention used by the Solaris Security Toolkit software is to store all of the audit scripts in the Audit directory. However, for flexibility, the JASS_AUDIT_DIR environment variable is available for administrators who need to store audit scripts in different locations. By default, this variable is set to JASS_HOME_DIR/Audit.

This variable should not normally require modification.

JASS_CHECK_MINIMIZED

This variable is used in audit runs only. The value of this variable determines how the Solaris Security Toolkit software performs the check_minimized function that is included in many of the audit scripts. If this variable is set to 0, then the check_minimized function responds immediately without performing any of its checks. Otherwise, the check_minimized function operates as normal. This variable is included to permit the exclusion of these checks from a software run when a system has not been minimized. Otherwise, the check_minimized functions would result in failure messages on non-minimized systems, thereby precluding the ability of ever successfully passing an audit run. By default, this variable has no value and, therefore, the check_minimized function operates as normal.

JASS_CONFIG_DIR

Starting with version 0.3 of the Solaris Security Toolkit software, the variable JASS_CONFIG_DIR was renamed to JASS_HOME_DIR to provide a clearer meaning as to its use. The JASS_CONFIG_DIR variable is deprecated and should no longer be used. Refer to "JASS_HOME_DIR" on page 309.

JASS_DISABLE_MODE

This variable defines the approach used by the Solaris Security Toolkit software to disable services that are started from run-control scripts. For Solaris OE versions 9 and newer, this variable is assigned the default value of conf, whereas all earlier releases default to the value of script.

Note – If a particular service does not use a configuration file, or it does not check for its existence prior to starting, then the software uses the script method when disabling the service.

When the JASS_DISABLE_MODE variable is set to conf, the software disables a service by moving aside its configuration file. This approach is effective on services that first check for the existence of a configuration file prior to starting. This approach leads to a more supportable and sustainable configuration because Solaris OE patches rarely replace these disabled configuration files.

When this variable is set to script, the software disables services by moving aside their respective run-control scripts. This approach is also effective because a service is not able to run, if it is never permitted to start. This configuration is less supportable, however, because Solaris OE patches install run-control scripts, re-enabling services that were disabled.

We recommend that you do not change the default settings. Note that if security scanners are used, they should be adequately tested using this configuration. Setting this variable to conf could result in false positives, because most scanners typically (and erroneously) check only for the existence of run-control scripts. Note that the audit function does not have this limitation.

JASS_DISPLAY_HOSTNAME

This variable controls the display of host name information during audit runs. You can select the level of verbosity to be used by the Solaris Security Toolkit software. In single-line output modes (refer to "JASS_VERBOSITY" on page 320), you have the option of tagging each line with the host name of the system on which the software is being run. This value is the same as JASS_HOSTNAME. Including this information can be useful when processing runs from multiple systems. If this variable is set to 1, then the software prepends the host name of the target system to each line of output. Otherwise, the software does not include this information. By default, the software does not display this information.

Note – The JASS_DISPLAY_HOSTNAME variable is used only when JASS_VERBOSITY is less than or equal to 2.

JASS_DISPLAY_SCRIPTNAME

This variable controls the display of the current script name during audit runs. You can select the level of verbosity to be used by the Solaris Security Toolkit software. In single-line output modes (refer to "JASS_VERBOSITY" on page 320), you have the option of tagging each line with the name of the current audit script being run. Including this information can be useful when attempting to determine the source of failure messages. If this variable is set to 1, then the software prepends the current audit script name to each line of output. Otherwise, the software does not include this information. By default, the software includes this information.

Note – The JASS_DISPLAY_SCRIPTNAME variable is used only when JASS_VERBOSITY is less than or equal to 2.

JASS_DISPLAY_TIMESTAMP

This variable controls the display of timestamp information during audit runs. You can select the level of verbosity to be used by the Solaris Security Toolkit software. In single-line output modes (refer to "JASS_VERBOSITY" on page 320), you have the option of tagging each line with the timestamp associated with the software run. This value is the same as JASS_TIMESTAMP. Including this information can be useful when processing multiple runs from a single system or set of systems. If this variable is set to 1, then the software prepends the timestamp of the run to each line of output. Otherwise, the software does not include this information. By default, the software does not display this information.

Note – The `JASS_DISPLAY_TIMESTAMP` variable is used only when `JASS_VERBOSITY` is less than or equal to 2.

JASS_FILES

This variable specifies a list of file system objects that are copied to the target system. Specify each of the objects listed in this variable by using its absolute path name. Each object is stored in a file system hierarchy under the root directory of `JASS_HOME_DIR/Files`.

Specifying Files With the `JASS_FILES` *Variable*

File lists are added to the contents of the general file list only when the Solaris Security Toolkit software is run on a defined version of the Solaris OE. A version-specific list is created by appending the major and minor operating system version to the end of the `JASS_FILES` variable, separated by underscores. The Solaris Security Toolkit software currently supports the options listed in TABLE 13-1.

TABLE 13-1 Supporting OS Versions in the `JASS_FILES` Variable

`JASS_FILES`	Applies to any version of Solaris OE
`JASS_FILES_5_5_1`	Applies only to Solaris OE version 2.5.1
`JASS_FILES_5_6`	Applies only to Solaris OE version 2.6
`JASS_FILES_5_7`	Applies only to Solaris OE version 7
`JASS_FILES_5_8`	Applies only to Solaris OE version 8
`JASS_FILES_5_9`	Applies only to Solaris OE version 9

For example, the `/etc/logadm.conf` file is only applicable to the Solaris 9 OE. To install the `Files/etc/logadm.conf` file only on the Solaris 9 OE, use the following syntax.

```
JASS_FILES_5_9="
        /etc/logadm.conf
"
```

Note – Note that this functionality is basically equivalent to the `JASS_FILES` "+" function.

You can use the JASS_FILES variable to specify files in the following ways:

Specify the file that is copied from the Solaris Security Toolkit software to the client.

The following example is from the hardening.driver:

```
JASS_FILES="
        /etc/motd
"
```

By defining the JASS_FILES environment variable to include this file, the /etc/motd file on the client is replaced by the JASS_HOME_DIR/Files/etc/motd file from the Solaris Security Toolkit software distribution. You can copy any file, directory, or symbolic link this way by simply including it in the Files directory and adding it to the JASS_FILES definition in the appropriate driver.

Specify host-specific files.

Host-specific files are those that are only copied if the host name of the target system matches the host name assigned to the object in the Files directory. To use this capability, simply create files in the Files directory of the following form:

```
/etc/syslog.conf.$HOSTNAME
```

In this scenario, the JASS_HOME_DIR/Files/etc/syslog.conf.HOSTNAME file is copied to JASS_ROOT_DIR/etc/syslog.conf on the target system only if its host name matches the value defined by *HOSTNAME*. When there is both a syslog.conf and syslog.conf.*HOSTNAME*, the host-specific file takes precedence.

Specify OS release-specific files.

OS release specific files are similar in concept to host-specific files, but are copied to the target system only if the target's version of the Solaris OE matches that assigned to the object in the Files directory. To use this functionality, create files in the Files directory with the following form:

```
/etc/syslog.conf+$OS
```

In this example, the JASS_HOME_DIR/Files/etc/syslog.conf+OS file is copied to the target as JASS_ROOT_DIR/etc/syslog.conf only if the version of the Solaris OE on the target system matches the value defined by OS.

The OS variable should mirror the output produced by the uname -r command. For example, if OS version 5.8 were being secured, then a file with the name of JASS_HOME_DIR/Files/etc/syslog.conf+5.8 would be copied. This file would not be copied to any other OS release. The OS-specific files take precedence over generic files, but host-specific files take precedence over OS-specific files.

Also, the JASS_FILES variable supports OS-specific extensions. Use these extensions to specify a list of file system objects that should be copied only for certain versions of the Solaris OE. The OS-specific JASS_FILES extensions are supported for Solaris OE versions 5.5.1, 5.6, 5.7, 5.8, and 5.9. For example, to copy a list of files only for Solaris 8 OE, define the JASS_FILES_5_8 variable and assign to it the list of files to be copied.

Customizing the JASS_FILES Variable

In this section, we describe and illustrate how to customize the JASS_FILES environment variable. The following code examples are taken from the Drivers/ config.driver file. This profile file performs basic configuration tasks on a platform. We use this profile as an example because it provides clear examples of how file templates, drivers, and finish scripts are used.

In the following example, this driver is configured to copy the /.cshrc and / .profile files from the JASS_HOME_DIR/Files directory onto the target platform when the driver.run function is called.

```
JASS_FILES="
/.cshrc
/.profile
"
```

To change the contents of either of these files, modify the copies of the files located in the JASS_HOME_DIR/Files directory. If you only need to add or remove file templates, simply adjust the JASS_FILES variable accordingly. We strongly recommend that you track changes to the Solaris Security Toolkit configuration using a change-control mechanism. For more information, refer to Chapter 1, "Maintaining Version Control" on page 14.

The software supports operating system-version specific file lists. For detailed information, refer to the previous section "Specifying Files With the JASS_FILES Variable" on page 306.

JASS_FILES_DIR

This variable points to the location of the Files directory under JASS_HOME_DIR. This directory contains all of the file system objects that can be copied to the client.

To copy objects to a system, you must list a file in a JASS_FILES variable or one of its OS-specific extensions. These objects are copied to the client during hardening runs by the install-templates.fin script. Set the JASS_FILES variable within an individual driver. This variable is not defined by any other configuration file. For other methods of copying files using this variable, refer to "JASS_FILES" on page 306. By default, this variable is set to JASS_HOME_DIR/Files.

This variable does not normally require modification.

JASS_FINISH_DIR

The convention used by the Solaris Security Toolkit software is to store all finish scripts in the Finish directory. However, for flexibility, the JASS_FINISH_DIR environment variable is for storing finish scripts in different locations. By default, this variable is set to JASS_HOME_DIR/Finish.

This variable should not normally require modification.

JASS_HOME_DIR

This variable defines the location of the Solaris Security Toolkit source tree. In JumpStart mode, the JumpStart variable SI_CONFIG_DIR sets the JASS_HOME_DIR variable. In standalone mode, it is set by the jass-execute script, which is included in the base directory.

This variable should not normally require modification, except when the Solaris Security Toolkit software is installed into a subdirectory of a pre-existing JumpStart installation. For these cases, append the path of the Solaris Security Toolkit source to SI_CONFIG_DIR, as in SI_CONFIG_DIR/jass-*n.n*, where *n.n* is the current version number of the software.

JASS_HOSTNAME

This variable contains the host name of the system on which the Solaris Security Toolkit software is being run. This variable is set during software runs through the Solaris OE uname -n command within the driver.init script.

This variable must not be changed, because several components of the framework rely on this variable being set properly.

JASS_ISA_CAPABILITY

This variable defines the Solaris OE instruction set potential of the target system. Use this variable to determine if the system has the potential of operating in 32- or 64-bit mode. This task is done to provide instruction set architecture (ISA) information for use by finish scripts. The value of this variable is defined based on a check for the existence of the Solaris OE package, SUNWkvmx. If this package is installed, then the system is assumed to be 64-bit capable, and this variable is set to "64." Otherwise, the system is assumed to be only 32-bit capable, and this variable is set to "32."

This variable should not normally require modification.

JASS_LOG_BANNER

This variable controls the behavior of the logBanner function. The logBanner function generates all of the banner messages used by the Solaris Security Toolkit software. If this variable is set to 0, then the logBanner function responds immediately without displaying any information. Otherwise, the logBanner function displays the information passed to it as an argument. Use this variable to adjust the output of the software to better suit your needs. By default, this variable has no value and, therefore, the logBanner function operates normally.

Note – The logBanner function only displays output when JASS_VERBOSITY variable is 3 or higher and the JASS_LOG_BANNER variable is not 0.

JASS_LOG_ERROR

This variable controls the behavior of the logError function. The logError function generates messages with the prefix [ERR]. If this variable is set to 0, then the logError function responds immediately without displaying any information. Otherwise, the logError function displays the information passed to it as an argument. Use this variable to adjust the output of the software to better suit your needs. By default, this variable has no value and, therefore, the logError function operates normally.

JASS_LOG_FAILURE

This variable controls the behavior of the logFailure function. The logFailure function generates messages with the prefix [FAIL]. If this variable is set to 0, then the logFailure function responds immediately without displaying any information. Otherwise, the logFailure function displays the information passed to it as an argument. Use this variable to adjust the output of the software to better your needs. By default, this variable has no value and, therefore, the logFailure function operates normally.

JASS_LOG_NOTICE

This variable controls the behavior of the logNotice function. The logNotice function generates messages with the prefix [NOTE]. If this variable is set to 0, then the logNotice function responds immediately without displaying any information. Otherwise, the logNotice function displays the information passed to it as an argument. Use this variable to adjust the output of the software to better suit your needs. By default, this variable has no value and, therefore, the logNotice function operates normally.

JASS_LOG_SUCCESS

This variable controls the behavior of the logSuccess function. The logSuccess function generates messages with the prefix [PASS]. If this variable is set to 0, then the logSuccess function responds immediately without displaying any information. Otherwise, the logSuccess function displays the information passed to it as an argument. Use this variable to adjust the output to suit your needs. By default, this variable has no value and, therefore, the logSuccess function operates normally.

JASS_LOG_WARNING

This variable controls the behavior of the logWarning function. The logWarning function generates messages with the prefix [WARN]. If this variable is set to 0, then the logWarning function responds immediately without displaying any information. Otherwise, the logWarning function displays the information passed to it as an argument. Use this variable to adjust the output to suit your needs. By default, this variable has no value and, therefore, the logWarning function operates normally.

JASS_MODE

This variable defines the way that the Solaris Security Toolkit software operates. This variable accepts one of six values: APPLY, UNDO, AUDIT, HISTORY_LAST, and HISTORY_FULL. Normally, this variable is set in standalone mode by the jass-execute command. In JumpStart mode, it defaults to APPLY. For the purpose of this variable, APPLY refers to hardening runs.

This variable must not be changed.

JASS_OS_REVISION

This variable is a global variable specifying the OS version of the client on which the Solaris Security Toolkit software is being used. This variable is set automatically in the driver.init script through the uname -r command and exported so that all other scripts can access it.

Caution – This variable must not be changed.

JASS_OS_TYPE

This variable determines if the system being hardened or audited is a Solaris OE system or a Trusted Solaris OE system. If the system is running a generic version of Solaris OE, it is set to "Generic," otherwise it is set to "TS8." This variable is in the driver.init file.

Note – Only Trusted Solaris 8 OE is supported by the Solaris Security Toolkit.

JASS_PACKAGE_DIR

The convention used by the Solaris Security Toolkit software is to store all software packages to be installed in the Packages directory. However, for flexibility, the JASS_PACKAGE_DIR variable is available to store packages in a different location. By default, in standalone mode, this variable is set to JASS_HOME_DIR/Packages.

In JumpStart mode, however, this variable is defined as a transient mount-point, JASS_ROOT_DIR/tmp/jass-packages. The package directory, stored on the JumpStart server, is mounted as this directory on this client during a JumpStart installation.

This variable should not normally require modification.

JASS_PATCH_DIR

The convention used by the Solaris Security Toolkit software is to store all of the software patches to be installed in the Patches directory. However, for flexibility, the JASS_PATCH_DIR variable is available to store patches in a different location. By default, in standalone mode, this variable is set to JASS_HOME_DIR/Patches.

In JumpStart mode, however, this variable is defined as a transient mount-point, JASS_ROOT_DIR/tmp/jass-patches. The actual package directory, stored on the JumpStart server, is mounted as this directory on this client during a JumpStart installation.

This variable should not normally require modification.

JASS_PKG

This variable defines the Solaris OE package name of the Solaris Security Toolkit software. This variable has a value of SUNWjass.

Caution – This variable must not be changed.

JASS_REPOSITORY

This variable is part of the execution log and undo functions. The path specified by JASS_REPOSITORY defines the directory where the required run information is stored. This functionality facilitates the capture of information related to each script that is run, the resulting output of each, and the listing of files that were installed, modified, or removed during a run.

This variable is dynamically altered during the execution of the software. Any values assigned to this variable in any of the init files are overwritten. By default, this variable is assigned the value of JASS_ROOT_DIR/var/opt/JASS_PKG/run/JASS_TIMESTAMP.

Caution – This variable must not be changed.

JASS_ROOT_DIR

This variable defines the root directory of the target's file system. For JumpStart mode, this directory is always /a. For standalone mode, this variable should be set to / or the root directory of the system.

Solaris Security Toolkit software versions 0.2 and newer automatically set this variable's value in the jass-execute script, so manual modification is no longer required.

Caution – This variable must not be changed.

JASS_RUN_AUDIT_LOG

This variable is part of the execution log. This variable defines the name and absolute path to the file that stores the output generated during an audit run. This information is collected to document which scripts were executed, in addition to the output of each audit check tested during the course of the run.

Any errors or warnings generated are stored in this file. The information stored in this file is equivalent to the output displayed on the screen during an audit run. By default, this variable is set to JASS_REPOSITORY/jass-audit-log.txt.

Caution – This variable must not be changed.

JASS_RUN_CHECKSUM

This variable is part of the execution log and undo functionality. This variable is also used by the jass-check-sum program included in JASS_HOME_DIR. This variable defines the name and absolute path to the file that stores all of the checksum information used by the software. This information records the state of files both before and after modification. This information is used to determine if files changed since they were last modified by the software. This information is stored within the JASS_REPOSITORY directory structure and has a default value of JASS_REPOSITORY/jass-checksums.txt.

Caution – This variable must not be changed.

JASS_RUN_FINISH_LIST

This variable's name was changed. Refer to "JASS_RUN_SCRIPT_LIST" on page 315.

JASS_RUN_INSTALL_LOG

This variable is part of the execution log. This variable defines the name and absolute path to the file that stores the output generated during hardening runs. This information is collected to document which scripts are executed, in addition to listing any files that were installed, removed, or modified during a run.

Any errors or warnings generated are stored in this file. The information stored in this file is equivalent to the output displayed on the screen during a hardening run. By default, this variable is set to JASS_REPOSITORY/jass-install-log.txt.

Caution – This variable must not be changed.

JASS_RUN_MANIFEST

This variable is part of the execution log and undo functionality. This variable defines the name and absolute path to the file that stores the manifest information associated with a run. The manifest file records the operations conducted as part of a hardening run. This file is also used in undo runs to determine which files must be moved, and in what order, to restore a system to a previous configuration. By default, this variable is set to JASS_REPOSITORY/jass-manifest.txt.

Caution – This variable must not be changed.

JASS_RUN_SCRIPT_LIST

This variable is part of the execution log. This variable defines the name and absolute path to the file that stores a listing of all finish or audit scripts executed during a run. This information is collected for informational and debugging purposes and is stored within the JASS_REPOSITORY directory structure. By default, this variable is set to JASS_REPOSITORY/jass-script-list.txt.

Caution – This variable must not be changed.

JASS_RUN_UNDO_LOG

This variable is part of the execution log. This variable defines the name and absolute path to the file that stores the output generated during an undo run. This information is collected to document which scripts were executed, in addition to listing any files that were installed, removed, or modified during a run.

Any errors or warnings generated are stored in this file. The information stored in this file is equivalent to the output displayed on the screen during an undo run. By default, this variable is set to JASS_REPOSITORY/jass-undo-log.txt.

Caution – This variable must not be changed.

JASS_RUN_VERSION

This variable is part of the execution log. This variable defines the name and absolute path to the file containing the version and associated information for a run. This file typically includes information about the version, mode, and security profile used by the Solaris Security Toolkit software during its run. This information is collected to document the manner in which the software was used on a system. By default, this variable is set to JASS_REPOSITORY/jass-version.txt.

Caution – This variable must not be changed.

JASS_SAVE_BACKUP

This variable controls the creation of backup files during hardening runs. The default value is 1, which causes the software to create a backup copy of any file modified on the client. If the value is changed to 0, then all backup copies created during a run are removed at its completion.

Modify the user.init script if you want to prevent the creation of backup copies of files. The value in the user.init script overrides any value set in the variable.

Caution – The Solaris Security Toolkit undo feature is not available if you define the value of JASS_SAVE_BACKUP as 0.

JASS_SCRIPTS

This variable specifies a list of finish scripts to execute on a target system when you want to use a specific driver. For each entry, make sure you provide a corresponding finish script with the same name located in the JASS_FINISH_DIR directory.

In addition, we recommend that you also have an audit script, stored in JASS_AUDIT_DIR, corresponding to each finish script that is stored in JASS_FINISH_DIR.

Specifying Files With the JASS_SCRIPTS Variable

The JASS_SCRIPTS variable supports OS-specific extensions. Use these extensions to specify a list of finish scripts to execute only when the target system is running certain versions of the Solaris OE. Create a version-specific list by appending the major and minor operating system version to the end of the JASS_SCRIPTS variable, separated by underscores. The Solaris Security Toolkit software supports the options listed in TABLE 13-2.

TABLE 13-2   Supporting OS Versions in the JASS_SCRIPT Variable

JASS_SCRIPTS	Applies to any version of the Solaris OE
JASS_SCRIPTS_5_5_1	Applies only to the Solaris OE version 2.5.1
JASS_SCRIPTS_5_6	Applies only to the Solaris OE version 2.6
JASS_SCRIPTS_5_7	Applies only to the Solaris OE version 7
JASS_SCRIPTS_5_8	Applies only to the Solaris OE version 8
JASS_SCRIPTS_5_9	Applies only to the Solaris OE version 9

For example, to use the disable-something.fin script only on the Solaris 9 OE, you would add the following to the driver.

```
JASS_SCRIPTS_5_9="
disable-something.fin
"
```

Note – The OS-specific file and script lists are always appended to the generic list of files and scripts. As a result, they are always executed after their more general counterparts.

Customizing the JASS_SCRIPTS *Variable*

To add or remove finish scripts from a driver, modify the JASS_SCRIPTS variable as needed. Drivers provide a mechanism for grouping file templates and scripts into a single security profile. These profiles allow you to logically group customization. For example, a single profile could be used to define a baseline that is applied to all of the systems within an organization. Alternatively, a profile could define the modifications that are done to secure systems operating as database servers. These profiles can be used individually or combined into more complex profiles.

```
JASS_SCRIPTS="
print-jass-environment.fin
install-recommended-patches.fin
install-jass.fin
set-root-password.fin
set-term-type.fin
"
```

In this example, five different scripts are configured to run when the driver.run function is executed. These five scripts are grouped together because they represent system configuration changes that are not directly related to hardening, which is why they are grouped into the config.driver.

JASS_STANDALONE

This variable controls whether the Solaris Security Toolkit software runs in standalone or JumpStart mode. This variable defaults to 0 for JumpStart installations and 1 when the jass-execute command is used to initiate a run.

This variable should not normally require modification.

JASS_SUFFIX

This variable determines which suffixes must be appended onto backup copies of files. By default, this is set to JASS.JASS_TIMESTAMP. During a run, the value of the timestamp field changes to reflect the time a file is created. This action guarantees that all backup file names are unique.

This variable is dynamically altered during runs. Any value assigned to this variable in the init files is overwritten.

This variable must not be changed.

JASS_TIMESTAMP

This variable creates the `JASS_REPOSITORY` directory, `/var/opt/SUNWjass/run/` `JASS_TIMESTAMP`. As noted previously, this directory contains the logs and manifest information for each run of the Solaris Security Toolkit software. This variable contains the timestamp associated with the start of a run, and its value is maintained for the entire run. As a result, its value is unique for each run. This unique value allows information for each run to be clearly separated from all others, based on the time that the run was started. By default, this variable is set to `date` `'+%EY%m%d%OH%OM%S'`. This command creates a timestamp of the form YYYYMMDDHHMMSS. For example, a run started at 1:30 p.m. on April 1, 2003 would be represented by the value 20030401013000.

This variable should not normally require modification.

JASS_UNAME

This variable was renamed to `JASS_OS_REVISION`. Refer to "This variable is a global variable specifying the OS version of the client on which the Solaris Security Toolkit software is being used. This variable is set automatically in the `driver.init` script through the `uname -r` command and exported so that all other scripts can access it." on page 312.

JASS_USER_DIR

This variable specifies the location of the configuration files `user.init` and `user.run`. By default, these files are stored in the `JASS_HOME_DIR/Drivers` directory. Use these files to customize the Solaris Security Toolkit software to meet the needs of your organization.

If you need to customize the Solaris Security Toolkit software, do so in these files to minimize the impact of Solaris Security Toolkit software upgrades in the future.

Global variables should be created and assigned either in the `user.init` file or within a driver. New functions or overrides of existing functions should be implemented in the `user.run` file. All variable or function overrides take precedence over their counterparts defined in the Solaris Security Toolkit software.

JASS_VERBOSITY

This variable controls how the Solaris Security Toolkit software displays its results when running during audit runs. The software currently supports five different verbosity levels: 0 through 4. Set this variable to any of these values using the -V option with the jass-execute command. Do not modify this variable directly. The verbosity levels used during audit runs are as listed in TABLE 13-3.

TABLE 13-3 Verbosity Levels for Audit Runs

Level	Description
0	Final. This mode results in only one line of output that indicates the combined result of the entire verification run. This mode is useful if a single PASS or FAIL is needed.
1	Consolidated. In this mode, one line of output per audit script is generated indicating the result of each audit script. In addition, subtotals are generated at the end of each script, as well as a grand total at the end of the run.
2	Brief. This mode combines the attributes of the Consolidated verbosity level and includes the results of the individual checks within each audit script. This mode is useful for quickly determining those items that passed and failed within a single audit script. The format of this mode still represents one result per line.
3	Full. This is the first of the multiline verbosity modes. In this mode, banners and headers are printed to illustrate more clearly the checks that are being run, their intended purpose, and how their results are determined. This is the default verbosity level and more suitable for those new to the Solaris Security Toolkit verification capability.
4	Debug. This mode extends upon the Full verbosity mode by including all entries that are generated by the logDebug logging function. Currently, this is not used by any of the Solaris Security Toolkit audit scripts, but it is included for completeness and to allow administrators to embed debugging statements within their code.

Note – In hardening runs and other operations, this variable is set to 3 and typically should not be changed.

In the least verbose mode, level 0, only a single line is displayed representing the overall result for a run. The output at this level would look like:

```
# ./jass-execute -a starfire_ssp-secure.driver -V 0
starfire_ssp-secure.driver [PASS] Grand Total : 0 Error(s)
```

JASS_VERSION

This variable defines the version of the Solaris Security Toolkit software associated with the software distribution being used. This variable documents the version of the software and permits its use with logging and other functions.

Caution – This variable must not be changed.

Define Script Behavior Variables

Script behavior variables are those that are defined and used by the Solaris Security Toolkit software to affect the behavior of finish and audit scripts. The Solaris Security Toolkit software provides a robust and flexible framework for customizing its functionality to suit individual site requirements. One of our design goals was to limit the amount of source code that had to be modified for users to implement site-specific customization. The script variables provide an easy to use method for altering the behavior of a script without modifying the script's source code.

These variables are defined in the JASS_HOME_DIR/Drivers/finish.init file. Although they are global, their use is typically limited to a small set of finish and audit scripts. As described earlier in this chapter, you can customize these variables using techniques such as static, dynamic, and complex assignment in either the user.init file or within an individual driver.

We recommend that you tune these variables, where necessary, to meet organizational or site security policy and requirements. Used in this manner, the software provides the greatest value in helping you improve and sustain the security posture of your environment.

JASS_ACCT_DISABLE

This variable contains a list of user accounts that should be disabled on a system. During hardening runs, these accounts are disabled by the disable-system-accounts.fin script. During audit runs, the disable-system-accounts.aud script inspects the accounts defined by this variable, to ensure that they are disabled.

By default, the following accounts are assigned to the JASS_ACCT_DISABLE
variable:

```
daemon
bin
adm
lp
uucp
nuucp
nobody
smtp
listen
noaccess
nobody4
smmsp
```

The default shell used by the Solaris Security Toolkit to disable accounts is /sbin/
noshell, which is installed by the software.

JASS_ACCT_REMOVE

This variable contains a list of user accounts that should be removed from a system.
During hardening runs, these accounts are removed by the remove-unneeded-
accounts.fin script. During audit runs, the remove-unneeded-accounts.aud
script inspects the system to ensure that the accounts do not exist.

By default, the following accounts are assigned to the JASS_ACCT_REMOVE variable:

```
smtp
listen
nobody4
```


JASS_AGING_MAXWEEKS

This variable contains a numeric value specifying the maximum number of weeks
passwords remain valid before they must be changed by users. The default value for
this variable is 8 (weeks). This variable is used by the set-user-password-
reqs.fin script and the set-user-password-reqs.aud script.

JASS_AGING_MINWEEKS

This variable contains a numeric value specifying the minimum number of weeks
that must pass before users can change their passwords. This variable is used by the
set-user-password-reqs.fin script and the set-user-password-reqs.aud
script. This variable has a default value of 1 (week).

JASS_AGING_WARNWEEKS

This variable contains a numeric value specifying the number of weeks before passwords expire and users are warned. This warning is displayed to users upon login during the warning period. This variable is used by the `set-user-password-reqs.fin` script and the `set-user-password-reqs.aud` script. The default value of this variable is 1 (week).

JASS_AT_ALLOW

This variable contains a list of user accounts that should be permitted to use the `at` and `batch` facilities. During hardening runs, the `install-at-allow.fin` script adds each user account defined by this variable to the `JASS_ROOT_DIR/etc/cron.d/at.allow` file, if not already present. Similarly, during audit runs, the `install-at-allow.aud` script determines if each user account defined by this variable is listed in the `at.allow` file. Note that for a user account to be added or checked, it must also exist in `JASS_PASSWD`. By default, this variable contains no user accounts.

JASS_AT_DENY

This variable contains a list of user accounts that should be prevented from using the `at` and `batch` facilities. During hardening runs, the `update-at-deny.fin` script adds each user account defined by this variable to the `JASS_ROOT_DIR/etc/cron.d/at.deny` file, if not already present. Similarly, during audit runs, the `update-at-deny.aud` script determines if each user account defined by this variable is listed in the `at.deny` file. Note that for a user account to be added or checked, it must also exist in `JASS_PASSWD`. By default, this variable contains all of the user accounts defined on the system in the `JASS_PASSWD` file.

JASS_BANNER_DTLOGIN

This variable contains a string value that represents a file name containing a banner message to be displayed to users after logging into CDE. During hardening runs, this banner is installed by the `set-banner-dtlogin.fin` script. During audit runs, the existence of this banner is checked by the `set-banner-dtlogin.aud` script. The default value of this variable is `/etc/motd`.

JASS_BANNER_FTPD

This variable contains a string value that is used as a banner displayed to users prior to authenticating for FTP service. During hardening runs, this banner is installed by the `set-banner-ftpd.fin` script. During audit runs, the existence of this banner is checked by the `set-banner-ftpd.aud` script. The default value of this variable is `\"Authorized Use Only\"`.

Note – The back slash characters are required in this string to prevent the quote characters from being interpreted by the command shell. When installed in the relevant FTP configuration file, the string displays as "`Authorized Use Only`."

JASS_BANNER_SENDMAIL

This variable contains a string value that is used as a banner displayed to clients immediately after connecting to the sendmail service. During hardening runs, this banner is installed by the `set-banner-sendmail.fin` script. During audit runs, the existence of this banner is checked by the `set-banner-sendmail.aud` script. The default value of this variable is `Mail Server Ready`.

JASS_BANNER_SSHD

This variable contains a string value that represents a file name containing a banner message to be displayed to users prior to authenticating the Secure Shell service. During hardening runs, this banner is installed by the `set-banner-sshd.fin` script. During audit runs, the existence of this banner is checked by the `set-banner-sshd.aud` script. The default value of this variable is `/etc/issue`.

JASS_BANNER_TELNETD

This variable contains a string value that is used as a banner displayed to users prior to authenticating for Telnet service. During hardening runs, this banner is installed by the `set-banner-telnetd.fin` script. During audit runs, the existence of this banner is checked by the `set-banner-telnetd.aud` script. The default value of this variable is `\"Authorized Use Only\"`.

Note – The back slash characters are required in this string to prevent the quote characters from being interpreted by the command shell. When installed in the relevant Telnet configuration file, the string displays as "`Authorized Use Only`."

JASS_CORE_PATTERN

This variable contains a string value that represents the path name and core file naming pattern used by the coreadm facility. This variable is used to configure coreadm to restrict core files generated on the system to the specified directory and name based on the file pattern defined by this variable. During hardening runs, coreadm is configured by the enable-coreadm.fin script. During audit runs, the coreadm configuration is checked by the enable-coreadm.aud script. The default value of this variable is /var/core/core.%f.%p.%n.%u.%g.%t. For more information on the file naming options, refer to the coreadm(1M) manual page.

JASS_CPR_MGT_USER

This variable contains a string value that defines which users are permitted to perform checkpoint and resume functions on a system. During hardening runs, this restriction is implemented by the set-power-restrictions.fin script. During audit runs, this restriction is checked by the set-power-restrictions.aud script. The default value of this variable is "-," indicating that only the root account is permitted to perform these management functions. For more information, refer to the /etc/default/power information in Chapter 9.

JASS_CRON_ALLOW

This variable contains a list of user accounts that should be permitted to use the cron facility. During hardening runs, the update-cron-allow.fin script adds each user defined by this variable to the JASS_ROOT_DIR/etc/cron.d/cron.allow file, if not already present. Similarly, during audit runs, the update-cron-allow.aud script determines if each user defined by this variable is listed in the cron.allow file. Note that for a user account to be added or checked, it must also exist in JASS_PASSWD. By default, this variable contains only the root account.

JASS_CRON_DENY

This variable contains a list of user accounts that should be prevented from using the cron facility. During hardening runs, the update-cron-deny.fin script adds each user defined by this variable to the JASS_ROOT_DIR/etc/cron.d/cron.deny file, if not already present. Similarly, during audit runs, the update-cron-deny.aud script determines if each user defined by this variable is listed in the cron.deny file. Note that for a user account to be added or checked, it must also exist in JASS_PASSWD. By default, this variable contains all of the user accounts defined in the JASS_PASSWD file with user identifiers less than 100 and greater than 60000. Typically, these ranges are reserved for administrative access. Note that by default, the root account is explicitly excluded from this list.

JASS_CRON_LOG_SIZE

This variable contains a numeric value representing the maximum size, in blocks, that the cron facility log file can be before it is rotated. During hardening runs, this setting is installed by the update-cron-log-size.fin script. During audit runs, this setting is checked by the update-cron-log-size.aud script. The default value of this variable is 20480 (or 10 megabytes). This size is an increase over the default Solaris OE value of 1024 (or 0.5 megabytes).

JASS_FIXMODES_DIR

This variable contains a string value representing the absolute path to the FixModes software distribution, if present. If the FixModes software is installed from the tar distribution by the Solaris Security Toolkit, it is installed into the directory defined by this variable. During hardening runs, this variable is used by the install-fix-modes.fin script to install and run the FixModes software. During audit runs, the FixModes software is run by the install-fix-modes.aud script. The default value of this variable is /opt.

JASS_FIXMODES_OPTIONS

This variable contains a list of options that are passed to the FixModes software when it is run during hardening runs from the install-fix-modes.fin script. This variable is not used during audit runs. By default, no options are specified by this variable.

JASS_FTPD_UMASK

This variable contains a numeric (octal) value that represents the file creation mask (umask) to be used by the FTP service. During hardening runs, this setting is installed by the set-ftpd-umask.fin script. During audit runs, this setting is checked by the set-ftpd-umask.aud script. The default value of this variable is 022.

JASS_FTPUSERS

This variable contains a list of user accounts that should be prevented from using the FTP service. During hardening runs, the install-ftpusers.fin script adds each user defined by this variable to either the JASS_ROOT_DIR/etc/ftpusers file (Solaris 8 OE or earlier) or the JASS_ROOT_DIR/etc/ftpd/ftpusers file (Solaris 9 OE) if not already present.

Similarly, during audit runs, the `install-ftpusers.aud` script determines if each user account defined by this variable is listed in the `ftpusers` file. By default, this variable contains all of the user accounts defined in the `JASS_PASSWD` file with user identifiers less than 100 and greater than 60000. Typically these ranges are reserved for administrative access.

JASS_KILL_SCRIPT_DISABLE

This variable contains a Boolean value that determines whether the kill run-control scripts should be disabled or simply left in place when a service is disabled. The start run-control scripts are always disabled. Some administrators prefer to have the kill scripts left in place so that any services that are started manually can be properly terminated during a system shutdown or reboot. By default, this variable is set to 1 indicating that the kill run-control scripts should be disabled. Setting this variable to 0 configures the software to ignore kill run-control scripts.

JASS_LOGIN_RETRIES

This variable contains a numeric value specifying the number of consecutive failed login attempts that can occur before the login process logs the failure and terminates the connection. During hardening runs, this setting is installed by the `set-login-retries.fin` script. During audit runs, the `set-login-retries.aud` script checks that this setting is installed. By default, this variable has a value of 3.

JASS_MD5_DIR

This variable contains a string value representing the absolute path to the MD5 software distribution, if present. If the MD5 software is installed from the `tar` distribution by the Solaris Security Toolkit, it is installed into the directory defined by this variable. During hardening runs, this variable is used by the `install-md5.fin` script to install the MD5 software. During audit runs, `install-md5.aud` script checks for the existence of the MD5 software at the location defined by this variable. The default value of this variable is `/opt`.

JASS_PASS_LENGTH

This variable contains a numeric value specifying the minimum length of a user password. The default value for this variable is 8 (characters). This variable is used by the `set-user-password-reqs.fin` script and the `set-user-password-reqs.aud` script.

JASS_PASSWD

This variable contains a string value that specifies the location of the password file on the target system. This variable is used in many of the scripts and for dynamic assignment of many variables. This variable has a default value of JASS_ROOT_DIR/etc/passwd.

This variable should not require modification.

JASS_POWER_MGT_USER

This variable contains a string value that defines which users are permitted to perform power management functions on a system. During hardening runs, this restriction is implemented by the set-power-restrictions.fin script. During audit runs, this restriction is checked by the set-power-restrictions.aud script. The default value of this variable is "-," indicating that only the root account is permitted to perform these management functions. For more information, refer to the /etc/default/power information in Chapter 9.

JASS_REC_PATCH_OPTIONS

This variable contains a string value that specifies options to be passed to the patchadd or installpatch commands when installing a Solaris Recommended and Security Patch Cluster on a system. For information on available options, refer to the patchadd(1M) manual page or the installpatch program code. During hardening runs, this variable is used by the install-recommended-patches.fin script when installing the patch cluster on the system. This variable is not used during audit runs. By default, no options are assigned to this variable.

JASS_RHOSTS_FILE

This variable contains a string value that specifies the file where the list of .rhosts or hosts.equiv files found on the system are stored. This variable is used during hardening runs by the print-rhosts.fin script. This variable is not used during audit runs. By default, no file name is assigned to this variable. As a result, the output of the print-rhosts.fin script is displayed on the screen.

JASS_ROOT_GROUP

This variable contains a numeric value that is used as the root user's primary group identifier (GID) value. During hardening runs, this setting is installed by the set-root-group.fin script. During audit runs, this setting is checked by the set-root-group.aud script. By default, this value is set to 0 (or root). This value overrides the Solaris OE default value of 1 (or other).

JASS_ROOT_PASSWORD

This variable contains a string value that is used as the encrypted password for the root account. During hardening runs, this setting is installed by the set-root-password.fin script. During audit runs, this setting is checked by the set-root-password.aud script. By default, this variable is set to JdqZ5HrSDYM.o. This encrypted string equates to the clear-text string t00lk1t.

Note – This script operates only when the system is running from a miniroot during a JumpStart installation, to prevent the root password from being accidentally overwritten with a widely known value.

Caution – We strongly recommend that you change the value of this string from the default value that ships with the Solaris Security Toolkit software. Failure to do so could leave systems vulnerable because the password is publicly known.

JASS_SADMIND_OPTIONS

This variable contains a string value specifying options to be used with the sadmind daemon that is executed from the inetd process. During hardening runs, this setting is installed by the install-sadmind-options.fin script. During audit runs, these settings are checked by the install-sadmind-options.aud script. By default, this variable has a value of -S 2 to instruct the sadmind daemon to use strong authentication (AUTH_DES) when communicating with clients.

JASS_SENDMAIL_MODE

This variable contains a string value specifying options to be used by the sendmail daemon to determine its operation. During hardening runs, the disable-sendmail.fin script configures the daemon for the operation specified by this variable. During audit runs, the disable-sendmail.aud script checks to ensure that the sendmail daemon is configured for the correct operation. The default value of this variable is \"\". This value indicates that the `sendmail` daemon should operate in queue-processing mode only. This value overrides the default value where the `sendmail` daemon is configured to operate as a daemon and receive incoming mail.

Note – The back slash characters are required in this string to prevent the quotation marks from being interpreted by the command shell. When installed in the relevant `sendmail` configuration file, the string displays as "".

Note – Due to changes in `sendmail` versions and configurations, this variable is applicable only to Solaris 8 OE versions. Other mechanisms are used for newer and earlier Solaris OE versions to achieve the same goal.

JASS_SGID_FILE

This variable contains a string value that specifies the file where the list of set-group-id files found on the system are stored. This variable is used during hardening runs by the `print-sgid-files.fin` script. This variable is not used during audit runs. By default, no file name is assigned to this variable. As a result, the output of the `print-sgid-files.fin` script is displayed on the screen.

JASS_SHELLS

This variable contains a list of shells to add to the `JASS_ROOT_DIR/etc/shells` file. During hardening runs, the `install-shells.fin` script adds each shell defined by this variable to the `JASS_ROOT_DIR/etc/shells` file, if not already present. Similarly, during audit runs, the `install-shells.aud` script determines if each shell defined by this variable is listed in the `shells` file.

The default value for this variable are as follows:

```
/bin/csh
/bin/jsh
/bin/ksh
/bin/sh
/sbin/sh
/sbin/jsh
/usr/bin/csh
/usr/bin/jsh
/usr/bin/ksh
/usr/bin/sh
```

For Solaris OE versions 8 and newer, the following shells are added to the default value:

```
/bin/bash
/bin/pfcsh
/bin/pfksh
/bin/pfsh
/bin/tcsh
/bin/zsh
/usr/bin/bash
/usr/bin/pfcsh
/usr/bin/pfksh
/usr/bin/pfsh
/usr/bin/tcsh
/usr/bin/zsh
```

JASS_SHELL_DISABLE

This variable contains a file name that specifies the location of the shell used when disabling user accounts. During hardening runs, this variable is used by the `disable-system-accounts.fin` script when installing the shell for the accounts defined by JASS_ACCT_DISABLE variable. During audit runs, this variable is used by the `disable-system-accounts.aud` script to check that the shell program exists on the system and that the accounts defined by JASS_ACCT_DISABLE are configured to use the shell.

The default value for this variable is `/sbin/noshell`.

JASS_SUID_FILE

This variable contains a string value that specifies the file where the list of set-user-id files found on the system are stored. This variable is used during hardening runs by the `print-suid-files.fin` script. This variable is not used during audit runs. By default, no file name is assigned to this variable. As a result, the output of the `print-suid-files.fin` script is displayed on the screen.

JASS_SUSPEND_PERMS

This variable contains a string value that defines which users are permitted to perform system suspend or resume functions. During hardening runs, this restriction is implemented by the set-sys-suspend-restrictions.fin script. During audit runs, this restriction is checked by the set-sys-suspend-restrictions.aud script. The default value of this variable is "-," indicating that only the root account is permitted to perform these management functions. For more information, refer to the /etc/default/sys-suspend file.

JASS_SVCS_DISABLE

This variable simplifies the removal of different services from the JASS_ROOT_DIR/etc/inet/inetd.conf file. During hardening runs, the update-inetd-conf.fin script disables each inetd service defined by this variable, unless it is also listed in the JASS_SVCS_ENABLE variable. Similarly, during audit runs, the update-inetd-conf.aud script determines that the appropriate inetd services are disabled on the system. By default, the list of services disabled by this variable includes all of the entries that are provided by default with the Solaris OE.

Caution – When using the default list of services, be certain to have either console access to the system, Secure Shell access (for Solaris 9 OE), or a nondefault remote access capability, because Telnet, RSH, and RLOGIN servers are all disabled by default.

The JASS_SVCS_DISABLE and JASS_SVCS_ENABLE variables provide a straightforward and easy-to-use mechanism for modifying the default behavior of update-inetd-conf.fin without requiring any modifications to the script itself. The four configuration possibilities for modifying these variables are as follows:

Example 1:

JASS_SVCS_DISABLE (defined)

JASS_SVCS_ENABLE (not defined)

This example is the default case for backward compatibility with older versions of the Solaris Security Toolkit software. In this case, the services listed in JASS_SVCS_DISABLE are commented out of the /etc/inetd.conf file when the update-inetd-conf.fin script is run.

Example 2:

JASS_SVCS_DISABLE (not defined)

JASS_SVCS_ENABLE (defined)

Only services listed in JASS_SVCS_ENABLE are left enabled. All other services, including those that are not Sun specific, are disabled. This example permits the implementation of the principle "all that is not explicitly permitted is denied."

Example 3:

JASS_SVCS_DISABLE (defined)

JASS_SVCS_ENABLE (defined)

The services in JASS_SVCS_DISABLE are disabled and JASS_SVCS_ENABLE are left enabled. Services not covered in the list are unaffected. If a service is listed in both JASS_SVCS_ENABLE and JASS_SVCS_DISABLE, then it is enabled because JASS_SVCS_ENABLE takes precedence.

Example 4:

JASS_SVCS_DISABLE (undefined)

JASS_SVCS_ENABLE (undefined)

In this example, none of the services are affected because there is no explicit direction defined.

JASS_SVCS_ENABLE

This variable contains a list of inetd services that are expected to be enabled on a system. During hardening runs, the update-inetd-conf.fin finish script enables any service listed in this variable that is currently disabled. If the service is already enabled, no action is taken. During audit runs, the update-inetd-conf.aud script determines if the services defined by this variable are enabled on the system. By default, this variable contains no services. As a result, the behavior of the update-inetd-conf.fin script and update-inetd-conf.aud script is controlled solely by the contents of the JASS_SVCS_DISABLE variable.

JASS_TMPFS_SIZE

This variable contains a string value representing the amount of space to allocate to the /tmp (tmpfs) file system. During hardening runs, this setting is installed by the set-tmpfs-limit.fin script. During audit runs, this setting is checked by the set-tmpfs-limit.aud script. This variable has a default value of 512 megabytes.

Note – This variable should be adjusted to ensure that it is large enough to meet the current and expected /tmp needs for system functions and applications running on the system.

JASS_UMASK

This variable contains a numeric (octal) value that represents the file creation mask (umask). During hardening runs, this setting is used by the set-system-umask.fin and set-user-umask.fin scripts. During audit runs, this setting is checked by the set-system-umask.aud and set-user-umask.aud scripts. The default value of this variable is 022.

JASS_UNOWNED_FILE

This variable contains a string value that specifies the file where the list of unowned files found on the system are stored. A file is considered unowned if its user or group assignment does not correspond to a valid user or group on the system. This variable is used during hardening runs by the print-unowned-objects.fin script. This variable is not used during audit runs. By default, no file name is. assigned to this variable. As a result, the output of the print-unowned-objects.fin script is displayed on the screen.

JASS_WRITABLE_FILE

This variable contains a string value that specifies the file where the list of world-writable files found on the system are stored. This variable is used during hardening runs by the print-world-writable-objects.fin script. This variable is not used during audit runs. By default, no file name is assigned to this variable. As a result, the output of the print-world-writable-objects.fin script is displayed on the screen.

Define JumpStart Mode Variables

JumpStart mode variables are those that are defined and used by the Solaris Security Toolkit software solely when operating in JumpStart mode. These variables facilitate the use of the Solaris Security Toolkit software either as a JumpStart framework or integrated as part of a larger build environment. These variables are mentioned separately because they are only relevant during a JumpStart installation.

These variables are defined in the `JASS_HOME_DIR/Drivers/user.init` file. They are in the `user.init` file because they typically require modification in contrast to most of the other variables that can be used as-is with no modification.

Note – In some cases, such as with multihomed JumpStart servers, special customization might be required.

We recommend that you tune these variables, where necessary, to best suit the environment in which the Solaris Security Toolkit software is used.

JASS_PACKAGE_MOUNT

This variable defines the named resource or location where the Solaris Security Toolkit software expects to find the software packages that it may be required to install onto a client. This resource is defined as an Networked File System (NFS) path of the form: `host name:/path/to/software`. This resource is mounted to `JASS_PACKAGE_DIR` by the `mount_filesystems` function during the execution of the `driver.run` script.

The location of this resource must be specified by host name or IP address, and the complete path must be listed to provide the NFS daemon enough information to mount the directory during a run. Because a host name or IP address can be specified in the value of the environment variable, it often requires modification.

The Solaris Security Toolkit software attempts to configure the correct host name and directory path automatically; however, this automatic configuration might not be applicable to your environment. By default, this variable is set to `HOSTNAME:/jumpstart/Packages`. The `HOSTNAME` variable is dynamically assigned to the address of the NFS server from which the client has mounted the `/cdrom` file system.

JASS_PATCH_MOUNT

This variable defines the named resource or location where the Solaris Security Toolkit software should expect to find the software patches that it may be required to install onto the client. This resource is defined as an NFS path of the form: *host name*:/*path/to/patches*. This resource is mounted to JASS_PATCH_DIR by the mount_filesystems function during the execution of the driver.run script.

The location of this resource must be specified by host name or IP address, and the complete path must be listed to provide the NFS daemon enough information to mount the directory during the Toolkit run. Because a host name or IP address can be specified in the value of the environment variable, it often requires modification.

The Solaris Security Toolkit software attempts to configure the correct host name and directory path automatically; however, this automatic configuration might not be applicable to your environment. By default, this variable is set to HOSTNAME:/jumpstart/Patches. The HOSTNAME variable is dynamically assigned to the address of the NFS server from which the client has mounted the /cdrom file system.

Index

extensions, 23
extracting patches, 12

F

-f option, undo, 75
FAIL messages, 150, 311
failed checks, 102
failed login attempts
    logging, 247, 254
    setting, 327
failure messages, 136, 137
failures, applications, 34
false-positive vulnerabilities, 93
fast track approach, installation, 63
faults, 34
feedback, providing, 40
file check, 138
file checksums, 73
file content, checking, 137
file content, variables, 298
file creation mask
    default, 254
    enabling FTP, 242
    protecting, 255
    umask, setting, 326, 334
file exists, 172
file header, 208
file length/size is zero, 164
file name extensions, 207
file not found messages, 141
file ownership check, 142
file permissions check, 140
file samples, sysidcfg, 13
file system objects
    backing up, 161
    copying, 164
    copying to client, 309
    copying, selectively, 164
    obtaining information, 25
    specifying list to copy, 306
    type, checking, 175

file systems
    integrity, 21
    mounting and unmounting, 204
    single, 133
    target, 314
file templates
    adding or removing, 308
    checking match on target system, 174
    directory, JumpStart client, 195
    installing, 249
    using, modifying, and customizing, 187
File Transfer Protocol (FTP), 242, 253
File Transfer Protocol (FTP) service, status, 278
file type check, 143
filenames, 44
files
    checking, 172
    checking ownership, 174
    content matching, 171
    copying, 204
    corrupted contents, 71
    determining usage, 31
    directory, 9
    directory, path, 309
    disabling, 167
    inconsistent, 75
    JumpStart clients, storing, 9
    listing and reviewing changes, 73
    matching, precedence, 164
    modifying, 16
    moving from one name to another, 169
    naming standards, 16
    permissions, checking, 173
    profiles, 86
    recording state, 314
    reviewing manually changed, 73
    rules for copying, 190
    specifying, 317
    specifying copies to clients, 307
    specifying list, 306
    sysidcfg, 17
    templates, checking match on target system, 17
files directory, 9
finish and audit script variables, 296
finish directory, 10

finish scripts
    adding or removing, 318
    configuration variables, 228
    convention for storing, 309
    conventions, for developing, 225
    corresponding audit scripts, 265
    creating new, 71, 131, 222
    customizing, 222, 228
    kill scripts, 224
    listing ones to execute, 317
    storing, 206
    storing in alternate locations, 309
    undo feature, 72
    using standard, 228
finish.init file
    defining behavior, 192
    driver flow, 8
    modifying, 192
    purpose, 192
finish_check function, 184
FixModes
    default directory path, 326
    FixModes.tar.Z file, 48
    options, 326
    software, 245
    software, downloading, 47
force option, 75
foreign agent functionality, 234
format, printing, 156
framework functions
    creating new, 132
    undo operations, caution, 132
    using, 131
    variables, 296
framework variables
    changing, caution, 303
    defining, 303
framework, customizing Solaris Security
    Toolkit, 72
frameworks, services, 28
FTP
    access attempts, logging, 242
    default configuration, 23
    ftpaccess(4) manual page, 253
    ftpusers file, 246
    service banner, 253
    services, enabled, case scenario, 120

functionality
    adding, 93
    detecting in multiple releases, 161
    extending, 132
    files, loading, 204
    patches, 45
    problems, 21
    testing, 34
functions
    common miscellaneous, 155
    new, 319
    overriding, 319
    site specific, 205

G

getusershell(3C), determining valid
    shells, 248
GID, 172, 329
global changes, 209
global environment variables, 300, 312, 319
graphical consoles, systems without, 256
group access, restricting, 249
group ID permissions, printing, 250
group identifier (GID), 172, 329
group membership check, 139
groups, caching, 235
guest account, 298

H

hardening a system quickly, 42
hardening runs
    core processing, 204
    executing Solaris Security Toolkit, 51
    listing for undo, 78
    reversing changes, 77
hardening, defined, 2
hardening.driver, 213
helper functions, 72
high-water mark, security, 51
history option, 57
host files, specifying, 307
host name, defining, 309

maximum size, `cron` log file, 326
MD5 binaries, 50
MD5 software
    default directory path, 327
    downloading, 50
    `md5.tar.Z` file, 50
memory exhaustion, preventing, 256
memory-resident mini-root, 222
messages, audits, 100
messages, displaying for users, 146
meta-services, 28
methodology, securing systems, 19
`mibiisa(1M)` manual page, 238
migration issues, minimizing, 228
`minimal-Sun_ONE-WS-Solaris*.profile`, 88
minimization, defined, 2
minimized installations, required link, 247
minimized platform, checking packages, 177
`minimize-Sun_ONE-WS.fin` script, 249
minimizing output, 101
minimizing, Solaris Operating Environment, 23
minimum password length, 256
miniroot, 329
MIP, 234
`mipagent(1M)` manual page, 234
mirror directory, 167
`mkdir_dashp` function, 168
Mobile IP, 234
mobile IP (MIP) service, status, 271
modes, 42
modifications, tracking, 70
modifications, validating, 61
modifying
    audit scripts, 261
    code, 15
    drivers, 131, 203, 221
    profile files, 86
    scripts, 131, 203, 221
monitoring security, 36
monitoring software, inventorying, 24
most recent execute option, 57

mount point
    implementing, finish script, 133
    permissions, 199, 200
    specifying, 205
mount removable media, 254
`mount_filesystems` function, 133
`mount_filesystems` routine, 205
`mount_tmpfs(1M)` manual page, 256
`mountall` command, 200
`mountd(1M)` manual page, 234
mounted filesystem, permissions, 199, 200
`move_a_file` function, 169
moving a file from one name to another, 169
moving patch files, 46
multihomed JumpStart server, 85
multiple runs, processing, 305
multiple systems, processing runs, 305
`mv` command, 131

N

name service cache daemon (NSCD), 235
name service databases, 235
name service requests, 235
naming files, standards, 16
naming services, 28
naming standards
    custom files, 16
    installations, 10
    Solaris OE, 11
`nddconfig` file, 198
nested or hierarchical security profiles, 33
`netstat` command, 30
network access, protecting, 48
Network File System (NFS), *See* NFS
network interfaces, configuring, 198
network settings, implementing, 198, 200
new directory, creating, 168
new functions, 319
`newaliases` symbolic link, 247

run directory, 70
run information, storing, 313
run-control
    file, disabling, 167
    scripts, 224
    scripts, disabling, 161, 304
    start script exists, determining, 152, 183
    stop script exists, determining, 152, 184
running processes, checking, 180
runs
    processing multiple systems, 305
    storing list of scripts, 315
    version information, path, 316
run-time
    configurations, 170
    process arguments, checking, 149
    setting, 278
rusers command, 29
rusers service, validating, 29

S

S00set-tmp-permissions file, 200
s15k-exclude-domains.aud script, 293
s15k-exclude-domains.fin script, 260
s15k-sms-secure-failover.aud script, 293
s15k-sms-secure-failover.fin script, 260
s15k-static-arp.aud script, 292
s15k-static-arp.fin script, 259
S70nddconfig file, 200
S73sms_arpconfig file, 201
sadmind daemon, 248
sadmind daemon, specifying options, 329
sadmind(1M) manual page, 248
safe file creation mask, 255
Samba file, disabling service, 237
Samba service, status, 273
samples, profile files, 86
SCCS, 14
scenario, securing a system, 107
score, adjusting, 156
scp command, 46
script behavior variables, 321
script method, 304

script names, displaying during audits, 305
scripts
    audit, 266
    default, 213
    disable audit scripts, listing, 267
    disable finish scripts, listing, 229
    enable audit scripts, 277
    enable finish scripts, listing, 241, 277
    finish, 228
    install audit scripts, listing, 279
    install finish scripts, listing, 245
    JumpStart mode, 88
    list, 7
    minimize finish script, 249
    modifying, caution, 85
    naming, 16
    output, 207
    print audit scripts, listing, 283
    print finish scripts, listing, 250
    processing flow, 204
    remove finish script, 251
    running, 204
    separating security and configuration, 212
    set audit scripts, listing, 285
    set finish scripts, listing, 252
    update audit scripts, listing, 289
    update finish scripts, listing, 257
Secure Shell
    building and deploying, 49
    commercial versions, compiling, 49
    configuration, automating, 260
    configuring, 239
    installing, case scenario, 121
    product requirements, 43
    service banner, 253
    software, downloading, 48
    software, obtaining commercial versions, 49
secure.driver, 215
secure.driver, executing, 53
securing a deployed system, 20
securing systems, methodology, 19
security assessments
    configuration, 62
    performing, 103
security configuration, assessing, 35
security modifications, validating, 266

informIT

www.informit.com

YOUR GUIDE TO IT REFERENCE

Articles

Keep your edge with thousands of free articles, in-depth features, interviews, and IT reference recommendations – all written by experts you know and trust.

Online Books

Answers in an instant from **InformIT Online Book's** 600+ fully searchable on line books. Sign up now and get your first 14 days **free**.

POWERED BY

Catalog

Review online sample chapters, author biographies and customer rankings and choose exactly the right book from a selection of over 5,000 titles.

Wouldn't it be great

if the world's leading technical publishers joined forces to deliver their best tech books in a common digital reference platform?

They have. Introducing
InformIT Online Books
powered by Safari.

■ **Specific answers to specific questions.**
InformIT Online Books' powerful search engine gives you relevance-ranked results in a matter of seconds.

■ **Immediate results.**
With InformIt Online Books, you can select the book you want and view the chapter or section you need immediately.

■ **Cut, paste and annotate.**
Paste code to save time and eliminate typographical errors. Make notes on the material you find useful and choose whether or not to share them with your work group.

■ **Customized for your enterprise.**
Customize a library for you, your department or your entire organization. You only pay for what you need.

Get your first 14 days **FREE!**

InformIT Online Books is offering its members a 10 book subscription risk-free for 14 days. Visit **http://www.informit.com/onlinebooks** for details.

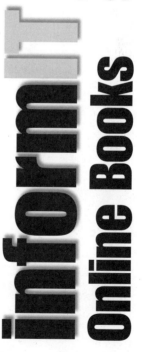

POWERED BY Safari™

InformIT Online Books

informit.com/onlinebooks

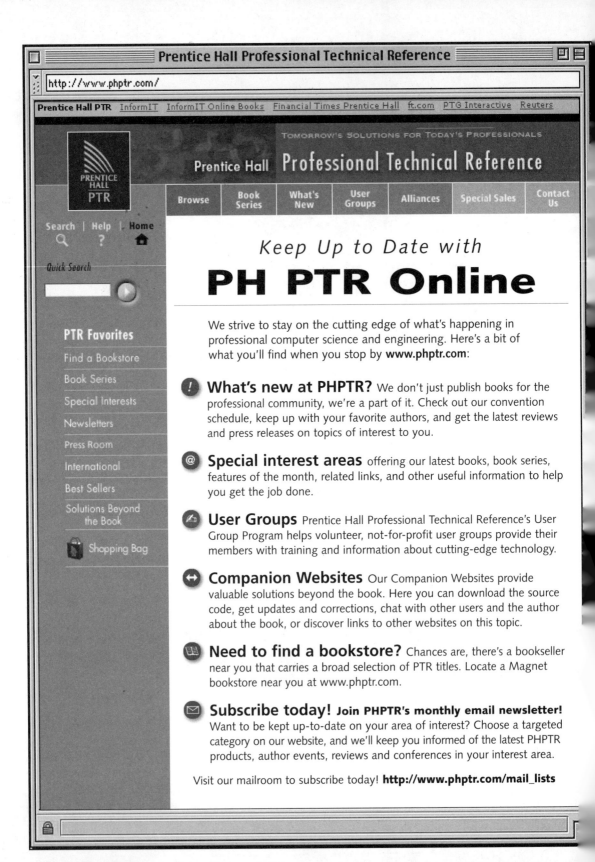

Prentice Hall Professional Technical Reference

http://www.phptr.com/

Prentice Hall PTR   InformIT   InformIT Online Books   Financial Times Prentice Hall   ft.com   PTG Interactive   Reuters

TOMORROW'S SOLUTIONS FOR TODAY'S PROFESSIONALS

Prentice Hall **Professional Technical Reference**

| Browse | Book Series | What's New | User Groups | Alliances | Special Sales | Contact Us |

Search | Help | Home

Quick Search

PTR Favorites

Find a Bookstore

Book Series

Special Interests

Newsletters

Press Room

International

Best Sellers

Solutions Beyond the Book

Shopping Bag

Keep Up to Date with

PH PTR Online

We strive to stay on the cutting edge of what's happening in professional computer science and engineering. Here's a bit of what you'll find when you stop by **www.phptr.com**:

What's new at PHPTR? We don't just publish books for the professional community, we're a part of it. Check out our convention schedule, keep up with your favorite authors, and get the latest reviews and press releases on topics of interest to you.

Special interest areas offering our latest books, book series, features of the month, related links, and other useful information to help you get the job done.

User Groups Prentice Hall Professional Technical Reference's User Group Program helps volunteer, not-for-profit user groups provide their members with training and information about cutting-edge technology.

Companion Websites Our Companion Websites provide valuable solutions beyond the book. Here you can download the source code, get updates and corrections, chat with other users and the author about the book, or discover links to other websites on this topic.

Need to find a bookstore? Chances are, there's a bookseller near you that carries a broad selection of PTR titles. Locate a Magnet bookstore near you at www.phptr.com.

Subscribe today! Join PHPTR's monthly email newsletter! Want to be kept up-to-date on your area of interest? Choose a targeted category on our website, and we'll keep you informed of the latest PHPTR products, author events, reviews and conferences in your interest area.

Visit our mailroom to subscribe today! **http://www.phptr.com/mail_lists**